Risks, Concerns,
and Social Legislation

Risks, Concerns, and Social Legislation

Forces that Led to Laws on Health, Safety, and the Environment

W. Curtiss Priest

Westview Press / Boulder and London

Westview Special Studies in Public Policy and Public Systems Management

This Westview softcover edition is printed on acid-free paper and bound in softcovers that carry the highest rating of the National Association of State Textbook Administrators, in consultation with the Association of American Publishers and the Book Manufacturers' Institute.

This volume copyright © 1988 by Westview Press, Inc.

Published in 1988 in the United States of America by Westview Press, Inc.; Frederick A. Praeger, Publisher; 5500 Central Avenue, Boulder, Colorado 80301

Library of Congress Cataloging-in-Publication Data
Priest, W. Curtiss
  Risks, concerns, and social legislation : forces that led to laws
on health, safety, and the environment / by W. Curtiss Priest.
      p. cm.—(Westview special studies in public policy and
public systems management)
   Bibliography: p.
   Includes index.
   ISBN 0-8133-7479-0
   1. Social legislation—United States. 2. Safety regulations—
United States. 3. Health risk assessment—United States.
I. Title. II. Series.
KF3300.P75 1988
344.73′04—dc19
[347.3044]
                                                                87-29531
                                                                   CIP

Printed and bound in the United States of America

The paper used in this publication meets the requirements of the American National Standard for Permanence of Paper for Printed Library Materials Z39.48-1984.

6   5   4   3   2   1

Contents

Acknowledgments

A team of fourteen people substantially contributed to the success of the research project on which this book is based. The original research was conducted at the Center for Policy Alternatives of the Massachusetts Institute of Technology, which was closed in 1986, in large part because the era of social legislation described in this manuscript had also come to a close. In memory of the Center I especially would like to recall the Center's founder, Dr. Herbert Hollomon -- an inspiration to all who would aspire to understanding a complex world of technology and mankind.

Also, without the unswerving dedication of Dr. Nicholas Ashford, this book would not be possible. Dr. Ashford assembled both many of the basic perspectives on health, life and regulation described here, and the research staff that conducted over ten years of support for the federal social regulatory activity.

The MIT students, both graduate and undergraduate, who worked on the project put in many hours performing content analysis, piecing together the account, and contributing pieces of this book. I had the pleasure of working, on this project, with some of the brightest and most perceptive students I knew during my days at the Center for Policy Alternatives. In particular John A. Smith, Jr. and Pamela Loprest contributed substantially and with dedication. Other contributors included Kyung Koh, Cindi Katz, Betsy Hanson, Helene Sperling, and Paul Jaminet.

My thanks also extend to Dr. Dale Hattis for his many insights into risk analysis, Dr. Caroline Whitbeck for her contributions to philosophy and values, and Dr. William White (University of Chicago) for consulting on the history of occupational safety concerns. Also, my thanks go to Ms. Rachelle Hollander of the National Science Foundation (Program on Ethics and Values in Science and Technology Program) and the peer reviewers for funding the project. Finally, I thank Eugene Narrett for helping take a rough initial manuscript and adding consistency and polish.

To complete the list, I also congratulate the congressmen, legislative aides, newspaper reporters, investigative writers, advocates, and others who helped translate the pain and suffering into legislative action.

W. Curtiss Priest
Lexington, MA

1

Introduction

Purpose

It has become easy to lose sight of the social forces that led to regulatory legislation during the late 60's and early 70's. As early as the Carter administration there had been a distinct shift in concern away from the original human concerns to the costs of regulation and by the Reagan administration hardly any vestige of the original concerns was left whatsoever.

These changes in political emphasis have obscured not only the generating forces but the goals of health, safety and environmental legislation. Regulatory impact analysis by its very nature is a value that competes with those that prompted such legislation. For example, while the Occupational and Safety Health Act mandates "safe and healthful working conditions for working men and women," the implementation of the legislation required cost-based definitions of "too much safety and health" and "adequate safety and health." The analytical tools available to the federal government and its contractors, moreover, could not measure the values that were contained within this act and others like it. Some government bodies, such as the Consumer Product Safety Commission, found themselves trying to justify control of hazards on the basis only of hospital costs and some arbitrary numeric representation of pain and suffering, a practice which consistently underestimated the impact of the injury on the person or family. In this way, during the 70's government analysts and economists placed monetary values on everything from chronic disease to loss of life. Regulatory impact analysis rationalized this process by focussing on secondary costs and issues and government agencies embraced it in order to justify their regulatory decisions.

These bureaucratic restraints on the goals of regulatory legislation have been accentuated by the current administration's championing of other competing values: market expansion and a severely curtailed role for government as protector of the public from industry-related hazards.

This book serves two major aims. First, it provides historical documentation of the social forces that lead to legislation and reviews values that have been important in shaping government's role as mediator between individual, family, community and industry. Second, the historical analysis verifies a prescriptive values framework. This verified values framework can inform future discussions, debates and legislation regarding not only health, safety, and environmental law and regulation but also the broad area of health policy.

<u>Scope of the Research</u>

The first part of our research identified "expressions of concern" about the issues and period in question. The second part sifted these remarks to derive the underlying values and "value phrases."

In order to survey a broad range of evaluative criteria, we studied legislation from five areas:

   o Air Pollution -- Including the Air Quality Act of 1967
   o Aviation Safety -- A series of laws from the 1920's to the present
   o Consumer Product Safety -- Including the Consumer Product Safety
       Act of 1972
   o Occupational Health and Safety -- Including the Occupational Health
       and Safety Act of 1970
   o Pesticide Control -- Including the Federal Insecticide, Fungicide, and
       Rodenticide Act of 1947, amended 1972

To document the social forces leading to legislation in these fields, we consulted:

   o Secondary Literature and Interviews
   o Content Analysis of five major indexes of popular and professional
       articles
   o Content Analysis of congressional hearings preceeding the enactment
       of legislation

The values framework presented in this book culminates twelve years of development at the MIT Center for Policy Alternatives. This framework was developed by a multidisciplinary group of professionals including lawyers, scientists, management scientists, economists, philosophers, and anthropologists who participated in the drafting of legislation. The group also developed trade-off analysis for analyzing proposed regulations and reviewed literature from the fields of philosophy, management and decision science, economics, sociology, socio-medical indicators, and others.

Organization of the Presentation

This book is divided into three major sections. The first section (2.1) discusses the methods used to glean information from our sources. The second section (2.2-2.6) presents our findings in each of the five areas of legislation -- air pollution, aviation safety, consumer products, occupational health & safety, and pesticides. In the third section (3.), we present a value framework for risks and concerns in the areas covered by such legislation and compare this framework with the values underlying the social forces we studied.

The historical record was consonant with a value framework that has been developed at our Center during the last decade. We have found it useful to add to the framework a few "critical distinctions" (see Section 3.1.5). In Section 3.2 (Values as Found in the Historical Review), we provide a map of the values found in the review.

2

Historical Review

The historical review covers the period from 1900 to 1973, by which date, legislation was in place covering the five areas in our study. The review stretches back to 1900 because social concerns about a number of these areas (especially Air Pollution and Occupational Health & Safety), date back at least to the beginning of the century.

2.1 Approach and Methods Applied in the Review

In contrast to anecdotal approaches to the history of social legislation, the approach here emphasizes structure and quantification. The use of techniques such as content analysis and an analytical framework for understanding human values helps make the process more explicit and reduces editorial bias.

2.1.1 Approach

Overview of Social Forces

The late sixties and early seventies proved to be important years for the passage of health and safety legislation. Robert B. Reich writing in The New York Times viewed the passage of regulatory legislation as occurring in peaks which he calls the "waves of regulation" (Figure 2.1.1-1). The health and safety legislation we studied is part of a wave occuring from 1965 to 1978. Like ocean waves, the waves of regulation develop momentum gradually.

6

The Waves of Regulation
Figure 2.1.1-1

Source: Robert B. Reich, 1981

Several primary groups influence the process leading to the enactment of legislation. The chart in Figure 2.1.1-2 diagrams the dominant interactions of these groups.

The public at large, made up of all the individuals in the country, includes a small sector that is active in the political process. James N. Rosenau describes this group as those who can be mobilized to give specific support, such as time or money, to an issue [Rosenau, 1972]. These people, the "participating public", write to congressmen, seek the help of advocates, or submit letters to the editor. They have input to the process through relationships with legislators, advocates or media representatives.

The public at large has a two-way relationship with the media (television, periodicals and radio). The media derive their material partially from what the public is doing and is concerned about. For professional and commercial reasons, it also covers what it believes is or will be of interest to the public. In this, media coverage is inflected by the discussions and rhetoric of politicians who not only reflect but try to anticipate or shape public opinion, sometimes seeking to meld it to the agendas of diverse and often hidden interest groups. These multiple inputs to media discourse are, for example, built into the practice of opinion polls. Thus, what the public knows and cares about is affected by the media through the amount and style of coverage and these are diversely shaped in ways whose details are beyond the scope of our study.

The media directly effects legislation by providing information to legislators and covering congressional events, such as hearings. Other effects come through the information it provides to advocates and concerned professionals, as well as the coverage it gives both of these groups.

Concerned professionals include the general groups of concerned scientists, concerned academics, and other professionals. They contribute through the media as described above, through advocates to whom they provide information, and directly to legislators through hearings, government reports, and studies.

Advocates (as regards the passage of legislation) are non-governmental professionals who represent a certain group or press for a certain issue. Besides trying to get media coverage for their cause and gaining information through media and concerned professionals, advocates gain input from the participating public. They have direct influence on the passage of legislation and sometimes provide specialized information to legislators.

It is interesting to contrast the process of social forces depicted in Figure 2.1.1-2 with a recent perspective presented in Chemical Week (Figure 2.1.1-3 [Chemical Week, 1981, p. 37]). The clear difference between the two is the "origins" of social laws. The Stanford Research International figure shows the forces beginning with "visionaries," proceeding to "radicals," then to academia, and then to the media. This perspective suggests that the origins are the imaginations of visionaries. In contrast,

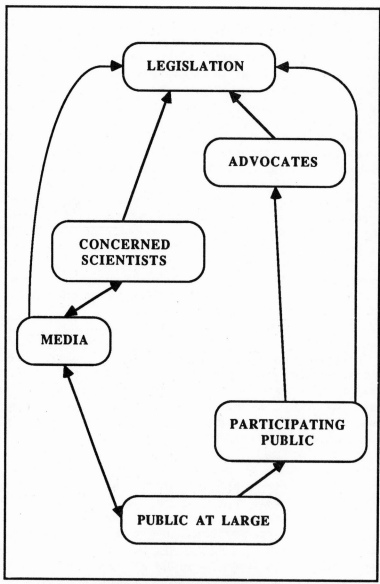

Social Groups' Input to Legislation
Figure 2.1.1-2
Source: MIT Center for Policy Alternatives, 1984

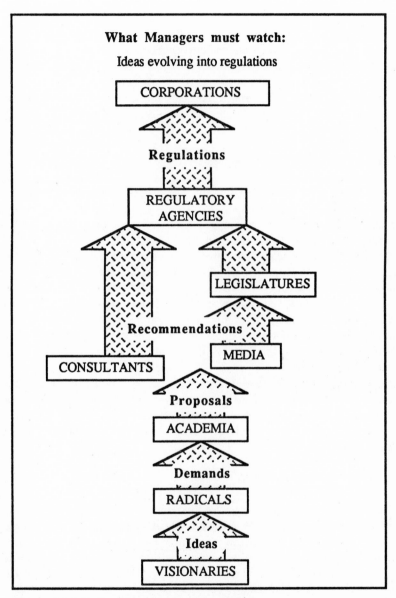

Figure 2.1.1-3 One Perspective of Social Forces

Source: Stanford Research International, 1981

the perspective of Figure 2.1.1-2 places the "public at large" as the origin of forces, and places the "advocates" in an active, interpretative role. To us, this latter view is the more plausible.

In summary, the dominant inputs to the process by which legislation is enacted are from the participating public, concerned professionals, advocates, and the media, through which the concerns of the "public at large" diffusely work. There are other factors that have not been addressed, and other relationships between the factors that have not been described. The forces we have discussed here are those crucial to the passage of legislation.

Expressions of Concern and Values

Social forces may be defined by "expressions of concerns" and our historical review concentrated on extracting expressions of concerns from the various sources. The relationship between expressions of concerns and values is close but not always self-evident.

Concern develops when the things we value are exposed to or suffer harm. Concerns and values are different but the relative strength of the concern can provide information about the underlying values. Only when one investigates the specific ways in which damage threatens or occurs can one pinpoint the values informing a specific expression of concern (for example, about pesticides. Expressions of concern about pesticides were strong and fairly constant from 1900-78 but the values involved changed drastically in the 1960s).

Statements of concern are pieces of a puzzle. While many statements together are sometimes enough to uncover an underlying value, other relevant technical and historical facts are useful. It is in this light that we offer the following description of values found by interpreting concerns voiced through the media.

2.1.2 Index Content Analysis

To identify the progression of sympathy for the social issues a quantitative approach of index content analysis was used. A large computer database was constructed which contained the results of many hours of reviewing article indexes. Only some of the many histograms produced from this analysis appear in this book and a reader interested in greater detail is invited to inquire with the author.

2.1.2.1 Origin of the Approach

To investigate trends of concern expressed in popular literature, we applied content analysis, referred to here as Index Content Analysis because the material we analyzed was the indexes of popular periodicals such as The Reader's Guide or The New York Times Index. This approach takes the titles of articles as sources for expressions of concern. Index Content Analysis recently has been used to study the origins of interest in public health [Vierthaler, 1981]. Vierthaler refers to the technique as "Wholesale Content Analysis" but his method is the same as that used here. The major points from Vierthaler's thesis that relate to the origin of Index Content Analysis are provided below.

Index Content Analysis: The Research Uses of Library Indexes

In order to study changes in topics of public interest, a new method of index content analysis was devised. The method may be considered a "wholesale" approach because it allows researchers to examine published communications on specific subject matters which remain in the mainstream of public discourse for long periods of time. Bibliographic indexes reference thousands of articles published in hundreds of magazines and arrange them under pertinent subject headings. These indexes are crucial to the study of print media because they readily make available massive amounts of data. Thus, they significantly aid investigations of cultural changes in American society -- especially, but not exclusively, elusive changes in public opinion.

Bibliographic indexes include such familiar reference works as The New York Times Index or The Social Sciences and Humanities Index. Most libraries also contain more specialized bibliographic indexes. These are valuable for social research because sources are referenced under topic headings that reflect the historical terms discussed in the periodicals. While a time lag must exist between the discussion of new issues in the literature and the adoption of corresponding subject headings, volumes of updated indexes are published continually to provide "living documents" of cultural change. The researcher who employs these subject categories does not impose an extrinsic structure of meaning upon communications [Cicourel, 1964:142-156] because the subject categories reflect mass media discussion. These "folk" categories are ideally suited for use as a data base to map the emergence of public issues covered in the indexed literature. Although the "public interest" is invoked frequently, insufficient effort has been made to gather evidence necessary to study changes in this important aspect of social organization.

An earlier monograph [Vierthaler, 1974a] examined the utility of The Readers' Guide to Periodical Literature as an instrument for investigating cultural change in American society. Begun by the H. W. Wilson Company, The Readers' Guide is a series of volumes which indexes popular American periodicals published since 1900. The indexed periodicals are chosen to represent areas of major interest to the general population. References to the articles published in this diverse collection of periodicals are indexed under alphabetically arranged categories that identify authors, article titles, and subject headings with subtopic headings. John Lawler [1950] attributes the growth of the Wilson Publishing Company to the parallel expansion in America of public education, public libraries, and the publishing industry. As subscribers to the service, librarians have traditionally been responsible for submitting requests to the Wilson Company for periodicals indexed in The Readers' Guide. Because periodicals are published on set schedules for circulation to national audiences, they are an excellent source for investigating changes in matters of public interest.

Thus, The Readers' Guide can be used to eliminate the most time-consuming segment of content analysis -- the encoding of texts. Because it lists references under subject categories, The Readers' Guide provides invaluable data for social research. Volumes in The Readers' Guide series index between 67 and 160 popular periodicals. Volume 31, for example, lists references for an estimated 70,000 articles published in 157 periodicals indexed from March, 1971 through February, 1972. The use of this resource for social research about communications during this century makes it unnecessary to identify a representative sample of older periodicals which must then be located to conduct an appropriate survey of articles. Moreover, The Readers' Guide is the oldest surviving index that employed professional indexers using standards developed and refined in the nineteenth century by librarians working at different sites in the coordinated effort of compiling Poole's Index [Bell, 1957]. The Guide's use of experienced personnel helped to establish its reputation for reliability.

Despite its reputation and demonstrable utility, a thorough search of the literature has disclosed only six studies that employ The Readers' Guide for sociological research. In the most recent study, Melvin Small [1975] makes use of references listed under the category "Russia" for the purpose of sampling original articles which he then submits to content analysis. To establish the origins of the Cold War, Small examines the seven-year trend of favorable, neutral, and unfavorable opinions expressed toward Russia in more than 1,200 articles published in a representative group of liberal, moderate and conservative periodicals. Small relies upon the indexers to provide the initial list of articles in order to choose a representative sample of published texts. He then analyzed these articles for content to identify even more specific categories selected for his own theoretical purpose. Despite the recognized advantage of using The Readers' Guide as a sampling frame for specific subject categories, the content analysis of primary texts remains a time-consuming procedure, especially for the large samples required to study long-term historical change. While it is recognized that content analysis of original materials provides evidence valuable for certain research purposes, the adherence to this conventional practice may lead social scientists inadvertently to omit the option of examining bibliographic indexes -- documentary texts themselves worthy of analysis as a source of data.

The six remaining studies found in the literature use The Readers' Guide as a documentary source of evidence more akin to index content analysis. That is, by using each volume in the series as a record of articles whose content already has been indexed under subject headings, the researcher may concentrate on changes in the frequency of references listed for specific subject categories as evidence of changing public attention to subject matters. To better understand the technique of wholesale content analysis, we will review closely the earliest and most extensive of these investigations.

A study by Hornell Hart [1933b] reports on "Changing Social Attitudes and Interests" that was part of a larger project commissioned by President Herbert Hoover to study social trends in America. Hart analyzes the listings of articles published in periodicals indexed from 1905 through 1930 to measure the trend of American concern in eight areas, namely:

1. Science and education
2. Religious interests
3. Sex and family relations
4. Prohibition sentiments
5. Uplift and social reform discussions
6. Scientific management
7. Business depression and prosperity
8. International relations including preparedness and disarmament,
   of Nations and international government, and trade.

For each of these categories, Hart examines specific subject headings and compares changes in the number of articles listed over the twenty-five years. The report's findings demonstrate a fairly consistent shift of public interest away from Biblical interpretations and religious authority toward scientific interpretations and empirical evidence as emerging sources of authority. Circulation figures for different types of periodicals, and the number of articles or the rate per 1,000 articles indexed on a given topic heading are presented to compare various trends over the period studied. These showed that discussions in the literature were shifting away from radical positions and absolute principles toward an emphasis on efficiency gained through cooperation.

Moreover, researchers collaborating with Hart used The New York Times Index, to conduct similar investigations on fictional characters and themes in books, short stories motion pictures and plays. These investigations provided Hart with additional substantiating evidence regarding the trends of attention for specific interest areas he found in the periodicals. Hart's research supports the concepts advanced in this dissertation: that popular periodicals tend to reflect shifts in attention given to topics in other types of mass communications. Even though audiences, as consumers, use the diverse communication sources for different personal or social purposes [Katz, 1973], changes in public attention occurring for subject categories in The Readers' Guide tend to be duplicated in other types of mass communications or cultural products. Whether this reflects a process of convergence among audiences toward shared topics of concern, or the competitive structure of different communication sources, the outcome is the same -- a high degree of consistency appears to exist in those subject matters gaining attention in different popular channels of communication.

A review of the four recent investigations may help explain why Hart's preeminent work was forgotten. Meg Greenfield [1961] uses The Readers' Guide to count the annual number of articles listed between 1945 and 1958 under the category "United States -- moral conditions," to locate the "periodic moral crises" occurring in American society. As literary criticism published in The Reporter, Greenfield's discussion would be less likely than academic journals to review Hart's precedent-setting research.

In the second recent work, Howard S. Becker [1963:135-146] investigates the historic social circumstances which led to the passage of the Marihuana Tax Act. Becker examines government documents to establish that the Treasury Department's Bureau of Narcotics was most involved in the enactment of this law. Because state governments in 1936 were not enforcing local laws, the Bureau argue the need for a federal law to ban marihuana which would be supported by "an educational campaign describing the drug, its identification, and evil effect" [quoted by Becker from a Bureau of Narcotics report]. A table showing the number of "marihuana" articles listed in eleven Readers' Guide volumes from 1925 to March, 1959, provide evidence about the success of the campaign to arouse public opinion against marihuana. Becker discusses the implications of the fact that peak attention to the danger of marihuana occurs with seventeen articles appearing between July 1937 and June 1939 -- the time when the federal statute outlawing the use of the substance was enacted. This case study is part of Becker's larger work which develops a theory to explain how people acquire a deviant label.

In the third study, John Mueller [1970: 32-33], extends Greenfield's indicator of "moral concern" to 1968, providing supplemental evidence to validate his main analysis and interpretation of public opinion data about "Presidential Popularity from Truman to Johnson." He finds that an eight-year cycle of heightened attention to moral conditions in the nation closely corresponds to the periods when second-term presidents lose public support. Recurring public anxiety about morals is closely related to a president's loss of popularity consistently followed by elections in which voters select a president from the party that has been out of office.

G. Ray Funkhouser [1973], in the fourth study, selects 12 issues of the 1960's that he determines are either unique for the decade, or appear in responses to the Gallup Poll question repeatedly asking Americans to name the most important problem facing this country. Matching the identified issues with appropriate subject categories in The Readers' Guide, he counts the number of articles that appear annually in Time, Newsweek, and U.S. News and World Report from 1960 through 1970 for an indicator of variations in news coverage. After discussing news reporting practices that can account for the wide range of news attention among issues, Funkhouser examines the relationship between news and peoples' opinions. Eight issues named by Americans since 1964, the first year Gallup includes the "problem" question, are examined to test the "agenda-setting" function of news coverage on public opinion. Chi square analysis indicates that issues receiving high news coverage are more likely to be identified by people as the most important issues. Funkhouser [1973:538] concludes with a statement of importance for future research: "Gallup data may be no more than an indirect content analysis of recent news coverage."

While this evidence suggests that the mass media determine public concern by highlighting certain issues, the finding is inconclusive for untangling the more complex dynamics of the relationship. Funkhouser uses a static form of analysis to verify a positive association between variations in news attention and opinion salience for the eleven-year period. Without comparing these variables for two or more time periods, he cannot distinguish which variable takes precedence in precipitating changes in the other. An adequate test of this crucial distinction requires time series data so that one can perform lead and lag analysis to determine whether or not one variable changes before the other with some degree of consistency. Only with this type of longitudinal analysis done for different issues can we begin to delineate whether increases in news coverage actually "reshape" people's judgment of salient issues, or whether attention in the news merely "reflects" people's concern for salient issues.

This brief review of previous research using Index Content Analysis illustrates that the efforts of investigators -- in developing theory, writing for different audiences, or concentrating on analysis of opinion poll data -- do not necessarily advance the scientific enterprise. But the evidence from these studies does illustrate the various ways in which wholesale content analysis can help to evaluate long-term cultural changes.

2.1.2.2 Strengths and Weaknesses

The most obvious strength of the method is efficiency. The technique of Index Content Analysis allows the researcher to look for trends in attitude shifts, emphasis of interest, emphasis of concern etc. by counting the titles of articles. Although the title of a single article may be misleading, it is assumed that in general the large numbers of titles used will offset these inaccuracies. Our review of previous work provides reason to accept this assumption as does the fact that the indexes are compiled and used by experts in the various fields covered. So there are strong reasons to believe that the articles do in fact correlate with the headings under which they appear in the indexes.

It is important to mention some of the weaknesses that may not appear upon initial consideration of the technique. The indexes place articles under headings if they are related to the heading in a significant way so articles may appear under more than one heading and, thus, overweight a count. This amplification effect, however, partly reflects expansion of interest in a topic and is counteracted by inevitable, accidental omissions in counting. Thus, the phenomena cancel each other.

The data collected from indexes is shaped by the specific index used. Expressions of concern about public health issues in The Readers' Guide to Periodical Literature differ considerably, both in substance and number, from those in The Index to Legal Periodicals. Our methodology accounts for such differences as described in the next section.

2.1.2.3 Application to Specific Indexes

We examined five indexes for expressions of concern relating to our areas of study. They were the Index to Legal Periodicals, The New York Times Index, the Public Affairs Information Service, The Readers' Guide to Periodical Literature, and The Washington Post Index. These indexes reference diverse groups of periodicals so the headings used to classify titles are different in each Index. Sometimes we modified headings to fit more accurately the concept "expression of concern". The index which represented a perspective most dissimilar to that we sought was the Index to Legal Periodicals. Since this index covers primarily professional journals, the headings and articles listed represent professional interest rather than personal concern. However, since trends in lawyer's professional interests may correlate with popular concerns, the Index to Legal Periodicals was examined using its own headings. The index which provided our richest source of data was The Readers' Guide to Periodical Literature. Every volume from 1919 through 1973 was examined extensively.

The indexes studied used different methods of cataloging article titles with respect to date of publication. In some indexes, the Public Affairs Information Service, The New York Times Index, and The Washington Post Index, a volume represented a twelve month period. However, the time periods in the Index to Legal Periodicals were thirty-six months long except for the one ending in 1922 (which was fourteen years long) and the one ending in 1961 (which was thirty-seven months long). The volumes examined in The Readers' Guide to Periodical Literature covered lengths of time varying from twelve months to forty eight months. The longer periods tended to be during earlier times (the forty eight month volume was the one ending in 1928), and the shorter periods were in later times (all volumes from the one ending in 1966 through the one ending in 1973 were twelve months long). We recorded the lengths of time represented by each volume examined in each index and factored these differences into our analysis of the data.

Although The Reader's Guide to Periodical Literature was examined exhaustively for the period from 1920-1973, the other indexes were not. The Washington Post Index currently starts in 1971, so it was examined only in the 1970s. The New York Times Index was examined from 1945 through 1975 in five year increments, except in two areas. The area of consumer products safety was also examined in 1966,1967,1968, and 1969, and the area of Air Quality was covered only through 1965, in The New York Times Index. The Public Affairs Information Service was examined essentially in five year increments from 1915 to 1965. The only exceptions were the first and last periods, 1916 and 1964, respectively. The Index to Legal Periodicals was examined completely from 1955 through 1973 and from 1908 through 1949. The first volume examined in that index was fourteen years long and ended in 1922. The other volumes examined in the Index to Legal Periodicals before 1950 were all thirty-six months long and ended in 1934, 1940, and 1949, respectively.

2.1.2.4 Method of Data Reduction and Analysis

The data provided by Index Content Analysis were counts of titles appearing under given headings in the indexes. The titles counted were only ones which appeared to represent relevant expressions of concern, that is, expressions of concern which might be related to at least one of the five areas studied. Since there were tens of thousands of such counts, they needed to be reduced to manageable size by a method which did not obscure the stories represented by the data. A reduction scheme based on placing counts into appropriate categories would have worked if the categories were known, but they were not. So our first task was to determine what the categories were.

An iterative process of establishing categories and subcategories was used, to reduce the data at each pass. Through this process a set of trees (Figures 2.1.2.4-1, 2.1.2.4-2, 2.1.2.4-3, 2.1.2.4-4, and 2.1.2.4-5) was developed. The categories for each area came from inclusive lists of possible concerns found in all the literature studied. The trees have more types of concerns than were found in the indexes since the process of refinement was stopped when the trees reached a manageable size.

Once the trees contained a set of categories and subcategories small enough to be handled by our data base management system, they were used to reduce the data. This reduction was accomplished by evaluating each expression of concern to determine which category or subcategory best captured the concern(s) involved. Expressions that did not relate to the areas studied were not counted. Expressions that fit easily into a category or subcategory were counted as a whole count in the appropriate part of the tree. Some expressions involved more than one concern and these were counted using a color-coded scheme. That is, if an expression went into more than one category or subcategory, it was recorded by using a color which represented the number of categories and subcategories involved.

A representation of the tree structures was created in an online data base management style. A profile of each time period in each index was then created by entering for each category and subcategory the sum of the counts for that time period and index. This sum was the total of all the counts in a category or subcategory with split counts (counts that went into more than one category or subcategory) divided by the number of categories and subcategories involved. Numbers were rounded up to integer values and entered into the computer. The data then was normalized for twelve month periods. Graphic representations of trends in emphasis of concern over time were then created. A compilation of significant examples of these representations of trends are presented in Appendix F of the report this book is based on [Priest, 1984].

2.1.3 Content Analysis of Legislative Hearings
2.1.3.1 Identification of Hearings

Congressional hearing records on air quality, aviation safety, consumer product safety, occupational health and safety, and pesticides control legislation were examined by content analysis. We used the Congressional Information Service index to locate hearings that preceded the passage of major legislation in each of our five categories. The index provided the name of the committee considering action on relevant legislation and the dates of the hearings. The hearing records, classified by committees, were available at the Government Document Depository of Harvard University. The appropriate hearing records were read for expressions of concern, which were recorded and later reduced and analyzed by the method discussed in

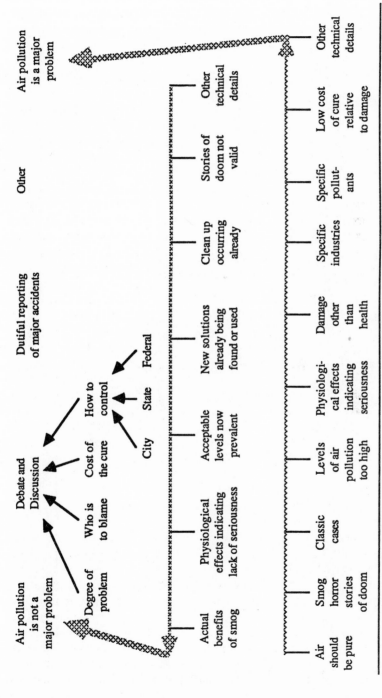

Figure 2.1.2.4-1 Air Quality Concerns
Source: MIT Center for Policy Alternatives, 1984

Each line of subcategories can be traced to a main category above.

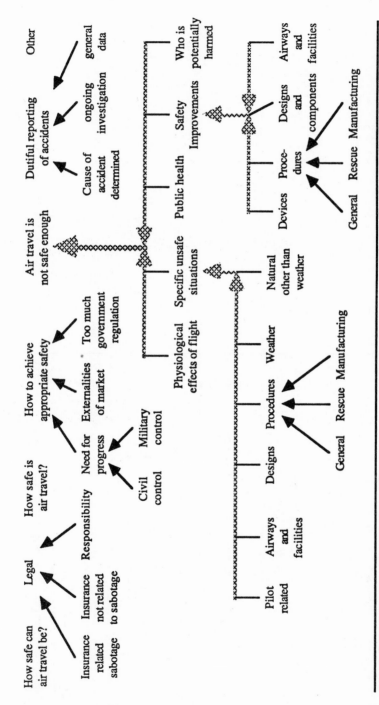

Figure 2.1.2.4-2 Aviation Safety Concerns
Source: *MIT Center for Policy Alternatives, 1984*

Each line of subcategories can be traced to a main category above.

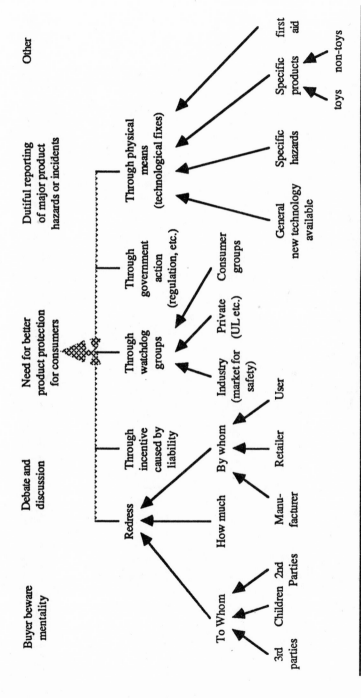

Figure 2.1.2.4-3 Consumer Product Concerns

Source: MIT Center for Policy Alternatives, 1984

Each line of subcategories can be traced to a main category above.

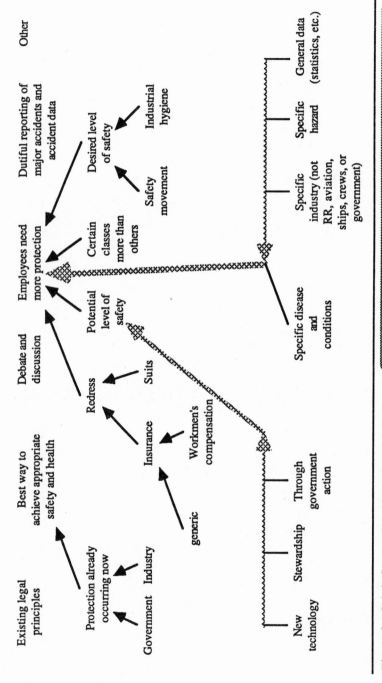

Figure 2.1.2.4-4 Occupational Health and Safety Concerns

Source: MIT Center for Policy Alternatives, 1984

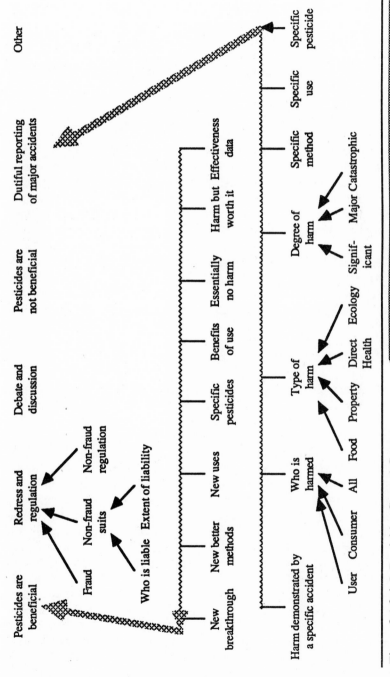

Figure 2.1.2.4-5 Pesticides Control Concern

Source: MIT Center for Policy Alternatives, 1984

Each line of subcategories can be traced to a main category above.

section 2.1.3.3.

Under consumer product safety, for example, the 1953 Flammable Fabrics Act (FFA) and the 1967 FFA Amendments were significant. The 1953 and 1967 House Committees on Interstate and Foreign Commerce, respectively, held hearings on these laws. Accordingly, the Committees' hearing records from the 83rd and 90th Congresses covering this topic were read for expressions of concern.

2.1.3.2 Application to Specific Hearings

After the hearings were selected by the procedure outlined in section 2.1.3.1, the committee records were examined for expressions of concern related to health, safety and the environment. The contents of the hearing records offered the verbatim testimony of witnesses as well as comments made by committee members and aides. The testimony reflected attitudes about different kinds of risks and about methods appropriate to their control.

At the initial stage, expressions of concern were extracted from the documents and recorded. We sought concerns in the form of factual statements, opinions and commentaries, and rhetorical statements. We also noted that questions asked during hearings often were disguised expressions of concern.

2.1.3.3 Method of Data Reduction and Analysis

The data from the hearings consisted of short paraphrases of statements of concern by the participants. We used a weighting scheme to reduce these to counts and place them into appropriate categories. We then totalled the counts in each category and plotted them as histograms.

The categories used to chart data from the hearings differed for each area studied but were uniform for all hearings in a given area. We used a two-step process to establish meaningful categories. We made an initial pass through the data and created an inclusive list of all the major concerns that were expressed. Then we reduced this list to a shorter one by placing similar concerns in the same category. A list of these final categories for each area are provided in the appendix.

The categories then were applied to the paraphrases from the hearings to quantify and locate emphasis of concern. Each statement of concern was read and evaluated for its particular concern components. This evaluation involved determining which type or types of category(ies) the statement belonged to and assessing the strength of the statement itself. If the statement was simply an expression of concern, it received a value of one. If it was a particularly clear statement, it received a two. If it was a persuasive argument, it received a four. If the statement was a convincing argument, it received an eight. To refine analysis further, counts could be split between categories. If a statement belonged to more than one category, the count was split using a color coded scheme.

The counts then were summed for each hearing in each category. We used the information provided by the color code to reduce the value of each count appropriately. If a statement had been placed into more than one category, its value was divided by that number of categories. The summation was accomplished by totalling these values and in all cases rounding up to an integer value. The total values were plotted for each category by hearing in the form of histograms. These are provided in the appendix.

2.1.4 Use of Secondary Literature

Additional knowledge of important events that preceded legislation in our five areas was obtained from secondary literature. We used Index content analysis to map changes in levels of concern and our analysis of the hearings themselves revealed the concerns of the participating Congresspeople and witnesses. Publicized incidents, executive actions, and activities of key individuals that helped shape or were influenced by the type of concerns found in both analyses also were uncovered by the use of secondary literature.

The term "secondary literature" is used to describe books and reports written by advocates and other individuals active in the areas studied. This literature ranges from Nader task force reports to key government reports (such as the National Commission on Product Safety final report) to objective academic histories of events.

An initial search was conducted to compile a working bibliography containing relevant health and safety literature for the five areas. Most books were selected by applying the list of The Reader's Guide search words that were pertinent to the catalogs of MIT libraries, Boston Public Library, and to five entire databases. As other sources were found and used they were added to the bibliography.

The first use of secondary literature was to establish a chronology of enacted legislation in each of the five areas studied. These laws were used to help determine which hearings would be analyzed and as a background to the chronological findings of the index content analysis.

The index content analysis revealed patterns relating the concerns expressed to the legislation passed. In some areas the relationship between the two was not clear and elicited questions about the particular character or intensity of the concerns expressed and about the success or failure of given legislation. To answer these questions it was necessary to research events and changes of attitude occurring at the time in relation to expressed changes in concerns.

Certain findings needed more explanation. In the area of pesticides, for example, content analysis verified that Rachel Carson's book, Silent Spring (1962), raised public concern but it was unclear why related legislation was not passed until ten years later. Concerns expressed about occupational safety and health peaked in the 1930s but the major piece of federal legislation in this area was not enacted until 1970. These anomalies were clarified with the aid of secondary literature.

Secondary literature also was used to uncover peripheral reasons for the passage of health and safety legislation. Societal expressions of concern were paralleled in many cases by extra-Congressional factors in the period prior to legislation being passed. Use of secondary sources uncovered relevant facts that enhanced understanding of the total social context for passage of legislation.

In summary, we used secondary literature to bridge concerns expressed in the index content analysis, views presented in the hearings, and in the actual passage of legislation. Findings from secondary literature contributed significantly to understanding the social forces leading to health and safety legislation.

2.1.5 Interviews

Questions that arose in the course of index content analysis were investigated by the use of secondary literature sources. When these proved insufficient to resolve an issue, we interviewed individuals involved in that particular area and period to gain additional information and, often, new perspectives. This procedure was particularly helpful in the area of occupational health and safety in which general trends in concern were clear but underlying factors often were not. Interviewing subcommittee chairmen present at hearings provided clarifying information.

Interviews followed a loose pattern. We used non-specific questions to guide interviewees toward the general area of concern so that they would speak freely about their involvement. Eventually they were asked about their specific involvement, why they thought the legislation was enacted or a commission created, who was instrumental in these events, and what role the public and media played.

As the interviewees spoke, notes were taken and later transcribed. Information obtained from these people often was not available from other sources. Their personal impressions and first hand information were vital in clarifying the relationships between the concerns expressed in index content analysis, hearing analysis, and legislation.

2.2 Historical Review of Forces Leading to Air Quality Legislation
2.2.1 Historical Context from the Secondary Literature and Interviews (Air Quality)

Legislation to attain and maintain clean air originated on the local level as early as the 1860s but it was not until the latter part of the 1960s that the federal government undertook an active role in this area. This belated spread of jurisdiction from local and state governments to the federal level was prompted by growing scientific knowledge about the potential health risks of air pollution and by steadily rising levels of air contamination.

The earliest concerns about air pollution were provoked by visible particulate matter from factory stacks. In the late 1800s, this type of air pollution gave Pittsburgh the nickname of the "sooty city". Black soot from smoke blanketing industrial areas encouraged local officials to pass cleanup ordinances [Jones, 1975].

But this early legislation was weak: it was rarely enforced and, in any case, failed to provide penalties. One reason for the law's inutility was that areas needing air pollution laws were economically dependent on the industry causing the problem. Legislation was declared invalid by courts for reasons including "unreasonable exercise of police power" and technical impracticality [Jones, 1975]. This lack of legislative and judicial follow-through grew from the same sensibility that defined air pollution as a nuisance rather than as a serious health hazard. Discussions of the period focussed on the economic consequences of smoke, such as destruction of property and vegetation.

In 1940, Saint-Louis was the first city to pass an effective smoke control law. The city was referred to as "spotless" in 1941. Spotless was the adjective of choice because air pollution was identified with smoke and soot. Despite this limited understanding of the problem, there had been a genuine growth of health concerns since the nineteenth century as is shown in the wording of Pittsburgh's first major smoke control ordinance which states that "excessive emission of smoke and the resultant effect upon the public health and welfare require adoption of a comprehensive and integrated plan of smoke control" and that "dense smoke is prohibited and hereby declared a nuisance" [Jones, 1975, p. 23]. To determine density, this law used a visual estimate of the color of the smoke emissions compared to a chart. So while awareness had grown about the dangers to health posed by air pollution, only crude scientific information and technological controls were available.

The affect of air pollution on health was demonstrated to the country dramatically during the week of October 25-31, 1948. In the small town of Donora, Pennsylvania, just south of Pittsburgh, geography, temperature, and lack of wind combined to trap smoke from nearby mills. Production in the mills continued and, by the end of the week, normal town activity had ceased. The air not only had a foul smell and color, it contained dangerous amounts of sulfur dioxide. The US Public Health Service reported that the smog had affected 5,910 people, 42.7 percent of the total population. Of these 2,322 were moderately affected, and 1,440 were severely affected with various degrees of nausea, headaches, abdominal pain, choking, and coughing up blood. Twenty people died during or shortly after the disaster which was highly publicized [Esposito, 1970].

Air pollution in the worst areas spread beyond city boundaries calling for intervention on the state level. California was the first state to pass an air pollution law. As individual areas successfully reduced smoke and large particles in the air, the extent and complexity of the problem became more apparent, as in the awareness that invisible gases as well as particulate matter were implicated. Research was needed but state and local resources were inadequate [Esposito, 1970].

Harry Truman was the first president to recognize officially that the federal government should assist in research, noting however that "responsibilities for corrective action ... are primarily local in character" [Jones, 1975]. Ambivalence about the federal role postponed action until the next administration when the secretary of the Department of Health, Education, and Welfare appointed an Interdepartmental Committee on Community Air Pollution. The Committee recommended that a federal program of research and technical assistance be set up in the fall of 1954. Buttressed by the interest of some senators and President Eisenhower, a bill asserting state and local "rights and responsibilities" to control air pollution passed with little debate and was signed on July 14, 1955. The extent of Eisenhower's concern about the problem was reflected in his public health message to Congress on January 31, 1955, when he said "some population centers may be approaching the limit of their ability to absorb air pollutants with safety to health."

Concern, research, federal legislation: this abbreviates the process of implementing controls on air pollution which, at each stage, generated considerable debate. Discussion on the control of automobile emissions was a microcosm for the entire air pollution problem from the late '50s to mid '60s. On March 3, 1953, Ford Motor Company said that its engineering staff did not feel that exhaust gases represented an air pollution problem. Kenneth Hahn, a Los Angeles county supervisor, disagreed. In 1953 he said automobile emissions contributed to smog a "considerable degree"; in 1954, that they were "a major factor in producing smog"; in 1956, that "scientific evidence" determined they were "the largest single uncontrolled source of air pollution"; and, by 1958, that "harmful exhaust fumes from automobiles" were the "major source of pollution of the air in Los Angeles County" [Hahn, 1968].

While Hahn understood the nature of the problem, research on the effects of automobile exhaust was still needed. In 1958, congressional advocates of extended federal efforts to control vehicle pollution held hearings before the House Committee on Interstate and Foreign Commerce. Testimony by the Secretary of DHEW and the chief of its Air Pollution Medical Program suggested that there was not enough scientific information available to enforce the act and advised that it not be passed. The bill that finally passed in 1960 provided for more research by the Surgeon General and the Public Health Service on the health effects of motor vehicle emissions. By 1962 a report entitled "Motor Vehicles, Air Pollution, and Health" was finished. Surgeon General Luther L. Terry stated that the report made clear that "research has shown that automobile emissions do produce adverse effects on human health and other biological systems" [Esposito, 1970]. This report was instrumental in passing the 1965 Motor Vehicle Air Pollution Control Act, which gave federal government authority to set emission standards effective in 1968 for new automobiles.

The movement toward federal legislation was in part due to the increasing knowledge of how automobile emissions damage health. Support for regulation in this area also was swelled by the industry's desire for uniform standards between states so as to avoid manufacturing difficulties [Stewart, 1978]. In fact, industry pressure may explain the relative ease with which the 1965 legislation overturned the traditional jurisdiction of states in this area.

The federal role in comprehensive air pollution legislation developed in three successive acts. The Clean Air Act of 1963 was the first time the government advanced beyond its role as researcher. The act provides for grants to the states and provides an abatement procedure for use in interstate pollution incidents. Still, the Clean Air Act by itself was less an extension of the federal role than consistent with its traditional limits in that DHEW could provide only advisory rather than mandatory air quality criteria. The abatement procedure also was more symbolic than instrumental, providing a cumbersome line of enforcement. In seven years it was used only eleven times, and only once led to enforcement action [Esposito, 1970].

During the mid-sixties, Thomas Williams, the public information officer for the air pollution activities of DHEW, directed his efforts to raising citizen awareness of the problem so as to enlist support for stronger action. The Nader Task Force Report in 1970 commented that "much of our knowledge and concern about air pollution today is a direct result of his [Williams'] lonely campaign" [Esposito, 1970]. On Thanksgiving Day in 1966, these efforts coincided with specific air pollution hazards to call attention to New York City where unseasonably warm temperatures precipitated an air pollution disaster which claimed 150 to 175 lives.

Shortly after this event, S. Smith Griswold, federal abatement chief for the National Air Pollution Control Administration, convened a conference on air pollution in the New York City metropolitan area. The New Jersey-New York Abatement Conference, the first step in the Clean Air Act's abatement procedure, began January, 1967. The "New York Times" published the names of the 373 largest polluters in the area, which created considerable discomfort. The conference advanced public education, and led to new legislation in New Jersey and New York.

The year 1967 also marked the passage of the Air Quality Act which required states to adopt air quality standards and implementation plans to achieve these standards, both subject to DHEW approval. Although Senator Muskie, who chaired the hearings, proclaimed it to be comprehensive legislation, its enforcement provisions showed it to be more a compromise than a reform. For example, the Air Quality Act kept the 1963 abatement procedure and, while it reflected a belief that state and local pollution control was inadequate, it did not redistribute authority accordingly. Reasons for this included the feeling that the federal role still should be limited to directing state attention to the problem and that centralization would be both costly and inadequate because of varying local conditions. Some argued that rigid standards would be unenforceable [Stewart, 1978]. Moreover, the Public Health Service was reluctant to take power from states because of its desire to keep good relations with state and local officials [Jones, 1975].

Others (including Ralph Nader's foundation and some environmental groups) saw different reasons for congressional and state reluctance, for example, the dependence of certain areas on polluting industries for jobs and taxes. Also, it was felt that pollution control programs suffered from "lack of money, lack of personnel, lack of legislation, and lack of will." [Esposito, 1970]. In addition to these arguments, advocates of greater federal intervention noted that air pollution was getting worse and abatement was essential. But in 1969, the National Air Pollution Control Administration still maintained that air pollution was primarily the responsibility of state and local government.

While this debate continued, public concerns about the environment grew quickly and congressional interest followed. In 1969, the National Environmental Policy Act was passed, requiring environmental impact statements from all government agencies on the environmental effects of any new project. This was the period when the Nader report called the environmental bandwagon "the cheapest ride in town." Environmental degradation had become one of the "foremost topics of public concern" [Esposito, 1970, p. 305]. Lobbying by environmental groups, especially Environmental Action, was instrumental in 1970.

Structural reform of government agencies followed. Many Congressmen felt that NAPCA was ineffective for many reasons including insufficient and misapplied funds [Stewart, 1978]. With only two men on NAPCA's automobile surveillance, vehicle emissions still were not monitored adequately, much less controlled. Ad hoc House hearings held at the end of 1969 on automobile pollution reported that the automobile was predominantly responsible for air pollution. In 1969, an air pollution emergency in Chicago took approximately one hundred lives. Also important in sustaining the public's feelings of urgency was the formation, by executive action, of the Environmental Protection Agency in 1970.

President Nixon heightened public focus on the problem when, in February 1970, he mentioned air pollution in his State of the Union address and, shortly thereafter, proposed a new air pollution bill with strict enforcement. Senator Muskie followed by introducing his own bill and holding hearings. With much debate and compromise, a final bill was passed and signed on December 31, 1970.

The Clean Air Act Amendments of 1970 greatly extended federal responsibility for the control of air pollution. EPA was required to develop air quality standards and given a new mechanism for enforcement, more direct than that of the 1963 act. Stronger standards for automobile emissions were set, and control of new stationary source polluters was given to the federal government. This legislation was a watershed for federal control of air pollution.

2.2.2 Findings from Index Content Analysis (Air Quality)

The indexes demonstrated similar trends from 1960: growing concern, peaking in the early 1970s, that air pollution was a major problem. The Readers' Guide clearly also shows an earlier, qualitatively different wave of concern about air pollution peaking in 1935 (Figures 2.2.2-1 and 2.2.2-2). The following presentation discusses significant trends in this area by using the categories of the tree structures described in section 2.1.2.4. Numbers in parentheses represent expressions of concern for a typical year in the period described. They are presented here to provide a better sense of variations in the relative strengths of concerns about air pollution expressed during the time period described. The trends illustrated by these numbers are analogous to the trends graphically represented here and in appendix F. Statistically insignificant numerical differences result from the rounding off used to create the graphs.

The Index to Legal Periodicals showed no significant concerns through 1949. In the 1952-1955 period the first, small signs of interest were under 'air pollution is a major problem' (1). In 1955-1958 'debate and discussion' 3), all in or under 'how to control,' was the only significant area. The period of 1958-1961 saw a decrease in overall concern with the category,

Figure 2.2.2-1 Citizens' Concerns that Air Quality is a Major Problem
(Concern for Air Quality)
Source: The Readers' Guide to Periodic Literature index, Level 1

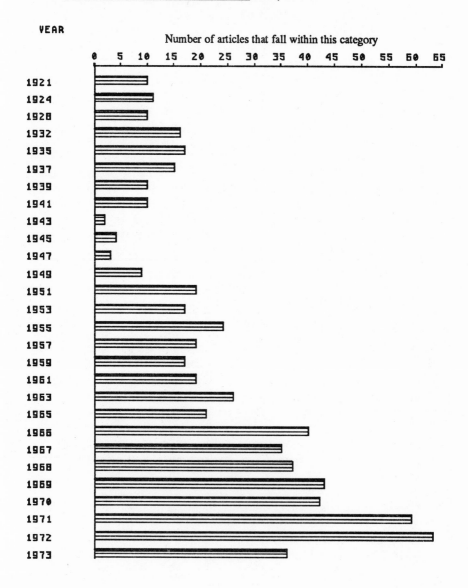

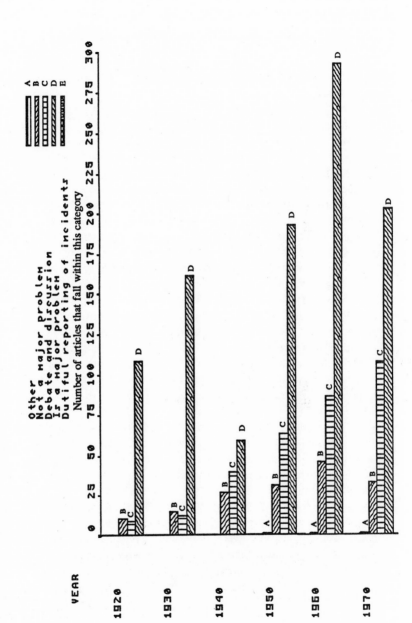

Figure 2.2.2-2 Citizens' Concerns about Air Quality
(Concern for Air Quality)

Source: The Readers' Guide to Periodic Literature index, Level 1

'debate and discussion' remaining most significant (1). The category, 'air pollution is a major problem' was small, but significant (1). The period of 1961-1964 saw further overall decreases. The category of 'debate and discussion' was the only area with expressions of concern (1), all in or under 'how to control.' The same trends continued in the 1964-1967 period. The period of 1967-1970 had dramatic change. The category of 'debate and discussion' was the main area (12), with essentially all the expressions of concern in or under 'how to control.' Most of this was direct, but a significant amount was in 'federal' (2). The only other significant general area was 'air pollution is a major problem' (5). The period of 1970-1973 saw overall decreases, with the two previous categories, 'debate and discussion' (6), and 'air pollution is a major problem' (4), still significant.

The New York Times Index had nothing in 1945. The period of 1950 was significant in all areas. The category of 'air pollution is not a major problem' (5) had essentially all (4) in direct expressions of concern. The category of 'debate and discussion' was the main area (70), most in direct expressions of concern (43), the rest under 'how to control,' split between 'city' and 'state.' The category of 'air pollution is a major problem' was substantial (18), most in direct expressions of concern (15). The period of 1955 was different than 1950. The category of 'air pollution is not a major problem' (9) had most of its expressions of concern in 'new solutions' (6), with the rest in direct expressions of concern. The category of 'air pollution is a major problem' (22) had most its expressions of concern in 'classic cases' (13), and the rest in direct expressions of concern. The main area was 'debate and discussion' (62), with the most in 'city' (40) under 'how to control.' Essentially the rest was split between 'degree of problem' (13), and 'federal' (7) under 'how to control.' The period of 1960 was similar to 1955 in character, but there were some differences. There were no direct expressions of concern in 'air pollution is not a major problem.' There were no expressions of concern in 'degree of problem,' or 'classic cases,' and there were expressions of concern in 'levels too high' (3). The category of 'debate and discussion' remained about the same. The category of 'air pollution is not a major problem' was cut in half. The category of 'air pollution is a major problem' dropped to 1/3 its previous value. The period of 1965 was quite different. There were only two (2) expressions of concern in 'air pollution is not a major problem.' The category of 'is a major problem' grew (32), with no direct expressions of concern. They were all in 'specific industries' (23), or 'physiological effects' (9). The category of 'debate and discussion' became quite numerous (130) with expressions of concern in the typical areas of direct, 'degree of problem,' and under 'how to control.' The emphasis was in the typical category of 'city' (81).

The Public Affairs Information Service had little until 1964. In 1964 'debate and discussion' (14) was the most numerous. Most expressions of concern were in or under 'how to control' (12). The category of 'air pollution is a major problem' (8) had the emphasis in 'physiological effects' (5).

The Readers' Guide had substantive expressions of concern in 1921 only in or under 'air pollution is a major problem' (10), with the majority of expressions of concern in 'specific pollutants' (6), and a substantial amount in direct expressions of concern. The period of 1924 was more typical of later periods, in that there were expressions of concern in all three main areas, with by far the most in 'air pollution is a major problem.' The periods of 1924 and 1928 were similar, (1,1) in the 'air pollution is not a major problem' and 'debate and discussion' areas. There were strong expressions of concern in the 'air pollution is a major problem category (10,8) spread out in many categories below, but primarily in 'specific pollutants' (6,8). The period of 1932 was similar to previous year, but with a resurgence of direct (2) 'air pollution is a major problem' expressions of concern, an increase in 'physiological effects' (2) under this category, and a slight growth in 'debate and discussion' (2). The period of 1935 was a cross between 1921 and 1924. It had very little in anything but 'air pollution is a major problem,' with an emphasis on 'specific pollutants' (8 out of 17).

The period of 1937 saw a decrease in 'air pollution is a major problem' (16), and an increase under 'air pollution is not a major problem' (2), all in 'new solutions.' Most of the expressions of concern under 'air pollution is not a major problem' had been in this category. The few that had not been were in 'clean up ' The spread under 'air pollution is a major problem' in 1937 was typical of previous years. The period of 1939 was similar to 1937 in the main areas except 'air pollution is a major problem' This area saw continued decrease (9), with spread similar to 1932. The period of 1941 was similar to 1939 in all main areas except 'debate and discussion,' which grew (9) to almost equal to 'air pollution is a major problem' (10). The category of 'air pollution is not a major problem' remained essentially unchanged (2). The spreads were typical, with the emphasis in 'debate and discussion' being 'city' (4) under 'how to control,' and 'degree of problem' (3) 1943 saw greatly reduced expressions of concern everywhere, except 'air pollution is not a major problem' (2), with all in 'new solutions' as usual. The other main areas were reduced drastically. These were the categories of 'debate and discussion' (1), and 'air pollution is a major problem' (2). These had the typical emphasis, as far as could be determined from the low activity. The period of 1945 was similar to 1941, with slight growth in 'debate and discussion' (3), with the emphasis in 'degree of problem' (2). The period of 1947 was similar to 1945, but with a shift of emphasis form 'degree of problem' to 'city,' under 'debate and discussion.' The period of 1949 was similar to 1947, but with some noticeable changes. The category of 'air pollution is a major problem' grew (9), with an emphasis in direct expressions of concern (3). Also 'debate and discussion' (3) was split evenly between 'degree of problem,' direct 'how to control,' and 'city' under 'how to control.' Also 'classic cases' (2) was as high as 'specific pollutants' (2).

The period of 1951 saw major increases in 'air pollution is a major problem' (13) and 'debate and discussion' (7). Spreads were typical, except for an emphasis in 'classic cases' (5) under 'air pollution is a major problem.' But, 'specific pollutants' (4) was still high. The period of 1953 had barely anything significant in any area or sub area, except in or under 'air pollution is a major problem.' In that category almost every subcategory was significant as were direct expressions of concern. The area was comparable in size to 1951. The period of 1955 was similar to 1951, but with an emphasis in 'physiological effects' (8) under 'air pollution is a major problem' (22). In 1957 'debate and discussion' remained about the same, 'air pollution is not a major problem' doubled (5), and 'air pollution is a major problem' remained almost as large (19).

The period of 1959 saw decreased expressions of concern all around. It looked very much like 1932, except for a shift of emphasis under 'air pollution is a major problem' away from 'specific pollutants' and 'physiological effects too high' to 'levels too high' and 'specific industries.' The period of 1961 was similar to 1959, except for nearly doubling (5) in 'new solutions under 'air pollution is not a major problem.' Also there was a focusing in 'physiological effects' and 'specific industries' under 'air pollution is a major problem' 1963 was similar to 1959 in the main areas, except that 'air pollution is not a major problem' contained no expressions of concern. Also the spreads were different. The category of 'debate and discussion' (3) was predominantly direct (2). The spread in and under 'air pollution is a major problem' (25) was in 'physiological effects' (9), 'specific industries' (6), direct expressions of concern (4), 'specific pollutants' (3). The period of 1965 saw a return to typical expressions of concern under 'air pollution is not a major problem' (2), mostly in 'new solution' (1). The category of 'debate and discussion' (4) was fairly typical, with most in 'how to control' (3). But 'air pollution is a major problem' (21) now emphasized 'specific industries' (8), and had very substantial activity in 'air should be pure' (5).

The period of 1966 showed increases in the overall numbers of expressions of concern. The category of 'debate and discussion' (7) was different in that it emphasized 'federal' (5) under 'how to control' (7) for the first time. The category of 'air pollution is a major problem (40) now emphasized 'air should be pure' (15). The category of 'specific industries' (11) was still high. The period of 1967 had almost nothing under 'air pollution is not a major problem' (2). The category of 'debate and discussion' (21) grew dramatically, with most in 'how to control' direct (14), but there was also an emergence of 'who is to blame' (5). The category of 'air pollution is a major problem' (35) dropped slightly, with a shift of emphasis away from 'air should be pure'

(0) and 'specific industries' (4), to 'physiological effects' (13) and direct (11). The period of 1968 saw a return to moderate expressions of concern under 'air pollution is not a major problem' (15), with most in 'new solution' (12) as usual. Expressions of concern in and under 'debate and discussion' and 'air pollution is a major problem' remained approximately the same as in 1967, but the expressions of concern were spread into almost all the subcategories. The only categories left empty in these main areas were 'city' and 'state' under 'how to control' under 'debate and discussion,' and 'smog stories of doom' and 'low relative cost of cure' under 'air pollution is a major problem.' The period of 1969 was similar to 1968, with reduced expressions of concern in and under 'air pollution is not a major problem' (6), slightly reduced levels in and under 'debate and discussion' (17), and slightly increased expressions of concern in and under 'air pollution is a major problem' (41). Also now the only empty categories under 'debate and discussion' and 'air pollution is a major problem' were 'state,' and 'levels too high' and 'low relative cost of cure.' Also there were no direct expressions of concern. The period of 1970 was a return to old patterns in and under 'air pollution is not a major problem' and 'debate and discussion,' with 'new solution' (5), and 'how to control' (3), and nothing else in or under these main areas. The category of 'air pollution is a major problem' (42) remained at 1969 levels, with a shift to direct (11) concern. The rest were spread out similarly to 1969.

The period of 1971 saw more than a doubling of expressions of concern in 'new solution' (13) under 'air pollution is not a major problem' (14). The category of 'air pollution is a major problem' (60) increased substantially, with a typical spread. But the big story in 1970 was a sudden dramatic increase in and under 'debate and discussion' (57). This was spread out, but with 'state' and 'federal' empty and 'who is to blame' (27) emphasized. The period of 1972 saw a return to almost typical expressions of concern in and under 'air pollution is not a major problem' (9), with 'new solution' (8), and almost typical expressions of concern in and under 'controversy' (21), and direct expressions of concern in 'how to control' (17). The category of 'air pollution is a major problem' (55) remained about the same, with a similar spread as in 1971, except for a moderate emphasis in 'specific pollutants' (23). The period of 1973 saw reduced levels in 'air pollution is not a major problem' (4). The category of 'debate and discussion' (23) remained about the same. Both areas had spreads similar to 1972. The category of 'air pollution is a major problem' (35) was also reduced from 1972 levels. The spread in this category was similar to 1972, except for an absence of expressions of concern in 'smog stories of doom' and an absence of direct expressions of concern.

The Washington Post Index had the area of 'air pollution is not a major problem' empty during the entire period studied. In 1971 'debate and discussion' (13), and 'air pollution is a major problem' (19) were both significant. The category of 'debate and discussion was dominated by 'how to control' direct (11). The category of 'air pollution is a major problem' had emphasis in 'physiological effects' (7), and 'damage other than health' (9). The period of 1972 was similar in and under 'debate and discussion' (21), but at higher levels. The category of 'air pollution is a major problem' (29) increased also, but saw a shift of emphasis to 'levels too high' (16). The category of 'specific industries' (6), and 'specific pollutants' (6) were also significant. In 1973 'debate and discussion was as in 1971. The category of 'air pollution is a major problem' (43) grew and had a shift of emphasis to 'specific industries' (24). The category of 'levels too high' (12) was also significant. The period of 1974 saw a drastic reduction in 'air pollution is a major problem' (12), with emphasis split between 'specific industries' (6) and 'physiological effects' (5). The category of 'debate and discussion' (28) grew substantially, with the emphasis still in 'how to control' direct (19), but with 'degree of problem' (9) playing a significant role. The period of 1975 was similar to 1974, except the emphasis in 'air pollution is a major problem' (13) shifted to 'levels too high' (8) and 'damage other than health' (4). Also direct expressions of concern in 'how to control' (13) were reduced slightly under 'debate and discussion' (24). The period of 1976 was similar to 1974 in 'debate and discussion' level and spread. The category of 'air pollution is a major problem' was similar to 1975. In 1977 'debate and discussion' (17) was reduced, but its spread remained the same. The category of 'air pollution is a major problem' (12) was reduced to a lesser extent, with the expressions of concern primarily split between 'levels too high' (5) and 'physiological effects' (5). The period of 1978 saw a sudden boost in 'how to control' (21) (20 in direct expressions of concern) under 'debate and discussion' (26). The category of 'air pollution is a major problem'(9) saw a further slight reduction. These expressions of concern were split between 'physiological effects' (4), 'damage other than health' (3), and 'levels too high' (2). The period of 1979 had a drastic reduction in 'debate and discussion' (6), split between 'degree of problem' (3) and 'how to control' direct (3). The category of 'air pollution is a major problem' (12) had moderate growth, but much of this was in 'other technical details' (6). Also 'physiological effects' (5) was significant.

2.2.3 Findings from Content Analysis of Hearings (Air Quality)

Hearings from the 1955 Senate Committee on Public Works centered on strengthening the water pollution control act. The latter parts of the testimony considered amending the water pollution control act in order to provide for the control of air pollution. Testimony stressed the availability of new technology and the need for administrative action to coordinate research and control. Primary concerns were inadequate data about the full extent of the physiological effects of air pollution and the dwindling supply of a precious natural resource (clean air). There was growing public concern that contaminated air was a dangerous problem.

In 1958, the House Committee on Interstate and Foreign Commerce held hearings on a bill that would prohibit motor vehicles from discharging dangerous levels of unburned hydrocarbons. Testimony and discussion stressed specific pollutants (unburned hydrocarbons and nitrogen oxide), their cause (motor vehicles) and physiological effects, and the need for administrative action.

The 1963 House Committee on Interstate and Foreign Commerce hearings focused primarily on the physiological effects and societal costs of air pollution. Fears were expressed about its worsening and there was increased awareness of its harmful effects on animals and vegetation as well as human beings. These hearings also discussed Federal responsibilities to protect clean air ("any pollution control which is to be really effective has to originate at the Federal level").

In 1963-1964, Edmund Muskie chaired hearings of the Senate Special Subcommittee on Air and Water Pollution. The hearings began in Washington and were continued in six different cities. Once again, the physiological effects of air pollution were a major topic of discussion: "Episodes of acute illness and death are serious but of even greater concern is the problem of the long-term effects." Speakers presented considerable data about the societal costs of air pollution and about the Federal Government's role in cleaning air. any specific pollutants were mentioned during the hearings.

The 1967 Senate Special Subcommittee on Air and Water Pollution hearings centered on efforts to remedy the costs to society from air contaminants, especially hydrocarbons from automobiles and waste from industrial plants. These hearings led to passage of the Air Quality Act of 1967.

The 1968 Senate Special Subcommittee on Air and Water Pollution conducted hearings to consider further regulatory action by the Federal Government. The premise of the hearings was that there was ample evidence about health damage to justify federal control of air pollution.

Costs to society and physiological effects from air pollution were discussed frequently throughout the 1969 Senate Special Subcommittee on Air and Water Pollution hearings (Figure 2.2.3-1) held in St. Louis. One emphasis was measures to protect the health of children. Consensus opinion favored intensive federal effort because of the severity of the problem and inadequate action by many States. Also emphasized was increased funding to research health effects.

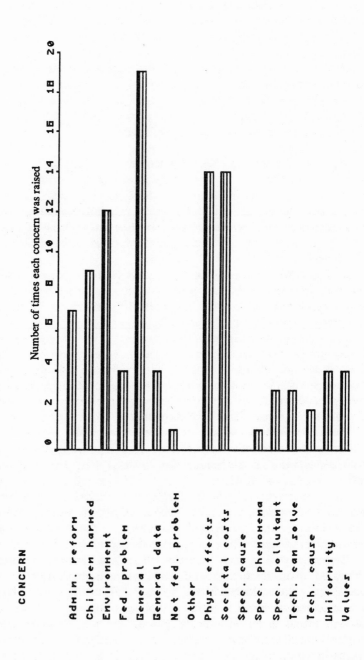

Figure 2.2.3-1 Legislators' Concerns about Air Quality
(Concern for Air Quality)

Source: 1969 Senate Hearings on Air and Water Pollution

The 1970 Senate Special Subcommittee on Air and Water Pollution hearings continued public discussion about the physiological and environmental effects and costs to society from air pollution. Social values, technological solutions, and the need for administrative action also were debated.

A large part of the hearing dwelt on the technical feasibility of reducing air pollution. One witness suggested that solving the pollution problem required considering the value of human life, of the environment, and of raw materials to future generations. Extensive concerns for the quality of life were expressed, especially for children and the elderly.

2.2.4 Summary (Air Quality)

The findings summarized in the three preceding sections show that a trend of growing concern about air pollution started late in the nineteenth century and continued, with only one interruption, into the 1970s. During this period the character of the concern changed: early concerns concentrated on the problems of urban centers and, although statements that air pollution could have serious health effects were found, the prevailing sense was that air pollution was merely a nuisance. This attitude gradually changed to awareness that air pollution was a not only a national but a global problem.

After a small peak in the mid 1930s, there was a lessening in expressed concern from the late 1930s through the 1940s. In addition to preoccupation with the economy and then, the War, the mid '30s saw the first successful efforts to control urban pollution and these may have persuaded people that the problem was being solved. In any case, it is clear that no such feeling existed after 1950, as evidenced by President Eisenhower's address of January 31, 1955, cited above.

From our analysis of congressional hearings, it is clear that by 1955 the Federal government felt it should participate in controlling air pollution. Its role initially was established by the 1955 Air Pollution Control Act, under whose provisions Washington would aid the states with research and technical assistance. By the late 1950s, even though the federal government had recognized that automobiles were a significant source of air pollution, the federal emphasis remained research (the 1960 Motor Vehicle Act provided for research only, on air pollution from autos).

During the 1960s, knowledge about the effects and causes of air pollution increased dramatically and environmental concerns became a significant social and political force. The 1960s also were marked by legislation which increased federal involvement in air pollution control. The first act to give an active role to the federal government was the Clean Air Act of 1963 whose limited abatement procedures were noted above as was the steadily increasing concern for air quality expressed in the popular literature. There were small peaks of concern at the passage of each act, but the overall trend of gradually increasing concern continued until 1970.

Following the Clean Air Act Amendments of 1970, there was a dramatic increase (nearly double that of the 1960s) in concerns expressed in the popular literature. Three aspects of this period distinguish it from earlier times.   First, it now was accepted that the federal government should control air pollution.   Second, pollution was identified not as a nuisance to be "absorbed" by the air but as something that "degraded the environment". Accordingly and third, air pollution had become a major political issue as part of what Ralph Nader referred to as 'the environmental bandwagon.' President Nixon reaffirmed the importance of the issue when he proposed a new strict air pollution bill early in 1970.

By 1970 the scientific community, the populace at large, and both the executive and legislative branches of the federal government seemed to agree that strict federal control of air pollution was needed and debate shifted to the appropriate means. By the end of 1970, executive and legis-lative efforts were coordinated.   Strict federal air pollution control measures became law and were implemented by the newly formed Environmental Protection Agency.

2.3 Historical Review of Forces Leading to Aviation Safety Legislation
    2.3.1 Historical Context from the Secondary Literature
        and Interviews (Aviation Safety)

As a transportation industry, aviation in the United States has been regulated and encouraged by the government almost since its inception early in the twentieth century. Early regulations served to speed industry growth; the rapid expansion of air traffic made them essential for safety as well.

World War I occasioned the first mass production of aircraft and pilots, resources which catalyzed commercial air travel. The federal government provided the first commercial use when the Post Office Department established a regular airmail service (staffed by army pilots) even before the war ended [Burkhardt, 1967]. At this time, the Post Office completely controlled airmail service: it owned the planes, hired the pilots, and, by 1924, ran regularly scheduled transcontinental flights. The success of airmail service proved the airplane's economic value and inaugurated commercial aviation.

Several groups with distinct agenda sought federal involvement in aviation in its early years. World War I had alerted the armed forces to the manifold uses of aircraft to wage and deter war. During hearings on civil aviation in 1921 before a Subcommittee of the Committee on Commerce, it was asserted that a strong civil industry would support the military's need for an established air infrastructure: trained pilots, operating runways, navigational aids, and ongoing technological improvements. The military urged government to encourage civil aviation.

Civilian pilots also sought federal aid in promoting and regulating aviation. In 1912, the Aero Club of America recommended that the government register aircraft and license pilots, practices fulfilled by the club until 1926 [Burkhardt, 1967]. Some aviators feared that their group as a whole was being discredited by accidents during barnstorming carnivals. In hearings before the House of Representatives in 1924, Godfrey L. Cabot, President of the National Aeronautic Association, testified that personal friends and fellow pilots, all good flyers, had crashed to their death due to structural defects in their airplanes. This testimony further boosted sentiment to require airworthiness certification.

In 1926, the federal government passed the Air Commerce Act which gave government the responsibility of operating and maintaining the nation's airways by providing navigational aids and safety regulations. To enact these provisions, the government established the Bureau of Air Commerce in the Department of Commerce. Registration of airplanes and licensing of pilots were among the first safety regulations [Kane, 1977].

The airmail service, which had been the economic engine of aviation, also led to a controversy which dramatized the need for better safety regulations. The Kelly Airmail Act of 1925 had provided for competitive bidding in granting airmail contracts. By 1930, Postmaster General Walter Brown believed that intense competition for contracts had led to price undercutting which diminished investment in new equipment and undermined safety and industry growth [Kane, 1977, p. 5-7]. To remedy this situation and to fulfill the government's mandate to encourage aviation, Brown supported passage of the Airmail Act of 1930 which provided for ten-year contracts to airmail carriers.

In 1933, a House Committee headed by Representative Hugo Black held hearings to investigate whether collusion on airmail contracts had taken place. The committee found that air commerce indeed had been poorly served by Brown's approach [Kane,1977]. In January 1934, Black asked President Roosevelt to suspend all contracts. James Farley, the new Postmaster General, duly so ordered and directed the army to fly the mail on a reduced schedule. From February 9 to June 1, the Army Air Corps carried airmail with disasterous results. Sixty-six crashes led to 12 deaths and an outraged country. Newsweek expressed this dismay in its story, "Airmail: Nation Protests Deaths of Army Postman as Congress Plays out Drama of Contracts" [Newsweek, 1934]. President Roosevelt called for a solution.

These policy reversals and accidents changed the structure of air traffic in America. The airlines decided that future growth lay not in airmail but in passenger service. Although passenger service revenues in 1934 were insignificant, by the end of 1936 they exceeded income from airmail [Kane, 1977]. Concomitantly, a need developed for a new regulatory system to serve an industry which had become a major part of American life.

To solve the airmail problem and consider future needs, the Airmail Act of 1934 was passed. This Act established new regulations on competition and also created a Federal Aviation Commission to study national aviation policy. Headed by Clarke Howell, the commission's report recommended the creation of an independent agency with the authority to regulate safety and marketing practices. But President Roosevelt did not support the call for this new agency and no legislation resulted.

At the same time, former Secretary of War, Newton Baker headed a committee to recommend improvements in the Army Air Corps. One concern leading to federal involvement was Europe's lead in aviation. The Committee's report, which showed that the US led in every area of aviation except military, led to more funding for the army but also revealed the rapid growth of America's civilian air industry.

From 1934-8 Congressional hearings continued on how better to regulate air travel for safety. The airlines worried that air travel was acquiring an image that intimidated potential passengers. Witnesses testified during 1936 hearings on air safety that regulations were needed to keep airlines from compromising safety to remain profitable.

On the other hand, the Aeronautical Chamber of Commerce, an association of airplane manufacturers, felt that uncoordinated government regulations that were difficult to implement threatened safety more than alleged structural defects. They argued that better regulation could solve the problem.

David L. Behcke, President of the Air Line Pilots Association, voiced the concern of his group that the government establish an independent board to promote safety regulations.

The result of these hearings was the Civil Aeronautics Act of 1938. Its stated purpose confirmed the traditional federal role: "the encouragement and development of a commercial air transportation system. . ." [Burkhardt, 1967]. This law empowered an independent agency, the Civil Aeronautics Authority, to regulate safety and economic issues. Within the Authority, an Air Safety Board was created to investigate accidents and to recommend safety regulations. However, it could not issue regulations. This consolidated oversight into one agency that would give its full attention to the needs of an expanding industry.

In 1940, the air regulatory system was reorganized. A five-member board, independent of any governmental agency, received authority to investigate accidents and create regulations. The Civil Aeronautics Authority became the Civil Aeronautics Administration (CAA). It was returned to the Department of Commerce and headed by an administrator who could not issue but, rather, executed safety regulations and operated the entire airways system [Kane,1977].

Meanwhile, industry expansion had created new safety issues. Airports that could handle more flights per day were needed. Navigational aids such as better radio communications were developed by the CAA which also standardized inspection and licensing procedures. In addition, public airports were deemed to be necessary for national defense (previously, airports had been owned and maintained privately or by local authorities) and, in October 1940, Congress appropriated funds for the construction and maintenance of public fields [Burkhardt, 1967, p.171].

As new issues were recognized and addressed, better coordination of government policies became necessary. President Truman accordingly created a study group in July 1947 to assist in formulating an integrated air policy. The commission's report "Survival in the Air Age" suggested strengthening of the military air services and incorporating all safety functions into one agency with an independent investigatory board. Another study group was set up by President Eisenhower in 1955. Its report stated that there was a crisis in air traffic management and recommended that an individual be assigned full-time to develop a program to deal with the complex problems facing the industry [Burkhardt, 1967]. The person selected was Edward P. Curtis.

During this period, airspace congestion increased as did the lack of coordination between military and civil flying. Government oversight did not keep up with "aviation's dynamic growth" [Burkhardt, 1967]. There were several major mid-air accidents in the mid-fifties, including, in June, 1956, a collision between two airliners. In May, 1957, Curtis submitted his report warning that the CAA's airspace management system was unable to cope with civil and military traffic. He recommended that an independent agency be formed to address civil and military needs.

In 1957 Congress responded (after hearings chaired by Senator Mike Monroney) by passing the Airways Modernization Act which provided for the development and modernization of traffic control facilities and navigational aids. The Federal Aviation Act was signed in August, 1958, forming the Federal Aviation Agency (FAA) whose purpose also was to improve aviation safety [Kane, 1977]. Formation of a new agency demonstrated the importance with which legislators viewed aviation.

The FAA remained an independent agency until 1966 when the Transportation Act renamed it the Federal Aviation Administration under the new Department of Transportation. This was the last major piece of legislation affecting aviation until the Airport and Airway Development Act of 1970. Other issues with major impact on aviation during the late fifties and sixties were handled by the FAA.

The beginning of jet travel caused safety concerns at the time of the Federal Aviation Act. The speed of jets and their aggravation of the congestion in the airways and at airports were all considered potential safety problems to be addressed by the FAA. Noise pollution from jets was the subject of congressional hearings.

Another problem was the increase in crimes aboard airplanes. In 1961, Congress convened hearings to discuss how to determine what state has jurisdiction when a crime is committed on board a plane during flight. The federal criminal code did not provide for this situation and concern was heightened by a attempted stabbing aboard a airliner prior to the hearings. A second aspect of airborne crime considered in those hearings and by the FAA throughout the sixties was the high incidence of hijackings. This highly publicized problem also received international attention which culminated in international meetings such as the International Convention for the Suppression of Unlawful Seizure of Aircraft held in December, 1970 [Kane, 1977].

Rarely the subject of hearings but often blamed for the majority of accidents was "general aviation" (private pilots and privately owned planes) whose interests are represented by associations such as the National Business Aircraft Association and Aircraft Owners & Pilots Associations. According to Senator Howard Cannon, speaking in 1969 hearings on general aviation, 98% of all aircraft and 71% of all air miles at the time were flown by private pilots. General aviation had been neglected by CAA and misrepresented as unsafe according to Max Karant, Vice President of the Aircraft Owners & Pilots Association. When the FAA was formed, general aviation was given more consideration as an important part of the economy and as a large part of civil aviation.

In summary, the government's role in civil aviation throughout its history has been to encourage the progress of the industry through economic and safety regulations. Legislation was enacted which made a place for the new and growing industry within the federal regulatory system. As growth occurred, new issues caused new safety problems which were addressed by the agency, bureau or administration in charge. Several times it was determined that administrative reform and better coordination was necessary, so a new agency was created. The Federal Aviation Administration is the most recent step in this evolution and has the power to promulgate and enforce new safety regulations.

2.3.2 Findings from Index Content Analysis (Aviation Safety)

The indexes studied showed different emphases in concern about air traffic safety. However they all showed cyclic waves of expressions of concern Figures 2.3.2-1 and 2.3.2-2). These waves of concern will be discussed in the following presentation using the categories of the tree structures described in section 2.1.2.4. Numbers in parentheses represent expressions of concern for a typical year in the period described. They are presented here to clarify variations in the relative strengths of concerns expressed about air safety during the time period described. The trends illustrated by these numbers are analogous with the trends graphically represented here and in appendix F, although the numbers stated may not match exactly those on a particular graph. This difference is caused by rounding errors resulting from the scheme used to create the graphs. These differences are small and do not affect the interpretation of trends.

The Index to Legal Periodicals showed substantial activity in the four areas of 'legal,' 'air travel is safe enough,' 'air travel is not safe enough,' and 'dutiful reporting of accidents.' There were cycles in the 'legal' category peaking in 1934, 1949, 1964, and building again in the late 1960s and early 1970s (possibly peaking in 1973, but the data stops there). The peaks are all roughly of the same level (6-9), with slight increases especially in 1960s and 1970s. "Valleys" of concern were 'higher' (1 in 1940, 3 in

48

Figure 2.3.2-1 Citizens' Concerns that Air Travel is Not Safe Enough
(Concern for Aviation)
Source: The Readers' Guide to Periodic Literature index, Level 1

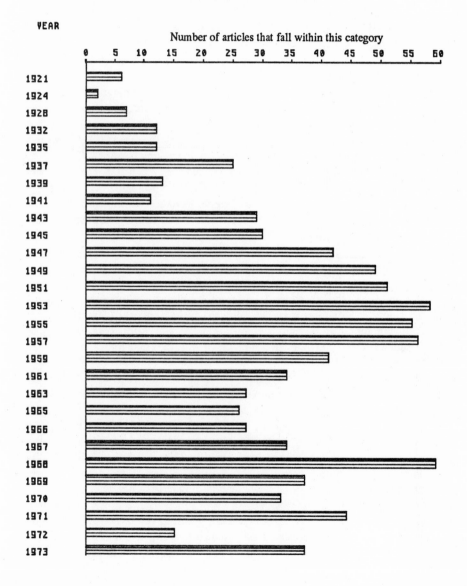

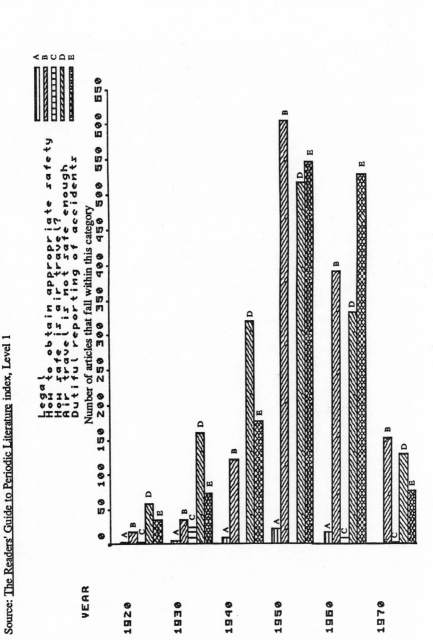

Figure 2.3.2-2 Citizens' Concerns about Aviation Safety
(Concern for Aviation)

Source: The Readers' Guide to Periodic Literature index, Level 1

A Legal to obtain appropriate safety
B How safe is air travel?
C Air travel is not safe enough
D Dutiful reporting of accidents

Number of articles that fall within this category

1955, 6 in 1967) during the time period studied showing an overall increase
in interest with a decrease in the degree of fluctuation. The category of
'how to achieve appropriate safety' also had cycles, but these were different
than those in 'legal.' There was nothing till 1949, then a jump (3), then a
decrease (1) in 1955. There was nothing in 1958, then a jump (3) in 1961,
decrease (2) in 1964 and 1967, then an increase (4) in 1970, and a decrease
(2) in 1973. The category of 'air travel is not safe enough' also had cycles.
These were different again. The first expressions of concern were in 1934
(3). There was an increase (4) in 1940 and 1949, and then a decrease (2) in
1955, and an increase (5) in 1958, and in 1961, and a decrease (4) in 1964.
There was a decrease again in 1967 (2), an increase in 1970 (7), and finally
a decrease in 1973 (3). The category of 'dutiful reporting of accidents' had
essentially nothing during the entire period studied in this index. The three
categories with expressions of concern did show some small increase over
time, but their overall characteristic was cyclical. The category of 'legal'
and 'air travel is not safe enough' were of the "rolling hills" variety (except
for the first instance of expressions of concern in 'air travel is not safe
enough' which went from nothing in 1922 to three in 1934, but this could be
due to the span from 1922 to 1934 or the fact that the industry was so
new in 1922, or both). The category of 'air travel is safe enough' had the
burst, decline,burst again variety of cycle (except for mid 1960s but this
looks more like a burst overlapped on a decline). In the 'legal' category,
"law of trespass" was typically the emphasized issue, however another very
significant one (almost as important as "trespass") was 'responsibility'; (3) in
1934, less than (1) through 1949, (1) in 1955, than (3),(2),(3),(2),(2),(3) through
1973. Also 'insurance not related to sabotage' appeared once (1) in 1955,
although some of the 'responsibility' expressions of concern must have been
related to this issue. Expressions of concern related to "enforcement"
appeared once (1) in 1949. And "crimes in general" became significant (2)
in 1970, and emphasized (4) in 1973. The expressions of concern under 'air
travel is not safe enough' were predominantly under 'specific unsafe
situations,' and those were typically in 'airways and facilities,' or under
'procedures,' or related to super sonic flight health issues (sonic booms etc).
Also there were direct expressions of concern in the 'air travel is not safe
enough' category in certain periods; 1961 (1), 1970 (2). And there were
expressions of concern in 'who is potentially harmed'; 1934 (1), 1955 (1),
1958 (1), 1961 (1). There were also expressions of concern (1) under 'safety
improvements' in 1970, mostly direct expressions of concern.

The New York Times Index was dominated with 'dutiful reporting of
accidents' expressions of concern. These were highest in the beginning of
the time period studied. Starting in 1945 (370), declining (190) in a lumpy
cyclic fashion to the end of the period 1975. (Lumpy means that there
were some hills and valleys.) The period of 1950 and 1960 were equivalent
(240), and were both less than 1955 (275). The period of 1965 was the

lowest (150), with an increase in 1970 (175). So the overall trend is one of lumpy decline. Also the area of 'air travel is not safe enough' (63) had expressions of concern in 1945, split between 'pilot related' (35) under 'specific unsafe situations,' and related to "research" (28). There were minimal expressions of concern (16) under 'air travel is not safe enough' in 1950 all in 'safety improvements' related to "research and development". There was nothing under that category from that point on. Also the categories of 'legal' and 'how to achieve appropriate safety' both had expressions of concern (8) in 1960, and (9) in 1965. These were the same articles and were related to politics and administrative issues.

The Public Affairs Information Service had nothing in 1916. There were small expressions of concern (4) in 1920 in 'legal' all in 'insurance not related to sabotage.' There were very low (2) expressions of concern in 'how to achieve appropriate safety,' all in 'civil control.' There was nothing 1920. In 1925 all the expressions of concern (5) were under 'how to achieve appropriate safety,' all in 'civil control.' In 1964 there was small activity in 'how safe is air travel?' (2), and under 'air travel is not safe enough' (2). The data from this periodical seems very sketchy, and is probably not a reliable source for detecting trends.

In The Readers' Guide the area of 'legal is either insignificant or minimal, except in 1951 (4), 1953 (2), 1961 (2), and 1968 (4), with most of the expressions of concern in 'insurance not related to sabotage.' The category of 'legal' was often empty especially in later years (nothing at all after 1968). The category of 'air travel is safe enough' starts in 1924 (1) all under 'need for progress' most in 'civil control.' The period of 1928 had (3) under the main category, with (2) in 'need for progress' and the rest (1) in 'civil control.' The period of 1932 had all in 'civil control' (3). There was nothing significant in 1935. There were small (1) under 'need for progress' most in 'civil control' (1) in 1937. The period of 1939-1943 had a few direct expressions of concern in 'how to achieve appropriate safety' but most in 'civil control':(7) in 1939, (9) in 1941, and only (1) in 1943. There was a return to typical expressions of concern (all in 'civil control') (9) in 1945, (2) in 1947, (35) in 1949, (32) in 1951.

The period of 1953 had by far the most (59) in 'civil control,' but also had a return to infrequent direct expressions of concern in 'how to achieve appropriate safety' (1). The period of 1955 also had by far the most in 'civil control' (64), but also had an increase in direct expressions of concern in 'how to achieve appropriate safety' (2). The period of 1957 (92) and 1959 (46) had all its expressions of concern in 'civil control.' Then there was a return to small, direct, main area expressions of concern (1) in both 1961 and 1963, but still by far the most (although significantly decreased) were in 'civil control' (28) in 1961 and (35) in 1963. The expressions of concern in 'civil control' were (44) in 1965, (102) in 1966, (27) in 1967, (42) in 1968, (9) in 1969, and (18) in 1970. The period of 1971 had most in 'civil control'

(62), but also had some in 'too much regulation' (3). The period of 1972 had most in 'civil control' (17), but also had some direct expressions of concern in 'need for progress' (2) (so total expressions of concern in 'how to achieve appropriate safety' was (19)). The period of 1973 had by far the most expressions of concern in 'civil control' (51), but also had significant expressions of concern in 'market externalities' (2).

Although 'how to achieve appropriate safety' and 'dutiful reporting of accidents' both show "lumpy" cycles, the trends are most clearly illustrated in or under the category, 'air travel is not safe enough.' In this area a small swell occurred in the 1930s, with a spike (30) in 1937. Another swell starts in the early 1940s, peaks (60) in the mid 1950s, and reaches a minimum in the mid 1960s. Apparently another swell starts in the mid 1960s and peaks at some unknown time later, with a conspicuous spike (58) in 1968, and a conspicuous low (15) in 1972. Until 1935 the category of 'air travel is not safe enough' emphasized 'safety improvements,' although there were significant expressions of concern elsewhere. The same was true for 1937 through 1949. The period of 1935 and 1951 had heavy expressions of concern (still less than 'safety improvements') in 'specific unsafe situation.' Also 'physiological effects of flight' became significant (1) in 1937, and again in 1941 (3), and substantial (8) in 1943, and significant (2) in 1945, and in 1947 (2). From 1953 through 1973 the two categories 'specific unsafe situation,' and 'safety improvements' were roughly equivalent and typically were by far the emphasized categories under 'air travel is not safe enough.' Direct expressions of concern under 'air travel is not safe enough' were significant in 1928, 1932, and 1937 (2), 1947 (3), in 1949 (9), 1953-1963 (2-10), and 1967, 1969, and 1970 (10). The category of 'public health' was significant (1) in 1939, and (1) in 1963. As mentioned above, 'dutiful reporting of accidents' shows cycles roughly corresponding to those of the two categories 'how to achieve appropriate safety' and 'air travel is not safe enough,' although this category is "noisier" than 'how to achieve appropriate safety.' The three categories under 'dutiful reporting of accidents' often were significant, with 'ongoing investigation' typically the least emphasized, and direct expressions of concern in 'dutiful reporting of accidents' typically outnumbering any subcategory in that main category.

The Washington Post Index had mostly 'dutiful reporting of accidents' expressions of concern in entire period studied. The patterns of these expressions of concern were jumpy. They were low (31) in 1971, then spiked (105) in 1972, went higher still (137) in 1973, then went down (66) in 1974, then jumped (117) in 1975, then decreased (62) in 1976, and had a small increase (80) in 1979. There also were small, but significant direct expressions of concern in 'safety improvements' (3) in 1971, 'specific unsafe situations' (8) in 1973, and (4) in 1974, 'safety improvements' (2) also in 1974, and 'who is potentially harmed' (5) in 1976, and 'who is potentially harmed' (2) in 1979 all under 'air travel is not safe enough.'

2.3.3 Findings from Content Analysis of Hearings (Aviation Safety)

The 1913 hearings of the House Committee on Military Affairs considered establishing a separate aviation corps in the armed forces. Most of the witnesses were military personnel who supported pilot training programs for national security.

The Committee's hearings in 1917 centered on improving air warfare capabilities which most of the witnesses believed would be crucial in future wars. According to one Congressman, the public wanted airplanes for fighting. There also was concern about the future development of "safe air machines" that would reduce the physical strain on aviators.

A 1917 House Committee on Rules hearing investigated the accelerating Congressional regulation of air safety. It also discussed how to keep pace with European aeronautical engineering and how to define the property rights of landowners over whose lands airplanes flew.

In 1921, a hearing of the Senate Committee on Commerce dealt primarily with a bill to create a Bureau of Civil Aviation "to encourage and regulate operation of civil aircraft." Lack of government regulation was believed to impede the progress of air traffic safety, since competition alone would not bring about safe machines. The great fear was that customers, in their search for cheap fares, would not understand the hazards of the machines.

In addition to establishing control standards, the development of aviation was another important concern. The nation's defense also would benefit from aviational progress. Reasons for flying accidents other than mechanical defects were listed by the Manufacturers' Aircraft Association.

The 1924 House Committee on Interstate and Foreign Commerce hearings focused on administrative reform within the Bureau of Civil Air Navigation (Department of Commerce) and on promoting aviation progress. The general sentiment was that safeguards initiated and enforced by the government were needed to gain the public's confidence.

The 1936 Senate Committee on Commerce hearings addressed the obstacles blocking "progress toward 100% safety in air travel." The lack of government regulation and support necessitated that airlines spend a great deal of money to insure safe navigation. Improvements in radio communication, airway and airport traffic control, inspection procedures, and weather reporting system were demanded. Some witnesses perceived lack of enforcement as the most serious weakness of the existing regulations.

Existing government agencies were setting rates too low and forcing airlines to spend meagerly on safety, according to airline officials. The president of the Air Transportation Association, an organization of major airlines, said that companies should not have to operate at a loss for safety's sake.

In these early decades, the public had little faith in the safety of air travel. To change this, the 1947 Senate Committee on Commerce considered bills providing for air traffic control, better training of personnel of the Civil Aeronautics Administration, and creation of an independent air safety board. Abundant data about aviation was offered by several witnesses, and several witnesses stressed the belief that the Federal Government could do the most to stimulate progress in airplane development and air traffic. There was also some consideration of air defense and specific dangers.

The 1958 House Committee on Government Operations addressed the increasing frequency of midair accidents and the possibility that jets would worsen air traffic control problems. The hearings focused on the need for improved air navigational facilities: better communication between pilots and controllers, more trained controllers, and better meteorological equipment. Specific accidents and dangers were discussed as were crashes between civilian and military aircraft. Civilian and military pilots failed to agree about air space use.

Federal financial and technical assistance for research and for the development of airports was discussed. Owners and pilots of small aircraft feared that regulations adopted as a result of highly publicized crashes would make general aviation more costly and complicated and, thus, more rare.

A 1961 hearing of the Senate Committee on Commerce discussed Federal jurisdiction of the airways. State laws could not adequately cover recent air crimes because the state in which the crime was committed could not be determined. Witnesses disagreed about whether the crew should be armed. Full enforcement of the laws was considered crucial by many witnesses.

The 1967-1968 House Committee on Interstate and Foreign Commerce hearings (Figure 2.3.3-1) were prompted by a midair collision in North Carolina which killed 82 people and by mail from the public to Congressmen about air safety. The hearings discussed efforts to improve air navigational facilities and addressed specific dangers like congestion in the airways and disorganization at airports.

According to most witnesses, more money was needed to hire and train capable air traffic controllers who were suffering aggravated stress as air traffic increased.

The subject of the 1969 Senate Committee on Commerce hearing was the role of general aviation in the overall transportation system. Although air traffic was congested, expanded airport construction and air traffic control were difficult to finance. The general opinion was that the Federal Government should not try to reduce demand but should provide a system able to handle efficiently the demands placed upon it. Generally, many witnesses discussed airports, air traffic control, funding, and general aviation restrictions. Several business interests wanted to expand aviational services even more.

Figure 2.3.3.-1 Legislators' Concerns about Aviation Safety
(Concern for Aviation)

Source: 1967-1968 House Committee Hearings on Interstate and Foreign Commerce

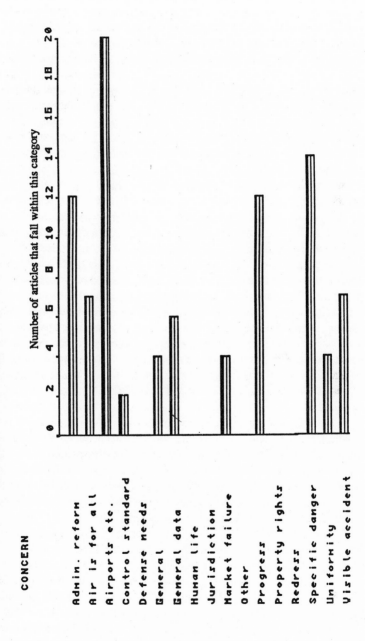

2.3.4 Summary (Aviation Safety)

The history of concern and legislation relating to air traffic safety is quite different from that of the other areas studied. Not only has the industry been regulated since its inception, it often sought regulation.

The index content analysis showed waves of concern which had characteristics specific to the index and category examined. Most of them seemed to correlate regulatory activity with factors like the introduction of new technology. Particularly interesting was the media's emphasis on specific physical or technological phenomena. Statements expressing safety concerns were typically about propellers, ice etc. while relating indirectly to the need for regulation.

Concerns about specific hazards of air travel also were expressed at the hearings, but the emphasis was on fears of inadequate industry progress and how regulation could help remedy this. Safety was a organizing issue which helped the industry to enlist government in controlling competition and other factors related to cost.

The analysis of secondary literature also showed an emphasis on the myriad benefits afforded by regulation to the industry and to the country as a whole. Defense needs were stressed in earlier hearings but later became less significant. The secondary literature also emphasized the importance of military needs to the growth of civil air regulation. The big difference in outlook between primary and secondary sources is that the latter tended to treat progress in the industry as good in its own right. The social benefits of such progress often were mentioned, but the overall sentiment was that progress in the industry was good and anything that slowed that progress was bad.

It might seem that the three sources of information used in this study conflict in the area of air traffic safety. It is more likely, however, that they are telling different parts of story which exceeds the scope of our study. and involving the ability of citizen concern to penetrate different areas of political discourse. While there were waves of concern associated with increased air traffic, technological change, and new legislation, the public consistently associated industry health with safety.

2.4 Historical Review of Forces Leading to Consumer Product
     Safety Legislation
     2.4.1 Historical Context from the Secondary Literature
           and Interviews (Consumer Product Safety)

The basic legislation in the area of consumer products safety is the 1972 Consumer Product Safety Act. This omnibus law differs strikingly from prior legislation which dealt piecemeal with specific products. This change from legislation that reacted to crises to legislation forming an independent agency to guide consumer production resulted from a slow transformation in social values and from the consequent progressive congress.

Early in this century, concern for consumer protection from unhealthy or unsafe products resulted in several different acts. The Pure Food and Drug Act of 1906 was supported initially by agricultural interests who were concerned about unfair competition from unscrupulous sellers. It received the necessary push to passage from President Roosevelt and from public concern aroused by journalists such as Upton Sinclair in his book The Jungle. During WWI, concern for consumer interests faded as the growth of industry commanded more attention. Legislation concentrated more on labeling requirements -- the Federal Hazardous Substance Act of 1927 -- but enforcement procedures were weak. The Food, Drug and Cosmetic Act of 1938, was considered needed reform to the outdated Pure Food and Drug Act by assistant secretary of Agriculture R.G. Tugwell, but it was difficult to get passage with scant media coverage and public concern.

The pattern for the next twenty-five years of consumer safety legislation emerged: a crisis accompanied by media coverage eliciting public outcry was necessary to get Congress to enact even limited legislation to control a given hazard. Illustrating this pattern was the process leading to the Flammable Fabrics Act of 1953. Concern was raised by a type of children's sweater that could easily ignite, nicknamed 'torch' sweaters. These brushed rayon sweaters, which would burn completely in twenty to forty seconds, caused many deaths and burns. Reacting to public concern, Congress passed the Flammable Fabrics Act which outlawed the use of highly combustible materials in wearing apparel. This law solved the immediate problem, but as Senator Warren G. Magnuson, a supporter of the 1953 bill and key figure in later consumer products legislation, stated, "the original Flammable Fabrics Act was inadequate and, in some ways, gave the public a false sense of security" [Magnuson, 1968, p.149]. The law's definition of "fabric" was narrow: it did not extend to upholstry, draperies, sheets, or blankets, so that the same 'torch' material still could be used legally in babies' blankets. Public concern died down with the passage of the Act, despite its ineffectiveness.

In 1956, public attention focused again on product safety when several small children suffocated in abandoned refrigerators. The Refrigerator Safety Act resulted, requiring manufacturers to produce refrigerators that opened from the inside.

What are the reasons behind this type of legislative action from WWI to the mid 60s? The forgoing examples indicate that the public became concerned when there was an easily identifiable crisis at hand (particularly one involving children) and publicized by the media. However, there was some general interest in consumer issues like product safety. Consumers Union (which publishes "Consumer Reports") was founded in 1936 to articulate consumer interests, but it was largely a "voice in the wilderness" in this period [Nadel, 1971]. An attitude of "let the buyer beware" was prevalent, leaving many people, including legislators, with the idea that consumer protection was less preferable than remedies. Reparations were awarded after injury in successful liability suits against the manufacturer, and legislation granted protection only after tragedy had struck.

After the New Deal, there was increased tolerance of government regulation, but industry still had more political power than did the consumer. The Commerce Committee in the 50s, with jurisdiction over many consumer issues, "was hardly noted for its enterprise in pursuing consumer interests. Indeed, its primary occupation was the protection of business interests ..." [Pertschuk, 1982, p.8]. Industry's resistance to regulation contributed to consumer education being pushed as the best way to prevent accidents. Labeling, as required in certain acts such as the 1960 Hazardous Substance Labeling Act, was a legislative attempt to educate consumers.

In 1966, Congress passed the National Traffic and Motor Vehicle Safety Act. Considered by many to be breakthrough legislation for consumer product safety, the law was the first to regulate the auto industry. It focussed on the product rather than the consumer in its attempt to reduce auto-related injuries. Moreover, the Act did not result from a specific tragedy but from the work of senators like Abraham Ribicoff and Warren G. Magnuson, consumer advocate Ralph Nader, and the enormous amount of publicity received by the hearings held. Following this Act, a series of consumer safety acts were passed including the 1966 Child Protection Act, the 1967 Amendments to Flammable Fabrics Act, the 1969 Amendments to the Federal Hazardous Substances Act, the 1970 Poison Prevention Packaging Act, and the 1971 Toy Safety Act leading up to the Consumer Product Safety Act in 1972.

What occasioned the outpouring of legislation in this area, in so few years? In 1969, the DHEW's National Center for Health Statistics and the National Safety Council estimated that in and around the American home each year, 30,000 people were killed and more than 20 million injured seriously enough to require medical treatment. By 1965, auto fatalities had risen to 55,000 per year and cigarette smoking had been linked to lung cancer. With the growth in product-related injuries and deaths, concerns to address the problem grew.

President Nixon, in his consumer message to Congress in February 1971, stated that the increasing complexity and sophistication of many consumer goods sometimes leads to inadvertent misuse resulting in physical danger to the consumer. The market mechanism of self-regulation did not seem to be working: "even the best-intentioned programs of industry advocates of safety fall afoul of the forces of competition" [NPSC final report, 1970, p.114]. Or, as Ralph Nader sarcastically noted, industry gave to consumers the "inalienable right to go through the windshield" [Pertschuk, 1982]. With President Nixon and Ralph Nader aligned on the issue, it was clear that sentiment for regulatory legislation was growing.

We can posit that consumerism became a movement when social consensus rejected the rhetoric of "let the buyer beware" and demanded consumer protection as a legislated right (an entitlement). This developing consensus had been prefigured by President John F. Kennedy's 1962 Congressional message spelling out a consumer bill of rights: the right to know, to choose, to be safe, and to be heard. Hearings held by Senator Estes Kefauver's Antitrust and Monopoly Committee on the prescription drug industry and Senator Paul Douglas' hearings on truth-in-lending heightened public interest and helped the movement to grow and, as it did, develop the issues of fair advertising, consumer fraud, and warranties. Product liability cases, although posing many difficulties for a consumer, were on the increase in the 1960s and in 1968 alone over 100,000 were filed [Nader, 1971].

In transforming consumer product safety into a viable political issue, presidential endorsement, consumer advocates, and individual members of Congress and their staffs played key roles. President Kennedy was the first president since the New Deal to deliver a consumer message to Congress. Although he had little involvement with consumer legislation, his endorsements were greeted with much public enthusiasm. President Johnson played an active role, delivering a consumer message in 1964, and every year from 1966 to 1968. The issue had grown in importance enough to be included in Johnson's state-of-the-union address in 1968. On January 3, 1964, Johnson appointed the President's Committee on Consumer Interests (PCCI) which included Kennedy's relatively inactive Consumer Advisory Council. The PCCI was not of great importance in the actual passage of legislation, but showed Johnson's interest in the consumer protection area.

Consumer advocacy was dominated by Ralph Nader whose researchers often were referred to as 'Nader's raiders.' His book Unsafe at Any Speed (1965), brought public attention to automobile safety; Beware, his commentary on the Final Report of the National Product Safety Commission, was published in 1971. Testifying at numerous hearings and writing investigative articles, he made consumer product safety a national issue. Advocacy groups like Consumers Union also brought the issue to the public with "Consumers Report" magazine. In November 1967, the Consumers Federation of America, an umbrella organization of national and local consumer groups, was formed to help give the consumer a stronger voice in government. Citizen advocates like these educated the public and lobbied effectively for legislation.

Some members of Congress and their staffs also played vital roles in passing consumer protection legislation. Senator Warren G. Magnuson identified himself with the issue beginning in 1964 and, as Chairman of the Commerce Committee, he had considerable power [Pertschuk, 1984]. His first major piece of legislation was the Flammable Fabrics Act Amendments of 1967, upgrading standards for safety protection. In 1967, Magnuson introduced a bill to create a commission to study the problem of consumer product safety, and at the end of that year the bill was signed into law. Although President Johnson had requested that research be done in this area, Robert Adler gives most of the credit for this bill to Michael Pertschuk, a member of Magnuson's congressional staff [Adler, 1984]. The bill gave authority to the National Commission on Product Safety (NCPS) to hold hearings and write a report on the condition of product safety. In June, 1970, the Commission made public its final report, including recommendations for legislation. Pertschuk stated that Magnuson and his staff expected the commission's report to lead 'inexorably to a legislative proposal for the creation of a permanent consumer product safety commission' [Pertschuk, 1982]. Senator Magnuson and his staff's creation of this committee was crucial to the eventual passage of the 1972 bill.

The NCPS final report reviewed the horrible accidents caused by many products and presented a list of the most hazardous ones. NCPS recommended the formation of an independent agency with authority to set product standards, to remove products from the market, and to enforce its decisions. The group reasoned that "with Government stimulation, manufacturers can accomplish more for safety with less effort and expense than any other body" [NCPS final report, 1970]. Ralph Nader concludes his book Beware by noting that "the NCPS report has provided an invaluable service to the nation. It remains now for those affected- all consumers- to take some action!" [Nader, 1971]. Action was taken, and the report became the catalyst for enacting the Consumer Product Safety Act of 1972.

On February 25, 1971, Senators Magnuson and Moss introduced the commission's bill. Hearings were held in 1971 and early 1972 by the House and the Senate and in 1972 Congress passed the Consumer Product Safety Act, creating an independent agency to promulgate and enforce product safety standards. This omnibus law was the first of its kind in consumer safety protection.

2.4.2 Findings from Index Content Analysis
(Consumer Product Safety)

When we tracked the tree structure of concerns for consumer products protection we discovered that concerns developed steadily from the 1920's through the early 1970's (Figure 2.4.2-1). The category of 'better protection is needed' typically contained almost all expressions of concern (Figure 2.4.2-2).

The data from The Readers' Guide most clearly illustrates the nature of the concern expressed (Figure 2.4.2-3). The other indexes show similar trends, graphs for which are provided in Appendix F for reference. The Index to Legal Periodicals follows The Readers' Guide closely. As expected, The New York Times Index shows a strong threshold effect. That is, minimal coverage until the issue became potent at which point there was a dramatic increase in reporting. Once The Times chose to cover the issue, it did so from many sides as demonstrated by the presence of articles in the high level categories of 'Other' and 'Debate and discussion,' with the latter being quite significant in 1970. The category of 'Other' was primarily related to such issues as 'the politics of consumer products safety.' The data collected from the Public Affairs Information Service followed what was found in The Readers' Guide. Since The Washington Post Index begins in 1971, we could compare it to The Readers' Guide only in the last three years. It seemed to follow The Readers' Guide in these years, except that the decline in concern expressed began in 1974 for the The Washington Post Index and in 1973 in The Readers' Guide. We noted also, in The Washington Post Index, that other general categories became significant in the period 1973-5, in particular, 'Debate and discussion.' After 1976 there was a return to pre-1973 degrees of concern about 'Better protection is needed' in The Washington Post Index.

An interesting phenomena appeared when the data in the various indexes were examined in the more specific categories -- the concerns which appeared in the branches of the tree structure described in section 2.1.2.4. All the indexes were dominated by increasingly specific concerns. Except for one time period studied in the Index to Legal Periodicals and two periods in The Washington Post Index, all the concerns counted in general categories came from more specific concerns. This suggests increasing sophistication in the public's and the media's understanding of the issue.

The Index to Legal Periodicals first showed expressions of concern in the early 1930's in the area of 'Redress.' This concern continued through the 1970's, with a significant drop in the 1940's. Activity in the 'Through physical means' category was present, but minimal from the late 1930's through the late 1950's. The 'Redress' concern was spread through the

62

Figure 2.4.2-1 Citizens' Concerns about Consumer Protection:
Better Protection Needed

(Concern for Consumer)

Source: The Readers' Guide to Periodic Literature index, Level 1

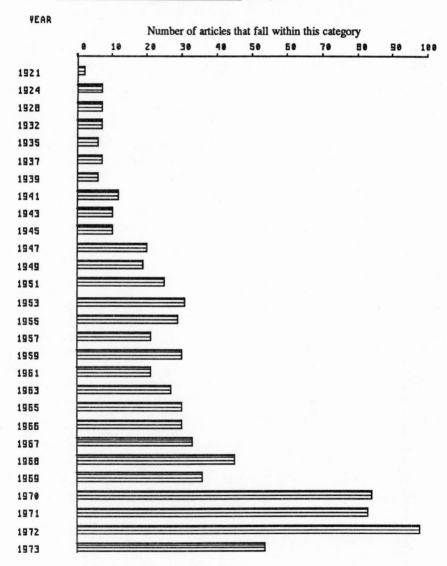

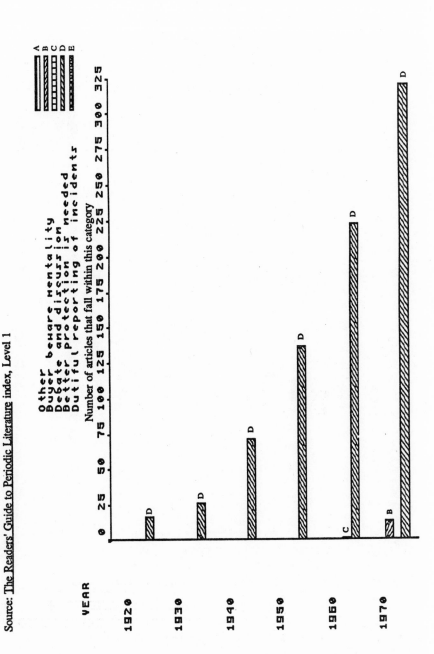

Figure 2.4.2-2 Citizens' Concerns about Consumer Protection
(Concern for Consumer)

Source: The Readers' Guide to Periodic Literature index, Level 1

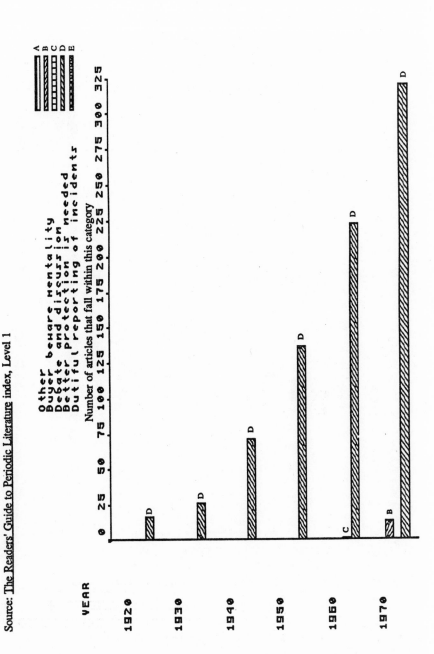

Figure 2.4.2-3 Citizens' Concerns about Consumer Protection
(Concern for Consumer)

Source: The Readers' Guide to Periodic Literature index, Level 2

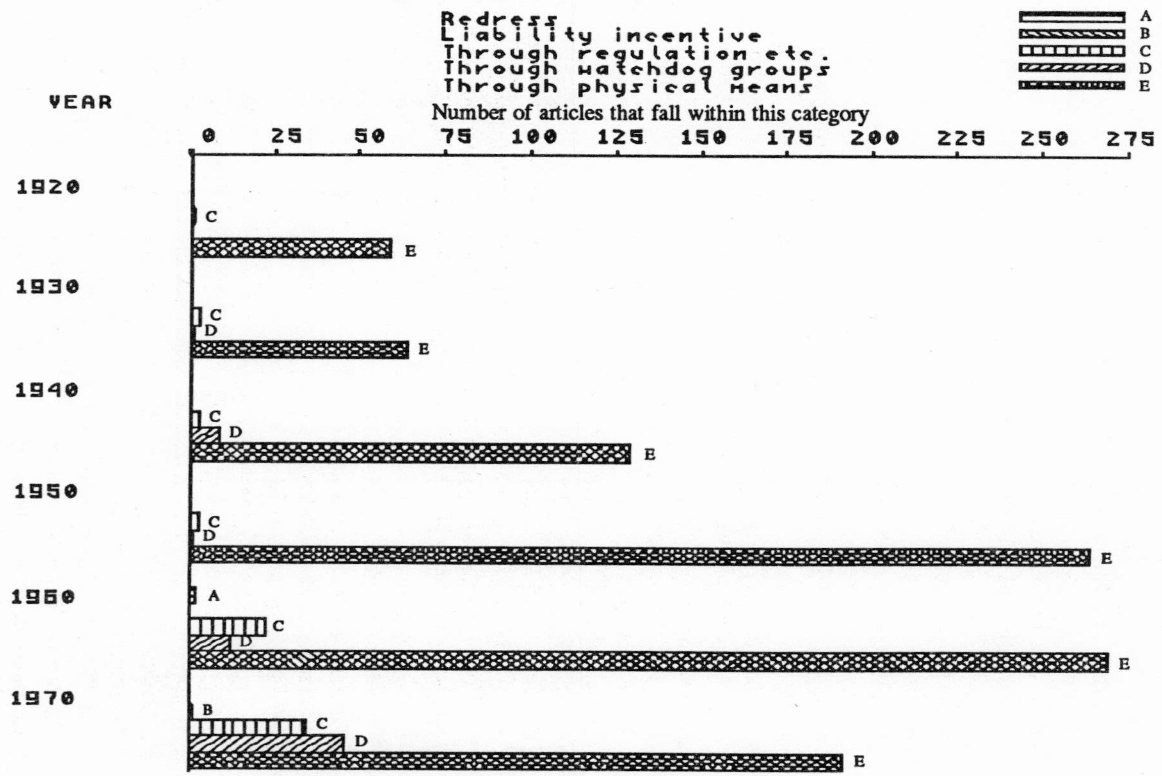

various branches below it, but was primarily in 'Redress' itself and in 'Manufacturer.' What concern there was under 'Through physical means' was in 'Specific products,' and that was in 'Non-toys.' In the 1960's 'Non-toys' became more significant, but never represented a major concern. In the early 1960's activity in the category 'Through regulation' appeared briefly and then reappeared in a significant way in the late 1960's and early 1970's. By far the major concern throughout the entire period studied was 'Redress.' This was expressed either directly or through the branches below it. The most significant of these branches was 'Manufacturer.'

The New York Times Index showed scant activity until 1967. In 1967 there was small but significant activity in the category of 'Through regulation.' There was very little in 1968. The year 1969 was very similar to 1967. In 1970 there was a major increase in the category 'Through regulation.' This increased activity remained in 1975. Also the areas of 'Consumer groups,' 'Industry,' and 'Redress' became significant in 1970 and 1975.

The Public Affairs Information Service showed slight activity in the area of 'Non-toys' and very minor activity in the area of 'Through regulation' in the early 1920's. Then in the mid 1960's there was significant activity in the areas of 'Non-toys,' 'Through regulation,' and 'Manufacturer.' There was also a very minor activity in the area of 'Debate and discussion' in the mid 1960's.

The Washington Post Index showed only moderate levels of expressed concern in 1971, with the greatest activity being in the 'Toys' category. There was a swelling of concern in the area of 'Through regulation,' peaking in 1973. This was matched by a sudden spike in the area of 'Watchdog groups' in 1973. From 1972 through 1974 there was continued concern in most of the branches under 'Physical means,' mostly in either 'Non-toys' or 'Specific hazards.' There was only slight activity in 1975 and 1976. Concern began to rise significantly again in 1977 in the areas of 'Through regulation' and 'Non-toys,' along with 'Specific hazards' in 1978. The year 1979 was similar to 1978.

The Readers' Guide demonstrated minor concern in 1921, split between 'Specific hazards' and 'Non-toys.' In 1924 the concern was essentially all 'Non-toys.' In 1928 and 1932 the main concern was in 'Non-toys,' with significant activity in the area of 'Specific hazards.' Also there was developing activity in the areas of 'New technology,' 'Through regulation,' and 'Toys.' These trends continued through 1943, except for a conspicuous absence of 'Through regulation.' Activity in 'Watchdog Groups' and 'Industry' appeared in 1941, and reappeared briefly in 1947 and 1949. These trends continued with little change through 1951. In 1951 there was a dramatic increase in the 'Non-toys' area. From 1953 through 1963 this trend continued. In 1965 the area of 'Through regulation' entered in a significant way although this area vanished in 1966 after which it saw moderate activity through 1970. There was little in the category 'Through regulation' in 1971 although it became significant in 1972 only to return to moderate levels again in 1973. There was a dramatic increase in the activity in 'Watchdog groups' in 1970, an area which had appeared slightly in earlier periods and also in 1958, 1961, 1968 and 1969. It tapered off again in the early 1970's. The area of 'Toys' appears early and then disappears from the period studied until the early 1970's. Activity built to a peak 1971 and then tapered, but remained strong though 1973.

2.4.3 Findings from Content Analysis of Hearings
(Consumer Product Safety)

The first set of hearings analyzed for expressions of concern about consumer product safety were those from the 1953 House Committee on Interstate and Foreign Commerce. These hearings considered legislation that later became the Flammable Fabrics Act (FFA). The need for legislation had surfaced in 1946 when there occurred incidents involving highly flammable fabrics that burst into flames causing injury and death. It was conceded by most witnesses that the textile industry had failed to protect the public adequately and that it was imperative to bar highly flammable merchandise from apparel.

The belief of the 1954 Senate Committee on Commerce was that government action was necessary to relieve the hazard of abandoned iceboxes and refrigerators into which children could lock themselves accidentally. Many of those testifying argued that it was mandatory that deaths of young children be prevented by imposing restrictions on the manufacturers. Industry interests advocated "free market" solutions to the problem along with extensive consumer education programs. These witnesses were confident that manufacturers, left unrestricted, could achieve satisfactory technological solutions.

The bill considered by the 1967 Senate Committee on Commerce would establish the National Commission on Product Safety (NCPS). The Committee chairman, Warren G. Magnuson, stated that two "essential rights" were paramount: (1) the consumer has a right to reasonable safety of products and (2) the manufacturer is entitled to reasonable uniformity in laws. A second major consideration was that technology could and should eliminate product hazards.

Other expressions of concern related to the role of consumer education, economic costs from increasing product safety, and problems associated with or caused by technological progress.

The 1967 hearings of the House Committee on Interstate and Foreign Commerce dealt with proposed amendments to the FFA of 1953 and the proposed establishment of the NCPS. Discussion of the hazards of flammable clothing and of preventive action to spare people from painful burns were the main topics of discussion. Several witnesses were dissatisfied with the patchwork of apparently inadequate laws for product safety regulation. There were expressions both extolling the virtue of the free market system's capability to solve problems and criticizing the market's failure to insure safety.

Concern also was expressed for consumers who might not be able to afford higher priced products with more safety features. Other concerns included promoting consumer education and encouraging manufacturers to employ technology to eliminate hazards.

Protecting children from a specific hazard was the main concern of the 1970 House Committee on Interstate and Foreign Commerce hearings. These hearings considered bills requiring child-resistant packaging to protect children from serious injury or illness. The Committee chairman deemed the legislation uncontroversial. Voluntary self-regulation had failed to provide adequately safe containers and supporters of the bills believed that laws would motivate manufacturers to resolve the problem through technological innovation.

The 1971-1972 House Committee on Interstate and Foreign Commerce hearings centered on an omnibus bill recommended by the National Commission on Product Safety to give the Federal Government authority to set safety standards for unreasonably hazardous consumer products and to create a new agency, the Consumer Product Safety Commission, to administer the law. The primary concern was to initiate governmental action; secondary concerns included providing technological solutions for specific hazards, protecting children, and educating consumers. An extensive amount of data was offered to support the call for governmental intervention.

The chairman of the NCPS declared that the laissez-faire approach to consumer product safety had hurt the American public and effective Federal regulation was the solution for reducing hazards. Many witnesses in the hearings agreed with the NCPS chairman that it was a right of citizens that hazards be controlled and limited.

The specific hazards considered in the 1971 Senate Committee on Commerce hearings (Figure 2.4.3-1) were clear -- a variety of dangerous consumer products, such as the power lawnmower. Considerable statistical evidence was displayed to support the call for administrative action. Denunciations of technological complexity in products went on record as several witnesses blamed it for causing an unreasonable number of deaths and injuries. Also, concern for buyers' rights was expressed several times, as were concerns about abandoned refrigerators, inflammable children's wear, etc. In fact, it was clear that protecting children was one of the prominent concerns of these hearings.

68

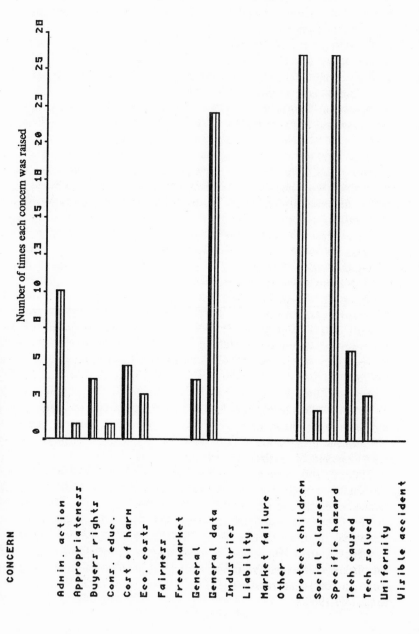

Figure 2.4.3-1 Legislators' Concerns about Consumer Protection
(Concern for Consumer)

Source: 1971 Senate Committee Hearings on Commerce

2.4.4 Summary (Consumer Product Safety Legislation)

The separate findings from the indexed content analysis, the content analysis of hearings, and the secondary literature and interviews show a clear trend of growing concern about need for consumer product safety over a period from the 1920's through the early 1970's. With the exception of several notable acts passed during the mid-1950's, the trend reached a peak in the period 1966-1972 when several major pieces of consumer protection legislation were approved by Congress. By that period, Presidential endorsement, consumer advocacy, and efforts by individual members of Congress and their staffs had consumer product safety a potent political issue.

Motivation to pass the Flammable Fabrics Act (FFA) of 1953 and the Refrigerator Safety Act of 1956 stemmed from the public outcry over incidents of burning or suffocation, usually affecting small children. In both cases, the free market was blamed for failing to uphold adequate safety standards. From 1956 to 1966, there was essentially no major Congressional action on consumer product safety.

President Johnson gave several speeches on the consumer's right to safety during the mid-1960's and helped lead the country to address the issue. The 1966 National Traffic and Motor Vehicle Safety Act may represent the breakthrough legislation for product safety, as the automobile industry became regulated by the Federal Government. The National Commission on Product Safety (NCPS) was established in 1967, and the out-of-date FFA was amended that same year.

The nature of the National Commission on Product Safety report submitted to the President in 1970 made it inevitable that the omnibus bill recommended by the report would become law (Consumer Product Safety Act of 1972). The chairman of the NCPS firmly stated that the laissez-faire approach to consumer products hurts the American public and that effective government intervention is the only way to reduce hazards. By 1971 a great amount of statistical evidence supported the call for governmental regulation, and several witnesses testifying in Congressional hearings denounced technological complexity in products for causing an unreasonable number of deaths and injuries.

The 1972 Consumer Product Safety Act was strikingly different from prior piecemeal legislation that dealt with specific product hazards. The changeover from legislation that responded to crises to legislation that established comprehensive product safety regulation was made possible by a slow but consistent transformation in societal attitudes and values from WWI to the mid-1960's.

2.5 Historical Review of Forces Leading to Occupational
     Safety and Health Legislation
     2.5.1 Historical Context from the Secondary Literature and
            Interviews (Occupational Safety and Health)

The Occupational Safety and Health Act of 1970 (OSHA) was the first
federal legislation providing health and safety protection for most American
workers. Yet occupational safety was not a new topic: legislative concern
about it was more than one hundred years old, beginning with Massachusetts'
1877 work safety law. OSHA was prompted by a few individuals who
perceived the nation's need for such a law and who had gained the power to
realize this goal.

Regulation of job hazards was traditionally a state duty. The rationale
for this delegation was that local politicians would know more about local
conditions and also would have greater incentive to correct injury to their
constituency [Page, 1972].   At the turn of the century, muckraking
journalists stimulated public outrage at unsafe working conditions which in
turn prompted a few states to pass work safety laws. By 1920 some form
of industrial health and safety law had been enacted by most states and
most regulated mining, but inspection and enforcement were haphazard
[Bureau of National Affairs, 1971].

The federal government's role began with selective involvement in certain
industries. The first laws passed concerned mine and railroad safety. In
1902, the Public Health Service was created and in 1910 the Bureau of
Mines was established, but these agencies only researched worker health and
safety.

The prevailing attitude in turn of the century America was that
occupational accidents resulted necessarily from "progress" [Page, 1972]. In
keeping with this attitude, the only recourse of injured workers was a
lawsuit for damages against the employer. The legal system, however,
afforded the employer three defenses which made it nearly impossible for a
worker to win redress: an employer could argue that the accident was partly
the fault of the employee; that the employee was voluntarily exposed to a
hazard; or that a fellow employee was responsible for the injury. Estimates
of claims left uncompensated by law ranged from 70 to 94 percent [Page,
1972, p.51] and efforts toward reform of this system were made as early as
1902.

Reform took the shape of laws that required unconditional, if partial,
compensation of workers by the employer, called workmen's compensation.
In 1902, Maryland passed the first workmen's compensation law. Although it
provided only for fatal accidents, the law was declared unconstitutional
because it denied the employer the right of trial by jury. In 1911, New
Jersey passed the first workmen's compensation law to be upheld, setting a
precedent. By 1920 all but eight states had passed workmen's compensation

laws, and by 1948 all forty-eight states had them.

The Federal government also passed a limited compensation law. In 1908, pressed by President Roosevelt, Congress passed a law covering some government employees. Not until the mid 1930s would the federal government again become involved with worker safety and health.

Workmen's compensation laws were not the same as health and safety laws which prevent hazardous work conditions and accidents from occuring. These laws did not provide full compensation, only partial, did not cover all workers, such as agricultural or domestic workers, and often had no provisions for industrial diseases even though there was some awareness about occupationally caused disease. In 1936, congressional hearings were held on the Gauley Bridge construction incident in which 476 died and 1500 were disabled from silicosis. At that time West Virginia, where the tunnel was being dug, did not cover silicosis in its workmen's compensation law. Senator Rush Dew Holt of West Virginia testified, "that company well knew what it was going to do to these men. (It) openly said that if they killed off those men there were plenty of other men to be had" [Page, 1971, p.63]. As a result, a few states included silicosis as compensable, but the laws still did not protect workers from chronic diseases.

In the late twenties and early thirties the labor movement grew rapidly. Organized labor and other advocates of working people made issues of child labor, long hours, low wages, the right to strike, and safe working conditions. This grassroots movement prompted the federal government to enter the occupational safety field once again. In 1936, the Walsh-Healey Public Contracts Act set health and safety standards for workers of Government contractors. The Bureau of Labor Standards was created in the Labor Department, helping to further the federal role as a consultant and information-provider to the states [BNA, 1971]. Public attention to the issue was great.

In the early forties, activity in the health and safety field was practically nonexistent. World War II and the "war effort" was commanding much of the nation's attention. A safety engineer, feeling a study of the present occupational safety field was needed, suggested that the President sponsor a conference. President Truman approved the idea and the conference was held. Similar conferences were held through the Eisenhower administration every two years although their results were less than job safety proponents had hoped for: no appraisal was conducted. Roland P. Blake, an organizer of the National Safety Council, says the conferences "had no discernible effect on annual death and injury tolls" [Blake, 1963, p.29]. No further action was taken.

Some congressional interest in the issue led to introduction of bills that never passed. In 1940 a bill to provide grants to state labor departments to establish industrial hygiene units failed in the Senate and in 1943 a bill to provide funds to states to improve safety and health conditions in industry failed in the House. Eight years later another Senate bill channeling funds to states for job safety failed to reach the floor. That same year Senator Hubert Humphrey introduced the Accident Prevention Act to establish a bureau to develop safety standards. The bill also failed to reach the floor. The Nader Task Force in its book Bitter Wages posed two reasons for failure as being unwanted encroachment on state's rights, and "bureaucratic jealousies" in putting public health activities under state labor departments [Page, 1971, p.64].

Several laws pertaining to specific industries with very high accident rates were passed during the fifties. These regulated longshoring and mining in particular.

The merits of occupational safety legislation were not totally unrecognized and knowledge of industrial disease was growing. Beginning with 1958, a sharp increase in industrial accidents, with a 29% increase from 1961 to 1970, was reported by the National Safety Council. Research in the sixties into new chemicals being used in the workplace revealed new hazards. In 1965, the Division of Occupational Health in the Department of Health, Education, and Welfare (DHEW) issued a report entitled "Protecting the Health of Eighty Million Americans: A National Goal for Occupational Health." This report, called the Frye report, provided clearer information on industrial chemical hazards, occupational disease, and outlined a national program to combat the problem with a recommended budget of fifty million dollars. No program emerged from lack of "any effective political support" [Page, 1971, p.90]. Knowledge of the problem was available and known by government officials.

Reasons for the delay of federal action are not fully clear. The traditional control of this area by the states was one stumbling block but it was known at the federal level that state safety laws were inadequate. Lack of funding and inadequate laws as well as the subservience of local politicians to industry all limited the strength of state programs. Outdated amounts of compensation, failure of coverage of certain workers, and inadequate provision for industrial diseases are well documented by the Nader Task Force using Bureau of Labor Standards' reports from as early as 1961. Only three years earlier, in 1958, Secretary of Labor James Mitchell refused to draft legislation setting mandatory standards for the safe use of hazardous materials, saying that the problem "did not warrant federal intervention" [BNA, 1971, p.16]. This attitude helped to defeat legislation like the 1962 Occupational Safety Act which provided only grants to states, with no federal regulation, but never got past the House Rules Committee.

Bureaucratic conflict contributed to the delay in federal action. Responsibility was fragmented between the Department of Labor, DHEW, Department of Interior and other agencies. The most pressing health hazards were ones which the Department of Labor knew little about. Data collecting and research by the Public Health Service has been greatly diminished by their lack of authority to enter work places: the Service had to ask management's permission to enter. DHEW never fought for this authority though it was considered a necessary aspect of fighting the problem [Page, 1971]. Pushing the debate for occupational safety and health laws was not a high priority for federal government until the mid to late sixties.

Concern became manifest with the introduction of more comprehensive legislation in 1968. President Johnson was an aggressive proponent of job safety and health. He showed interest in the issue as early as 1964 when he sponsored a President's Conference on Occupational Safety. In 1966 he established a special task force to study worker related problems including health and safety. On January 23, 1968 he delivered his Manpower Message to Congress in which he said, "It must be our goal to protect every one of America's 75 million workers while they are on the job" and he proceeded to propose a comprehensive program to do so. Johnson was a factor in having the Labor Department write a bill to submit to Congress [Harrison, 1984]. He included job safety as one of the many safety and health-minded pieces of legislation he backed.

Legislation on related issues began to pass in the mid-sixties. The McNamara-O'Hara Public Service Contract was passed in 1965 extending the Walsh-Healey Act to government service suppliers, and in 1966 the Metal and Non-Metallic Mine Safety Act was passed. After several big mining accidents including the Farmington, West Virginia coal mine accident in 1968 in which 78 died, dramatic hearings were held on worker health and safety in this industry. This resulted in the Coal Mine Safety Act of 1969. These acts showed an increasing governmental willingness to consider federal occupational safety and health legislation, even though they were in areas the federal government already regulated to some degree.

Other people were prominent in the passage of the 1970 act. Assistant Secretary of Labor Esther Peterson and Secretary of Labor Willard Wirtz showed particular interest in the issue. They began to draft legislation for an administration bill in the summer of 1967 and sent it to House Subcommittee on Labor. Instrumental in the initial consideration of this legislation and in reporting the bill out of committee were Representative James O'Hara and Senator Ralph Yarborough, each chairman of their respective Subcommittee on Labor.

Representative O'Hara had participated in health and safety legislation including the 1965 and 1966 acts mentioned above. He originally became interested in the field as a member of the Safety and Compensation Subcommittee. The administration, looking for someone to represent its bill, sent it to him [O'Hara, 1984]. The members of the Subcommittee liked the idea and held very extensive hearings in 1968. Although the bill was not acted upon in that Congress, its seeds were sown.

Senator Ralph Yarborough, who had long been a champion of public health, had a personal interest in calling hearings on an occupational safety and health bill: his experience as a trial lawyer in Texas and the terrible construction accident in Alexandria [Yarborough, 1984]. He had power as chairman to push the hearings and did so, even after he had lost the senatorial election in 1970. He and Senator Javits played a large part in seeing the bill through extensive debate. The personal interest these men had in getting what Yarborough called a "just" bill passed stems from events they had seen and from concerns sparked in the thirties and forties. It was not until the 1960s that people like Javits and Yarborough reached positions (like committee chairmanships) in which they had the influence and power to produce legislation [Harrison, 1984].

On December 8, 1970 the joint conference on the Senate and House bills began, and by December 17 a compromise had been fashioned and the bill passed. President Nixon signed the Occupational Safety and Health Act on December 29, 1970. Although there was no one particular incident creating a public outcry for this legislation, the context of a consumerist and safety minded Congress, president helped to pass an occupational safety and health bill.

2.5.2 Findings from Index Content Analysis
(Occupational Safety and Health)

The overall concern for occupational safety and health peaked in the mid 1930s. This is illustrated best by the data from The Readers' Guide (Figure 2.5.2-1). The nature of the concern is well illustrated also by the data from The Readers' Guide (Figures 2.5.2-2 and 2.5.2-3). Primary differences between this data and that from the other indexes were due to differences in the indexes themselves. Since The Washington Post Index only covered the 1970s, it could not test the phenomenon of concern peaking in the 1930s. The degree of concern shown by The New York Times Index was fairly constant from 1945 through 1960, with a slight increase in 1950 and very little in 1965. There was a large increase in 1970, and further increase in 1975. This was to be expected due to the tendency of The Times to publish "newsworthy" articles, and occupational safety and health issues were a topic of heated debate in the early 1970s. The Public Affairs Information Service largely confirmed what was found in The Readers' Guide. The Index to Legal Periodicals told a somewhat different story, showing a peak in professional interest in the mid 1930s, with steady growth from the early 1950s through the mid 1960s, then a sharp decrease in the mid 1960s, and a small increase towards the early 1970s. This might be explained by changes in state legislation dealing with workmen's compensation laws or with occupational safety and health. Since our project primarily studied the relationships of social forces to federal

Figure 2.5.2-1 Citizens' Concerns about Occupational Health and Safety:
More Protection is Needed
(Concern for Aviation)

Source: The Readers' Guide to Periodic Literature index, Level 1

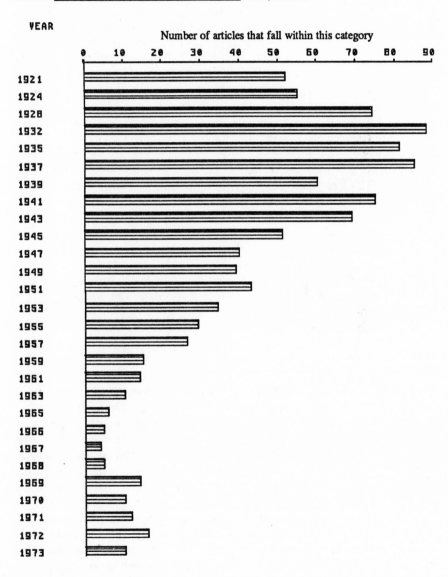

Figure 2.5.2-2 Citizens' Concerns about Occupational Health and Safety
(Concern for Occupational)

Source: The Readers' Guide to Periodic Literature index, Level 1

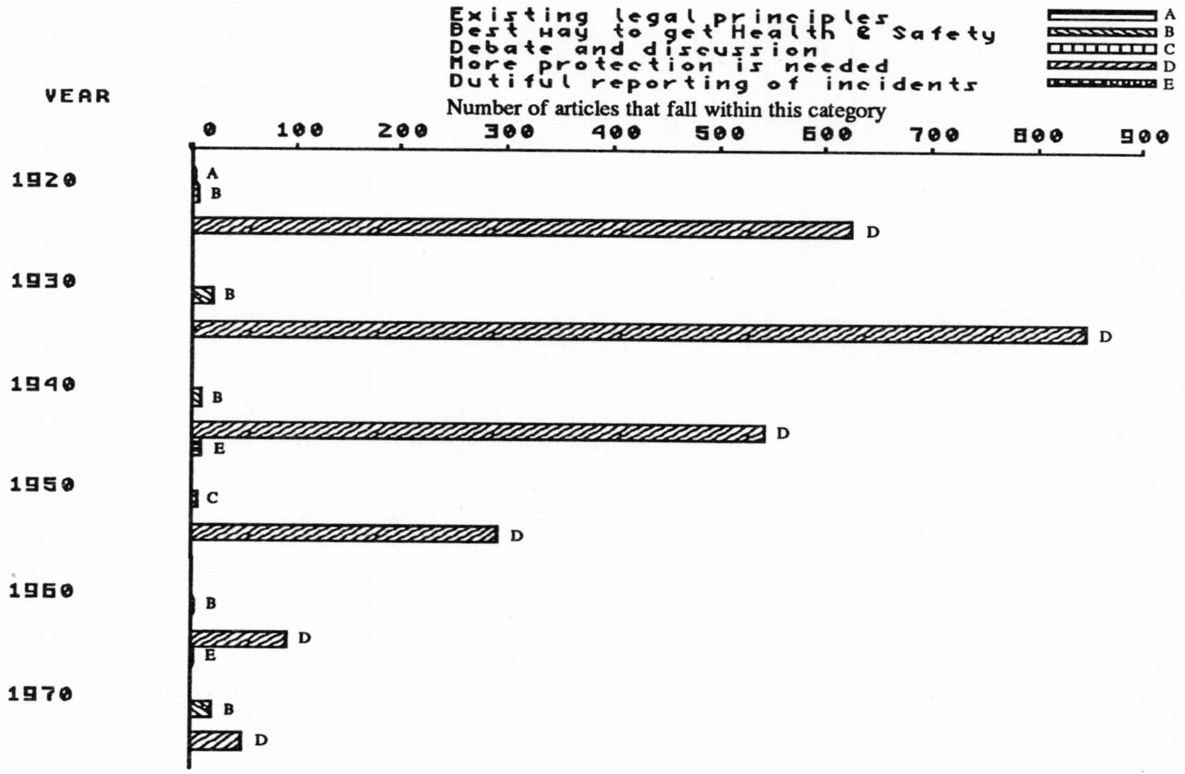
Existing legal principles A
Best way to get Health & Safety B
Debate and discussion C
More protection is needed D
Dutiful reporting of incidents E
Number of articles that fall within this category
YEAR
0
100
200
300
400
500
600
700
800
900
1920
1930
1940
1950
1960
1970
A
B
C
D
E

Figure 2.5.2-3 Citizens' Concerns about Occupational Health and Safety
(Concern for Occupational)

Source: The Readers' Guide to Periodic Literature index, Level 2

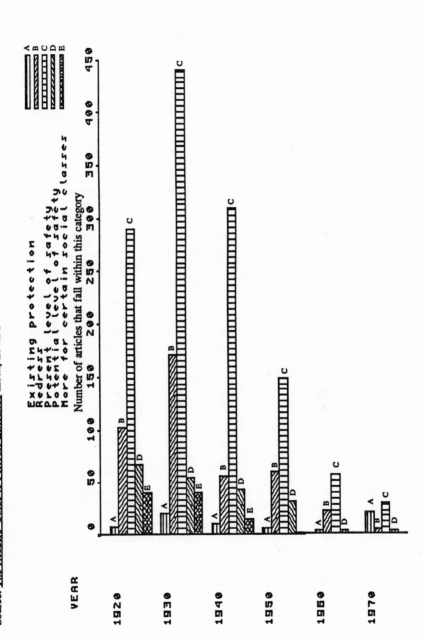

legislation, the effects of state legislation on social concern remains shadowy. A good overall picture of the trends in expressions of concern can be seen by examining the graph for The Readers' Guide of the categories under the category 'more protection is needed' mentioned above. This was the only main category with significant trends. A description of similar trends in the other indexes is provided here. The graphs for the other indexes are provided for reference in Appendix F.

In the Index to Legal Periodicals, the 1908-1922 period's concerns were primarily in 'workmens's compensation.' The second strongest area was 'legal' and most of this was related to FELA. There was also significant activity in 'through government action.' Overall levels peaked in the 1931-1934 period with very high concern in 'workmen's compensation,' high concern in 'through government action,' increased but still moderate concern in the 'specific ...' categories, and activity beginning in 'government' under 'existing protection.' Also there was activity beginning in 'redress,' during this time period. Through 1949 these were slightly decreased but activity remained strong in 'workmen's compensation.' There was moderate but continued concern under 'redress' along with 'legal' which was really related to accountability. There was an increase to moderately strong interest in 'government' in the 1937-1940 period which remained at that level until 1950. In the 1950's the area of 'workmen's compensation' returned to its very high levels and remained there. The area of 'government' under 'existing protection' grew in significance, becoming the second largest category. The area of 'legal' related to responsibility grew also towards the end of the 1950's. The area of 'redress' started out at zero at the beginning of the 1950's and grew to significance by that decade's end. The 'specific disease.' and 'specific hazard' categories grew. Also the areas of 'present level' and 'desired level' appeared along with all their branches except 'stewardship' which always contained zero expressions of concern. The 1961-1964 period still had strong concern in 'workmen's compensation' along with 'specific disease.' Most of the other areas were already declining rapidly. But FELA interest under 'legal' reappeared, and 'redress' remained at its moderate levels. The mid to late 1960's saw a decrease in concern in 'workmen's compensation,' but this still remained the most significant category. The areas of 'government,' and 'through government action' saw a rebirth of activity. The area of 'specific disease' also started to have activity in the late 1960's. In the early 1970's 'workmen's compensation' was still the strongest area, though it was still declining. The area of 'specific industry' was significant for the first time. The area of 'government' under 'existing protection' was continuing to grow, and was second only to 'workmen's compensation.'

In The New York Times Index the concern in 1945 was primarily in 'workmen's compensation,' and 'safety movement.' The period of 1950 saw a shift of emphasis from 'workmen's compensation' to 'safety movement' while 1955 reversed this. The year 1960 was very similar to 1955. The period of 1965 had almost everything in 'workmen's compensation,' with 'debate and discussion' beginning to show activity, and a decrease in the overall degree of concern. The period of 1970 showed dramatic changes. That year had almost all the expressions of concern in 'through government action,' with both a significant increase in 'debate and discussion' and in the overall degree of concern ('through government action' went from zero to 34). If one includes 'government' and 'through government action' together this still represents an order of magnitude increase in this area combination. The period of 1975 was similar to 1970 in the degree of concern in 'debate and discussion,' and 'through government action.' In 1975 'debate and discussion' was still, to a great extent, related to politics and administrative problems. The interesting aspect of 1975 is an increase in overall levels which occurred primarily in 'general data' and 'specific disease.'

In the Public Affairs Information Service the period of 1916 saw diverse activity. Almost all of the lowest level categories under 'more protection is needed' were significant (only 'generic,' and 'new technologies' were empty.). The other categories were not significant. The main activity was in 'through government action,' and 'workmen's compensation,' although this was not a major dominance over some other categories such as 'specific industry' or 'industrial hygiene.' The period of 1920 saw slight overall increases, primarily in the categories under 'present level of safety' (particularly 'specific hazards'). Also 'industrial hygiene' saw significant increase, although many of the other significant areas of 1916 had decreases. The period of 1925 blended the findings of 1916 and 1920. By 1964 there was dramatic decreases in overall levels, with most of the expressions of concern being in 'workmen's compensation' or in the categories under 'present level of safety,' in particular 'general data' and 'specific industry.' There were some expressions of concern in other typical areas such as 'industrial hygiene,' but these were very low and represented usually an order of magnitude decrease over the degree of concern shown in previous periods.

The Readers' Guide showed the cleanest trends in the more general concern categories. In addition the emphasis in the more specific categories did not change much over short periods of time. The period of 1919-1921 had significant expressions of concern in most of the lowest level categories, except 'generic' and 'stewardship.' Most of the expressions of concern went to the areas under 'present level,' 'desired level,' or 'workmen's compensation,' but the areas under 'potential level,' and 'certain classes' were not insignificant. The period of 1924 was very similar to 1921. The period of 1928 showed marked increases overall. These were taken up in all the previous areas, along with the first significant appearance of 'government' under 'existing protection.' The period of 1932 was very similar to 1928, with a heavier relative emphasis on 'workmen's compensation,' 'general data,' and a substantial increase in 'insurance' itself. The period of 1935 was similar to 1932, but with general decreases in the degree of overall concern, mostly felt in the categories under 'desired level,' and all the categories under 'present level' except 'specific disease.' There were decreases in the lowest levels under 'potential level,' but these were made up by new expressions of concern under that category directly. The period of 1937 saw continued decreases in essentially all areas. That trend continued in 1939.

The period of 1941 was similar to 1939, except for an absence of expressions of concern in 'government,' and except for a significant increase in 'workmen's compensation.' The period of 1943 was similar to 1941, except for a shift from 'workmen's compensation' to 'industrial hygiene.' The period of 1945 was similar to 1943, but with a decrease in the degree of overall concern, which occurred primarily in 'industrial hygiene.' Also there was small, but significant activity in 'government' again. The period of 1947 was similar to 1945. Also 1947 had the first significant expressions of concern in 'dutiful reporting of accidents.' The period of 1949 was similar to 1947, and 1945, with continued decrease in the degree of overall concern. The area of 'dutiful reporting of accidents' was significant. The area of 'government' doubled, but still was not a major area. The 1950s had a similar balance of concerns but with a general decrease in overall levels each year.

By 1961 the only areas with significant expressions of concern were the ones under 'present level,' 'workmen's compensation,' 'new technology,' and 'industrial hygiene.' By 1963 only 'insurance,' 'workmen's compensation,' and the areas under 'present level' were significant. The trend of general decrease in overall levels continued through 1965, when only the categories under 'present level' were significant. The period of 1966 was similar to 1965, but with lower overall expressions of concern. The period of 1967 was virtually empty. So was 1968, although there was a very small rebirth under 'desired level' directly and in 'industrial hygiene.' The period of 1969 showed slight growth. This was in the areas of 'specific disease,' and 'workmen's compensation' and 'redress' directly. The period of 1970 was similar to 1969, but with a shift from 'workmen's' compensation' and 'redress' to 'specific hazard' and 'more protection needed' directly. The period of 1971 showed slight growth in 'government' under 'existing protection.' 1972 showed slight growth in 'specific disease' and 'specific hazard.' The period of 1973 showed very little in any category other than 'government,' which grew to the largest it had ever been. There were also small but significant expressions of concern in 'safety movement,' 'workmen's compensation,' and directly in 'more protection needed.'

The primary period of popular concern about occupational safety and health was apparently in the 1930s so The Washington Post Index may not seem particularly helpful. However the data from this index did show a small resurgence in concern for occupational safety and health in the mid to late 1970s. The period of 1971 showed a small degree of concern, with essentially all in either 'present level' directly or in its branches of 'specific industry' and 'specific hazard.' The period of 1972 had a slight decrease in this area which was more than made up in 'redress.' In fact 'redress' and 'present level' were equivalent. So the net effect was an overall increase in 1972. The period of 1973 also had an increase in overall concern. The area of 'redress' stayed about the same, but 'present level' increased and 'safety movement' appeared. The period of 1974 had the same degree of overall concern as 1973, but there was a shift of almost all the expressions of concern into 'present level' while 'through government action' appeared in a small way. The period of 1975 had an overall increase in concern, predominantly due to a reappearance of 'redress.' Also there was a slight increase in areas under 'present level,' and return to nothing in 'through government action.' The period of 1976 had a big increase in overall concern, all in 'present level.' The period of 1977 had a decrease in overall concern due to large decrease in 'present level,' which was offset slightly by a doubling in 'redress.' The period of 1978 had a decrease in overall concern due primarily to a large decrease in 'redress.' The period of 1979 was similar to 1978, except for a first time appearance of 'debate and discussion.'

2.5.3 Findings from Content Analysis of Hearings (Occupational Safety and Health)

The first hearings we studied for this category were those of the 1968 House Committee on Education and Labor. Figure 2.5.3-1). These hearings were marked by great concern for administrative reform and increased technological development to solve problems. Several witnesses testifying before the Committee voiced the concern that society was not making an adequate effort to eliminate the problem of occupational hazards and injuries when compared to other governmental efforts. The general facts (14,000 workers killed annually and $1.5 billion lost in wages) justified concern for worker's safety and made it clear that industry was unable to police itself.

Not only were many of the existing standards outdated and inadequate, but understaffing vitiated their administration. Some states were notorious for not enforcing standards. Furthermore, there was strong concern that funding for research on occupational accidents and diseases was insufficient. These hazards included widespread use of toxic agents and lung disease among coal miners. Adequate information about industrial diseases was not

82

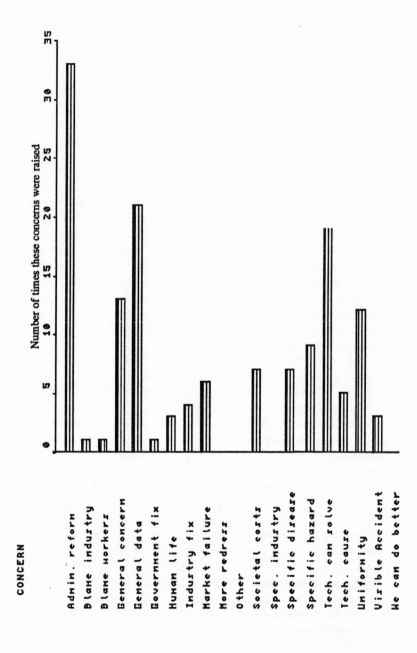

Figure 2.5.3-1 Legislators' Concerns about Occupational Health and Safety
(Concern for Occupational)

Source: 1968 House Committee Hearings on Education and Labor

always available, and some witnesses charged industry with withholding such data.

Hearings of the 1968 Senate Committee on Labor and Public Welfare paralleled House hearings and presented many statistics about occupational hazards and diseases. Experts like Ralph Nader conceded that the toll of job-related accidents had never been quantified accurately but that the public had been lulled by "mass statistics." Costs to society, solutions via technology, and the need for administrative reform were other important concerns at the hearings. Anxiety about the shortage of trained personnel in the field of occupational health and safety, and dissatisfaction with insufficient attention paid to worker's safety were also voiced. The general sentiment in the testimony was that society could and should make the workplace safer.

The National Consumers League asserted that assurance of safe and healthful working conditions was the right of every worker. Nonetheless, over thirty letters from industry leaders opposed the bill. Groups supporting the bill included organized labor, the medical profession, consumer groups, and concerned citizens.

Hearings of the 1969-1970 Senate Committee on Labor and Public Welfare emphasized the need for more administrative action. The AFL-CIO claimed the states had performed poorly, and supporters of OSHA urged the Federal Government to exercise more leadership in occupational health and safety. Blame was distributed between industry and workers for occupational accidents and injuries. More redress for injured workers, evaluation of societal costs, and solutions that technology could provide were discussed frequently.

Social attitudes had changed enough so that it was generally conceded that the contemporary worker could not alone secure his health and safety because of the complexities of his workplace. Moreover, new workers often lacked safety training and competition led industry to take dangerous shortcuts.

2.5.4 Summary (Occupational Safety and Health)

Occupational safety and health was the responsibility of state government until the Occupational Safety and Health Act (OSHA) of 1970 provided for a broad federal role in this area. The findings of the index content analysis shows a steady decline of concern (except for the Index to Legal Periodicals), starting from a peak in the mid-1930s decreasing to almost no popular expressions of concern at the time OSHA was passed.

Early in the twentieth century, public concern raised by several journalists about unsafe working conditions prompted some states to pass work safety laws. A viewpoint common among industrialists and government at the time was that the court system would answer justly any claim of an injured employee without need for legislation. Legal obstacles to prosecuting such suits and their prohibitive cost for many workers led to reform in the shape of workmen's compensation laws which provided unconditional partial damages for injured workers.

Popular periodicals reflected increasing concern in many different areas of occupational health and safety until the mid-thirties. This period was one in which the growing labor movement was fighting hard for child labor laws, an eight-hour work day, the right to strike, and safer working conditions. In 1936, the federal government passed the Walsh-Healey Act providing compensation to certain government contractors, another result of this grassroots political action.

As the thirties ended, popular concern overall as shown by the indexes gradually began to decrease. Paralleling this decrease, the secondary literature shows very little government activity until the late sixties. Some congressional interest led to the introduction of several bills none of which passed or even received much attention.

A strong feeling that legislation was the states' responsibility is part of the reason for this non-action, a feeling reflected by Secretary of Labor James Mitchell's remark in 1958 that setting mandatory standards for dealing with hazardous substances "did not warrant federal intervention" [Bureau of National Affairs, 1971, p.16]. The varying state laws resulting from this attitude help to explain the difference found in the index content analysis of the Index to Legal Periodicals. The analysis of this index showed steady and increasing professional interest from the early 1950s to the mid-1960s, especially related to workmen's compensation.

The decrease in popular concern shown in the analysis of the other indexes may also be part of the reason for the lack of action. Also, bureaucratic conflict and division of responsibility obstructed federal action. The Department of Labor traditionally administered the federal government's limited job safety role including the Bureau of Labor Standards; the Department of Health, Education, and Welfare was in charge of industrial disease and worker health.

Concern was still decreasing in the early and mid-sixties as shown by index content-analysis, but the actual need for effective occupational safety and health laws was growing. Research had increased the knowledge of occupational disease which was rarely covered under state laws. More complex industrial processes had introduced many hazardous new substances into the workplace as shown by a DHEW report of 1965. The National Safety Council reported a sharp increase in industrial accidents in 1958, increasing through the sixties. All of these exposed a need that certain key people perceived and acted on.

These people included Senator Ralph Yarborough, head of the Senate Subcommittee on Labor, Jim O'Hara, head of the House Subcommittee on Labor, and President Johnson, as well as members of organized labor. In 1968, bills on occupational safety and health were introduced in the House and the Senate, and hearings were held. At this point, during 1969, a slight increase in concern occurred, as shown in the indexes, mostly for specific diseases and workmen's compensation. The hearings presented new statistics and a desire for a more uniform method of dealing with the problem as well as concern over the cost to society of injury and disease among workers.

In 1970, more hearings were held. The attitudes expressed at this hearing contrasted sharply with those of the early part of the century, as all participants conceded that today's worker could not be insure his own health and safety. At the end of 1970, the Occupational Health and Safety Act was passed even though index content analysis reveals minimal popular concern at the time.

2.6 Historical Review of Forces Leading to Pesticides Control
     Legislation
     2.6.1 Historical Context from the Secondary Literature
            and Interviews (Pesticides Control)

Government regulation of pesticides has taken a variety of approaches. Early in the century, government standards promoted use; in recent decades, protection of humans and the environment have become prerequisite to marketing. Our study allowed us to map the shifting attitudes that produced this transition.

Pesticide legislation began with the Federal Insecticide Act of 1910. The main concern prompting this law was that farmers were being sold useless pesticides by certain manufacturers because of lack of information about the product. These fraudulent products affected not only the farmers but legitimate manufacturers also, who joined in lobbying for the bill which required labeling the contents on all insecticides and fungicides. The government's assumption was that accurate information best protects consumers.

Early concerns about the health hazards of pesticides appeared in the 1920s when the dangers of certain chemical residues were discovered. In 1927, the Food, Drug, and Insecticide Administration (FDIA) was established in the US Department of Agriculture (USDA). Even though it lacked an explicit legislative mandate, the FDIA set maximum levels for residues of arsenic, flourine, and lead on foods. Because USDA enforced the 1910 Insecticide Act, the guidelines of FDIA initiated the separation of regulatory activities protecting farmers and consumers [Blodgett, 1974, p.206]. Following the Food, Drug, and Cosmetic Act of 1938, the first legislation allowing tolerance setting for pesticides, the FDIA became the Food and Drug Administration (FDA) and, in 1940, it was moved out of the USDA.

During WWII, the first synthetic pesticide, DDT was tested and used to counter malaria. Previous to this, pesticides were organic and primarily not as complex. Acute toxicity was the biggest threat to health [Touhey, 1984]. By 1945, DDT had effectively controlled pests and was recommended for civilian use. Chemical manufacturers were excited by this new market and expanded their search for synthetic pesticides.

As new pesticides entered the market, health dangers multiplied. The labeling requirements of the Federal Insecticide Act did not specifically require efficacy information but only contents on labels, making it difficult for farmers to determine if a product would be effective. This, combined with the increased complexity and number of new pesticides, made it difficult for users to assess the efficacy, much less the safety, of a product [Blodgett, 1974]. In 1947, Congress passed the Federal Insecticide, Fungicide, and Rodenticide Act (which replaced the 1910 act) to deal with these problems. The new law provided for premarket testing and registration of pesticides by USDA, to determine efficacy and safety. Labels were required to indicate appropiate uses and possible health hazards.

After WWII concern for the effects of pesticides on human health grew. The House created a Select Committee, headed by Rep. James J. Delaney, to Investigate the Use of Chemicals in Food. In 1952 and 1953, the Committee recommended that additives in food be tested for safety prior to marketing. An amendment to the Food, Drug, and Cosmetic Act was passed in 1954 to address this concern with respect to pesticides. Called the Miller Amendment, it prohibited registration of a pesticide by the USDA if it did not comply with tolerances for residues in agricultural food products set by the FDA. There was still no way US Public Health Service (PHS) could effect any registration for non-food crop uses, USDA had sole authority.

The USDA has always been responsible primarily for the concerns of one group, the farmers. It is not surprising that with the increased number, uses, and effectiveness of chemical pesticides, the USDA became closely involved with pesticide promotion.

With the growing use of more complex and persistent pesticides, concern developed about the effect of pesticides on the environment. An illustration of this concern is the events surrounding the USDA's fire ant eradication program, begun in 1958. The USDA began using two of the most potent of the persistent hydrocarbon insecticides, dieldrin and heptachlor, with known toxicities higher than DDT, but with little data on the effects of their use. The program proceeded at great expense and with significant damage to wildlife yet Florida and Louisiana reported in 1962 that there were more fire ants than when the program started. Dissatisfaction with the program by farmers, state officials and ecologists grew. Rachel Carson wrote about the urgent requests to USDA made by conservationists and ecologists asking for at least a delay of the program until more research was done. "The protests were ignored ... It was clear that any research would be in the nature of a post mortem" [Carson, 1962]. Even as the destruction progressed, in 1958 the US Department of the Interior had received a legislative mandate to conduct research on pesticides' effect on the environment.

While environmentalists were being aroused by the fire ant program, the public learned about the dangers of pesticides by an event called the cranberry scare. In 1958, the USDA registered the pesticide aminotriazole for use on cranberry bogs a few days after harvesting. The FDA was asked to set a tolerance level so that the bogs could be sprayed at other times. The FDA announced in 1959 that there was no safe tolerance since the pesticide had caused thyroid cancer in some laboratory rats. On November 9, 1959 the Secretary of the Department of Health, Education, and Welfare (DHEW) issued a statement urging no further sales of cranberries grown in certain areas because of the possibility of contamination. The contaminated berries were seized by the FDA. Consumers had nothing to fear from those available, yet "the spectre of cancer" made cranberries unsellable. USDA, which had not been forewarned of FDA's announcement, was upset and paid $10,000,000 to cranberry farmers [Blodgett, 1974]. This government controversy attracted media exposure, alerting the public to the possibility of cancer from pesticides, and showing the lack of coordination between the USDA and the FDA.

Public awareness of pesticides' dangers continued to grow with professional controversies over their use. Rachel Carson's Silent Spring, a book promoting the careful use of pesticides, especially persistent pesticides, and the need for more research on their effect on the environment, was important in the early stages of this process. Beginning on June 16, 1962, a condensed version of the book appeared in "The New Yorker" magazine in three weekly installments. Attacks and praises came from all sides. Prominent biologists and other scientists concurred with Carson's thesis, while others vehemently criticized it, including George C. Decker chairman of the NAS-NRC Subcommittee on the Evaluation of Pesticide-Wildlife Problems who called the book "science fiction". The chemical and agricultural industries and all those with a vested interest in pesticides interpreted Silent Spring as an attack on any use of chemical pesticides rather than the call for caution it was [Graham, 1970]. Media coverage of the controversy went from technical journals to periodicals like "Reader's Digest" and "Time", with technical experts quoted on both sides.

As public concern grew over possible long-range effects of pesticides like DDT, President Kennedy requested the President's Advisory Committee make a study of pesticide use. The report of this Committee came out in 1963, during the heat of the controversy occasioned by Carson's book. The Committee reported that there were inherent hazards in the current approved uses of chemical pesticides. The report recommended that more research be done on pesticides' effect on the environment, that alternative methods of pest control be developed, that departments coordinate their activities and information, and that residues be controlled by 'an orderly reduction in the use of persistent pesticides.' There was heavy media coverage of the report with a headline in "The Christian Science Monitor" reading "Rachel Carson Stands Vindicated" [Graham, 1970].

The effects of the report were far-reaching. President Kennedy ordered that its recommendations be implemented, resulting in an interagency agreement signed by USDA, USDI, and DHEW in 1964, providing for greater coordination between the agencies. The report had called for revising FIFRA, the 1947 act, to include environmental protection. Senator Ribicoff of the Committee on Government Operations' Subcommittee on Reorganization held oversight hearings on the subject. In 1964, DHEW contracted with the National Cancer Institute to perform a long-range study on the chronic effects of pesticides. In 1965, the research budget for pesticides of the USDA almost doubled. Concerned citizens and professionals had brought the hazards of pesticides to the attention of the public and the government, and research to mitigate the damage had begun.

As research was being done on the environmental effects of pesticides, especially DDT, the Environmental Defense Fund (EDF) was formed. This private group, composed of lawyers and scientists, was created to combine the techniques of law with the knowledge of science to "defend" the environment. In 1969, EDF sued USDA and and DHEW over the registration of DDT. EDF also sued the EPA in 1971, with the Court ruling that EPA must hold cancellation proceedings on all DDT uses and consider whether DDT uses should be immediately halted [Blodgett, 1974]. EDF fought for the cancellation of the registration of other pesticides as well.

While scientific evidence on the dangers of certain pesticides was capturing attention, Congress attended to problems with administering FIFRA. Late in 1968 and early 1969, Representative H.L. Fountain, Chairman of the Subcommittee on Interdepartmental Relations, held hearings on this topic. Impetus for the hearings came from two GAO reports about the regulations and uses of the pesticide, lindane. J.R. Naughton, counsel for the Subcommittee, recommended that hearings be held after reading the reports, saying he found the present state of pesticide regulation to be an "indefensible situation" [Naughton, 1984]. According to Naughton, the hearings greatly heightened Congressional awareness of the problems of FIFRA.

Two other factors in 1969 heightened congressional concern. First, on March 27, 1969 the FDA seized some Coho salmon caught in Lake Michigan because they were thought to contain DDT residues. The controversy surrounding this event received a lot of public attention [Mrak, 1983]. At about this time, the National Cancer Institute issued a report on the chronic health effects of pesticides which suggested that DDT was carcinogenic.

These events stimulated Robert Finch, Secretary of DHEW, to form a commission to study pesticides. Commission member Dr. Dale Lindsay stated that the reason for its creation was "definitely public pressure" [Lindsay, 1983]. The Mrak commission, headed by Dr. Emil Mrak, issued its report "Pesticides and their Relationship to Environmental Health" by the end of 1969. This comprehensive document made many recommendations including a stronger interagency agreement; that all uses of DDD and DDT be stopped in two years and requiring unanimous agreement by USDA, USDI, and DHEW on any uses of DDT until then; minimizing human exposure to pesticides considered a potential health hazard; review of the adequacy of existing regulations and legislation. Research was producing a torrent of legislation.

That same year, 1969, certain uses of DDT were cancelled by the USDA which included persistence as an explicit criterion to be considered in registration. The National Environmental Policy Act was passed requiring statements from all government agencies on the environmental impact of any new project. Environmental concerns were further incorporated into government with the creation of the Environmental Protection Agency in 1970, by an executive reorganization plan. Environmental interests now had specific representation in government, and there was enough concentrated effort to push Congress to consider legislative reform of FIFRA rather than administrative solutions.

The Federal Environmental Pesticides Control Act of 1972 (FEPCA) is the legislation that was eventually passed to replace FIFRA. Early in 1972 the Nixon Administration proposed a bill form of FEPCA to Congress. The great controversy which lead to the cancellation of DDT revealed the inadequacy of FIFRA. Four sets of hearings were held in the House and Senate. Consideration of the bill was transferred in 1971 from the Senate Agriculture Committee, the traditional seat of agricultural interests, to the Senate Commerce Committee, allowing more of a voice for labor and environmental concerns. The bill passed with concessions by all sides in the last six days of the 92nd Congress. FEPCA rewrote FIFRA, including most of the suggestions of the Mrak report, and was signed on October 21, 1972.

The enactment of FEPCA was not the last instance of legislative reform regarding pesticides. The re-registration of pesticides required by FEPCA was called impossible and was changed in 1978 [Touhey, 1984]. Yet FEPCA was the legislation that embodied the awakening the country had gone through about the harmful effects of pesticide usage.

2.6.2 Findings from Index Content Analysis (Pesticides Control)

The trends found in expressions of concern relating to the use of pesticides were very similar in all the indexes. Early concerns about pesticides displayed the attitude that pesticide use was a good. These concerns emphasized protecting the farmer from fraudulent producers of pesticides and making sure that industry could provide adequate supplies of efficient pesticides. These concerns gradually gave way, from 1945-1960, to general unease about the bad side effects of pesticide use. In the early 1960s there was a sudden increase in concern about the ill effects of pesticide use. This was best shown by The Readers' Guide (Figures 2.6.2-1 and 2.6.2-2). This concern died in the mid 1960s and returned in the early 1970s. Although the indexes tell the same story in the more general categories, there were differences in subcategories. These differences and significant trends are discussed in the following presentation using the categories of the tree structures described in section 2.1.2.4. Numbers in parentheses represent expressions of concern for a typical year in the period described. They are presented here to provide a better sense of variations in the relative strengths of concerns expressed in this area during the time period described. The trends illustrated by these numbers are analogous with the trends graphically represented here and in appendix F, although the numbers stated may not be exactly the same as that

Figure 2.6.2-1 Citizens' Concerns that Pesticides are Not Beneficial
(Concern for Pesticides)

Source: The Readers' Guide to Periodic Literature index, Level 1

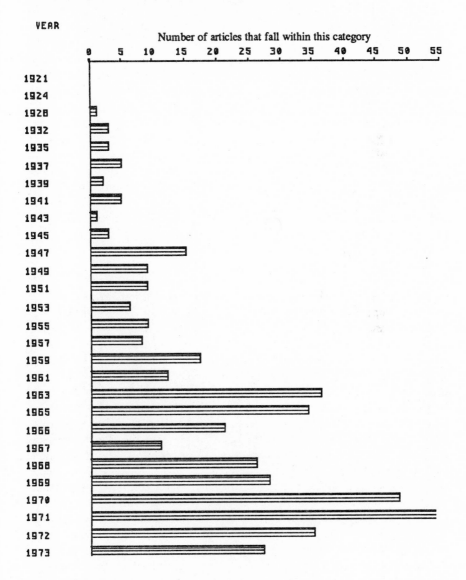

Figure 2.6.2-2 Citizens' Concerns about Pesticides
(Concern for Pesticides)

Source: The Readers' Guide to Periodic Literature index, Level 1

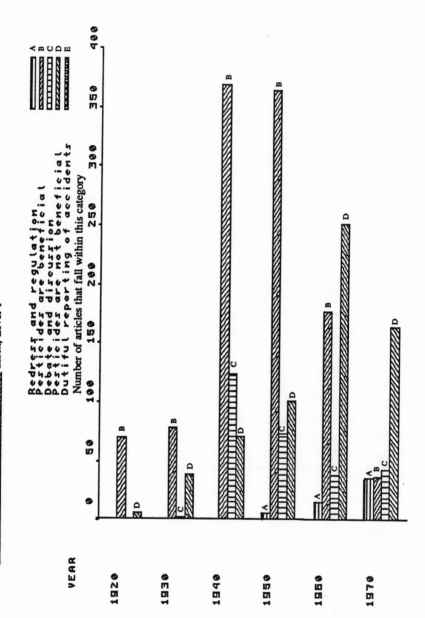

represented on a particular graph. These differences is caused by rounding errors which are due to the scheme used to create the graphs. These differences are small and do not affect the interpretation of trends.

The Index to Legal Periodicals showed remarkably little professional interest in the use of pesticides. The first significant expressions of concern were in or under 'pesticides are not beneficial' (1) in 1955-1958 period. There was significant concern under 'pesticides are not beneficial' (1) in 1967-1970. These expressions of concern were split between the main category itself, and 'ecology.' The period of 1970-1973 showed much growth with the heaviest category being 'redress and regulation' (2). Most of this was in 'non-fraud regulation.' The area of 'pesticides are not beneficial' was significant (1), with the emphasis being on 'ecology.'

In The New York Times Index 1945 was a very active period. Most of the expressions of concern were under 'pesticides are beneficial' (61). These were related predominantly to DDT. There also were significant expressions of concern (12) in 'general data' under 'debate and discussion.' There were small, but significant expressions of concern under 'pesticides are not beneficial' primarily in 'ecology.' These were at least partially related to DDT. There was not much activity in 1950, mostly in 'new breakthrough' under 'pesticides are beneficial' (10). The only other significant expressions of concern were under 'pesticides are not beneficial' (6). These were primarily in and under 'type of harm.' These were at least partially related to DDT. In 1955 the concern was insignificant in all but 'pesticides are beneficial' (3). The period of 1960 showed growth under 'pesticides are not beneficial' (6), primarily in 'food,' and 'ecology.' The period of 1965 was a year of marked growth. The area of 'pesticides are not beneficial' more than doubled (13). All of this concern was in 'food,' or 'consumer,' except for one direct general category count. The area of 'redress and regulation' appeared (6), with most of the concern in 'non-fraud regulation' (5). The area of 'pesticides are beneficial' was barely significant (2). There was continued and even greater growth in concern in 1970. The category of 'redress and regulation' increased (12), with most in 'non-fraud regulation' (11). The category of 'pesticides are beneficial' increased (9), but most of this was in 'harm but worth it' (6). The category of 'debate and discussion' reappeared with direct expressions of concern and in 'general data.' The category of 'pesticides are not beneficial' (42) grew both in the main category directly and in 'major' under 'degree of harm.' Many of these were related to a pesticide ban. The period of 1975 saw a large scale general decrease in concern, with expressions of concern under 'pesticides are beneficial' remaining almost the same as in 1970 (10). There was a shift of emphasis from ' harm but worth it' to 'new breakthrough.' The category of 'redress and regulation' was barely significant (2), as was 'debate and discussion' (2). The category of 'pesticides are not beneficial' dropped significantly (9), with a little more emphasis in 'major' though (5)).

In the Public Affairs Information Service there was little until 1964. In 1964 there was small but significant concern about pesticides. The category of 'redress and regulation' (4) was all in 'non-fraud regulation.' Nothing under 'pesticides are beneficial.' The category of 'debate and discussion' (3) was split between direct expressions of concern, 'general data,' and 'cost-benefit arguments.' The area of 'pesticides are not beneficial' (7) was primarily in 'ecology,' and 'direct health.'

The Readers' Guide told the most complete story about pesticide concern. The period of 1921 had significant expressions of concern in and under 'pesticides are beneficial' (8). The count under 'pesticides are beneficial' were in 'new methods,' 'effectiveness data,' and 'benefits of use.' The overall picture remained the same through 1935, with small but growing expressions of concern under 'pesticides are not beneficial.' These were 'food' related in 1928. In 1932 they were in 'user,' 'food,' and slightly in 'direct health.' In 1935 they were in 'food,' 'consumer,' and in 'specific pesticides.' The pesticide referred to seemed to be, at least sometimes, lead arsenate. The period of 1937 was similar to 1935, but with less in 'pesticides are beneficial' and a small appearance under redress and regulation in 'non-fraud regulation.' The period of 1939 similar to 1928. The period of 1941 saw general increase in both 'pesticides are beneficial' (17), 'pesticides are not beneficial' (5), but a greater relative increase in 'pesticides are not beneficial.' The expressions of concern under 'pesticides are not beneficial' were primarily in 'food,' and 'direct health.' But there was significant expressions of concern (1) in 'ecology.' The period of 1943 returned to scant (1) under 'pesticides are not beneficial.' The category of 'pesticides are beneficial' continued to increase (25).

The period ending in 1945 had a slight increase in 'pesticides are beneficial' (30), with many related to DDT. There were small but significant expressions of concern under 'pesticides are not beneficial' (3), with expressions of concern in 'user,' and 'ecology' (1). The ones in 'ecology' were related to DDT. There was also a very marked appearance of expressions of concern in 'specific pesticides' under 'debate and discussion' (16) in 1945. These were all about DDT. The period of 1947 saw major increases overall. The category of 'pesticides are beneficial' almost tripled, 'debate and discussion' almost doubled, and 'pesticides are not beneficial' (15) increased the most dramatically compared to 1945. Most of this activity was related to DDT. The period of 1949 was essentially the same as 1947, with all the expressions of concern cut in half. In the complete period from 1945 through 1949 'ecology,' 'food,' and 'direct health' all play significant roles, although it was primarily 'user' that had the expressions of concern under 'who is harmed.' The period of 1951 was similar to 1949, but with continued decrease in 'pesticides are beneficial' (20). The expressions of concern under 'pesticides are not beneficial' were primarily split between 'direct health,' and 'ecology.' The period of 1953 saw shifts away from 'pesticides are not beneficial,' and 'debate and discussion' to 'pesticides are beneficial.' The emphasis under 'type of harm' was 'ecology.' Also, under 'pesticides are not beneficial,' 'specific pesticide' had significant expressions of concern for the first time since 1939, and 'specific use' had significant expressions of concern for the first time since the beginning of the whole time period studied. In 1955 'debate and discussion' went to zero. The category of 'pesticides are beneficial' increased (60). The category of 'pesticides are not beneficial' increased slightly (10), with the emphasis on 'specific pesticides.' But 'ecology' was still significant (1). In 1957 'pesticides are not beneficial' remained about as it was in 1955. But there was a shift from 'pesticides are beneficial' to 'debate and discussion.' This was primarily (13) directly in the main category, of 'debate and discussion.' There was also slight (1) activity in 'non-fraud regulation.' In 1959 there was less (5) in and under 'debate and discussion' this was mostly still in 'general data.' The two main categories of 'pesticides are beneficial' (22) and 'pesticides are not beneficial' (16) were almost even. The category of 'ecology' gained relative significance also (3). In 1959 the area of 'redress and regulation' was barely significant (1). The period of 1961 saw general decreases overall. The category of 'pesticides are beneficial' dropped (14). The category of 'debate and discussion' dropped (3). The category of 'pesticides are not beneficial' dropped (12). The category of 'ecology' was now the emphasis under 'pesticides are not beneficial' (5).

The period ending in the year 1963 had nothing under 'debate and discussion,' 'pesticides are beneficial' dropped dramatically (5), 'pesticides are not beneficial' increased dramatically (36). Most of the expressions of concern under 'pesticides are not beneficial' were in the category directly (21) with the rest spread out as in the past. The period of 1965 was different, showing a return to significant activity in and under 'debate and discussion' (9). This was primarily direct (6), and almost all the rest was in 'general data' (2). The category of 'pesticides are beneficial' increased slightly (8), with substantial direct expressions of concern (2), and the emphasis in 'essentially no harm story' (3). This category included stories relating to proper use. The category of 'pesticides are not beneficial' remained strong (34), with the emphasis split between direct expressions of concern (14) and 'ecology' (10). It is important to note that 1965 was the first time 'redress and regulation' was substantial. All of this was due to 'non-fraud regulation' (3).

In the period ending in 1966, 'pesticides are beneficial' increased dramatically (35). The emphasis was on 'benefits of use' (15). The only other significant main category was 'pesticides are not beneficial' (21). The emphasis was split between direct and 'ecology.' In 1967 'non-fraud regulation' under 'redress and regulation' returned (6), and 'debate and discussion' returned (5). The category of 'pesticides are beneficial' grew again (64), with the most in direct expressions of concern (56). The category of 'pesticides are not beneficial' decreased (11), with the emphasis in 'ecology' (8). In 1968 'non-fraud regulation' was minimal (2). The category of 'debate and discussion' was small (5). The category of 'pesticides are beneficial' decreased remarkably (14). And in 1968 'pesticides are not beneficial' increased markedly (26), with the emphasis in 'ecology' (11). The period of 1969 was similar to 1968, with the expressions of concern in and under 'pesticides are not beneficial' (28) remaining almost the same, with similar emphasis in 'ecology' (10), although 'specific pesticides' was significant here (6), and not in 1968. The category of 'redress and regulation' was zero. The category of 'debate and discussion' (2) was barely significant. The category of 'pesticides are beneficial' (9), had the emphasis in 'essentially no harm story' (6). The period of 1970 had nothing significant in 'pesticides are beneficial,' or 'debate and discussion.' The category of 'redress and regulation' returned (10), with emphasis in 'non-fraud regulation' (9). The big change was in 'pesticides are not beneficial' (48), with emphasis in 'specific pesticides' (29). The category 'ecology' was still strong (10). The period of 1971 had substantial expressions of concern under all the previous main categories of 'redress and regulation' (10), 'pesticides are beneficial' (14), 'debate and discussion' (14), and 'pesticides are not beneficial' (50). The spread between the lower categories were typical of recent times, except that 'specific accident demonstrating not beneficial' under 'pesticides are not beneficial' appeared in a significant way (7) for the first time. The period of 1972 similar to 1971 with slight reductions in the expressions of concern in 'pesticides are beneficial,' and 'pesticides are not beneficial.' The same general relative emphasis existed, however there was nothing significant in 'specific accident demonstrating not beneficial.' The period of 1973 was similar to 1972 in character, but with continued reductions in the degree of overall concern.

The Washington Post Index showed the concern about pesticide use in the 1970s. The period of 1971 had by far the most expressions of concern in the main category of 'pesticides are not beneficial' (9), essentially split between direct expressions of concern and 'type of harm.' There were also significant expressions of concern in 'redress and regulation' (4),' and 'debate and discussion.' The period of 1972 was similar to 1971, except that there was nothing significant in 'debate and discussion.' The category of 'redress and regulation' had a slight increase (5), as well as 'pesticides are not beneficial' (10). The period of 1973 was essentially the same as 1972 in all areas except 'pesticides are not beneficial.' This area showed marked growth (23). Also there was now significant interest in the categories 'specific accident demonstrating not beneficial,' and 'user.' The period of 1974 was similar to 1971. The period of 1975 was similar to 1972, with slightly less expressions of concern overall (a reduction of approximately 25%). The period of 1976 had marked increases overall. The category of 'redress and regulation' increased (10), with all in 'non-fraud regulation' as in the previous periods. The category of 'debate and discussion' (5) increased. The category of 'pesticides are not beneficial' (28) had a dramatic increase, with an emphasis in 'type of harm' (22). The period of 1977 had a decrease in 'redress and regulation' (3). The category of 'debate and discussion' remained the same (5). The category of 'pesticides are not beneficial' decreased, but was still the strongest (15). The period of 1978 was similar to 1977, except that 'pesticides are not beneficial' dropped again (8). The period of 1979 was similar to 1978, except for a shift of emphasis from 'debate and discussion' (2) to 'type of harm' (8) under 'pesticides are not beneficial.' By 1979 'redress and regulation' (3), and 'debate and discussion' were barely significant. Only 'pesticides are not beneficial' had anything substantial in it (11), and that was rather small.

2.6.3 Findings from Content Analysis of Hearings
       (Pesticides Control)

The 1910 House Committee on Interstate and Foreign Commerce hearing, which led to the Federal Insecticide Act of 1910, sought to eliminate the marketing of fraudulent products. There was concern that some farmers were being defrauded through an absence of reliable information so the bill required contents labels on all insecticides and fungicides. Safety was not a prominent issue in this hearing.

Some concern for the business of legitimate manufacturers and also for the environment was voiced during the hearing. The head of the Bureau of Entomology, Department of Agriculture, stated that some pesticides are not only worthless but also injurious.

The 1946 House Committee on Agriculture hearings mainly dealt with objections and amendments to the Act of 1910. Farmers were especially pleased with the legislation because it provided them with protection against loss or damage before it occurred. The pesticides industry supported a labelling requirement but balked at establishing rigid standards. What the chemical manufacturers did seek was protection from multiple suits and liability in cases where the product was misused. Uniformity of regulation was considered essential by several witnesses.

The 1947 House Committee on Agriculture hearing was held to scrutinize a bill to regulate the marketing of poisons. The primary concern was that old regulations did not effectively regulate new products and administrative reform was necessary. Cases of fraud were still occurring, and some concern for protecting the users of poisons from financial loss was evident. A second major concern was for uniformity in State and Federal laws and for coordinating the activities of the two levels. The passage of new laws regulating poisons in several States prompted the call for uniformity. Fears about damage to the environment were beginning to surface.

Administrative reform to fill societal needs was the primary topic of the 1954 House Committee on Interstate and Foreign Commerce hearings. A second major concern was the safeguarding of public health against dangerous pesticides. Other concerns expressed during the course of the hearings included helping small farmers, keeping poisonous chemicals out of food, and studying unknown effects of certain chemicals. Several witnesses testified that they were worried about the inadequate testing procedures of pesticides for safety. Asserting the necessity of pesticides, some witnesses express concern for protecting food producers. Strong concern for the environment was becoming evident.

The 1954 Senate Committee on Labor and Public Welfare hearings dealt with the Miller Amendment. The effects of pesticides on human life and the necessary utilization of pesticides were frequently discussed. Concern for the small farmer, the environment, and the safety of food also was expressed.

The 1969 House Committee on Government Operations hearings examined the deficiencies in the administration of the Federal Insecticide, Fungicide and Rodenticide Act. The "Fountain Hearings" examined the need for improvement in the administration of FIFRA. The Committee did not feel that the Agricultural Research Service of USDA had served the public trust adequately in scanning new products for hazards to the environment and human health.

The main concern of the 1971 House Committee on Agriculture hearing was protecting the environment and natural resources. A second important concern was the use of pesticides for serving societal needs. There also were worries about the threat to human life; the health of the people was considered paramount. Some calls for strengthening Federal control over pesticides were voiced.

The main concern voiced during the 1971 Senate Committee on Agriculture and Forestry hearings (Figure 2.6.3-1) was protecting the environment. Other prominent concerns were human health and societal needs and assurance of an adequate food supply. Some witnesses claimed we were still ignorant of pesticides' effects on human life and ecosystems.

The outstanding focus of the 1972 Senate Committee on Agriculture and Forestry hearings was the environment. There was fear that the environment had been saturated with deadly poisons that endangered many organisms, including man. The need for more selective control of pesticides was emphasized by EPA officials. Some concern for farmers and field workers who come into contact with pesticides also was expressed. Sickness, injury, and death had struck some workers handling pesticides.

Figure 2.6.3-1 Legislators' Concerns about Pesticides
(Concern for Pesticides)

Source: 1971 Senate Committee Hearings on Agriculture and Forestry

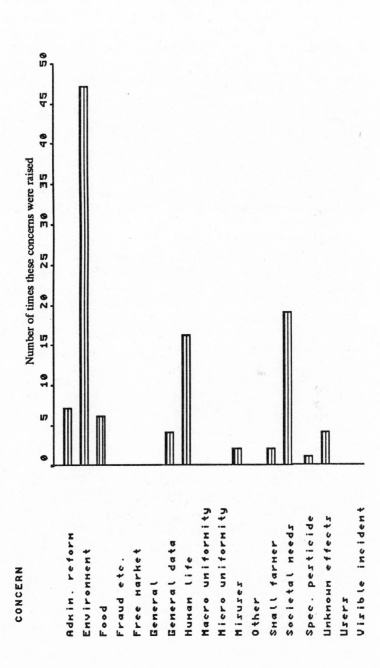

2.6.4 Summary (Pesticides Control)

The federal government has been involved in regulating pesticides since the turn of the century. The character of the concern expressed about this issue has changed dramatically from the farmers' wish for protection from unfair market practices to broadbased public concern for the environment and human health. Index content analysis shows an increasing number of articles, peaking in the 1950s and decreasing subsequently, that argue benefits to health from pesticide use. Concern that pesticide use is harmful was first present in the 1930s and escalated into the 1970s.

The year 1910 occasioned the first regulation of pesticides when content labels were instituted to protect farmers from fraudulent products. Lack of information leading to fraud against farmers was the primary concern voiced in hearings that led to this legislation which gave control over pesticides to the Department of Agriculture, whose main interest had been and continued to be the farmer and farm productivity.

Through the 1930s and into the 1940s the index content analysis reveals an increase of expressions promoting the use of pesticides as beneficial for health by controlling disease and providing plentiful produce through "winning the war on pests". During this period concerns about harmful effects of pesticides appeared as related to food, the consumer, and specific pesticides acutely toxic to humans such as lead arsenate. Expressions that pesticides should be used and are beneficial far outweigh concerns over harmful effects in the twenties and thirties.

World War II was a turning point in the development of pesticides. Synthetic organic compounds were introduced for use during the war and promoted heavily for civilian use afterward because they had impressive immediate effects. The first of these was DDT and the indexes record many articles extolling its attributes. As early as 1945, concern over harmful effects of DDT on the ecology was present but very small. Greater than concern over pesticides not being beneficial was the appearance in the indexes of articles questioning the relative harms and merits of pesticides in relation to health. As this questioning decreases steadily into the sixties, statements of concern about the dangers of pesticides increase.

In 1947 hearings were held to reform previous regulations that were not effectively controlling new products. Assuring uniformity between state and federal levels was another major concern. The result of these hearings was the Federal Insecticide, Rodenticide, and Fungicide Act (FIFRA) permitting the USDA to register and allow marketing of effective products. The indexes show concern almost tripling in this year relating to the benefits of pesticides. During the 1947 hearings, concerns over the effects of pesticides on the users' health and on the environment are found, although these are not the major issues.

Hearings leading to the Miller Amendment in 1954 which gave the Food and Drug Administration authority to set allowable tolerances of pesticides in food show increasing concern about pesticides' effects on human life and food. By 1957 the indexes showed approximately even concerns for the harms and benefits of pesticides. Chronic health effects of pesticides like DDT, known as persistent pesticides because they remain in the food chain, gained publicity.

There was heightened concern about the effects of pesticides in the early 1960s after Rachel Carson's book Silent Spring was published. This book, which urged that pesticides be used cautiously, ignited a controversy which brought the dangers of pesticides to the public eye [Graham, 1970]. Research into the effects of pesticides was sponsored by the government including a commission appointed by President Kennedy in 1963, a National Cancer Institute study appearing in 1969, and a commission set up by the Secretary of Health, Education, and Welfare known as the Mrak Commission in 1967.

Poor communication between the three federal agencies involved with pesticides impaired regulatory efficacy. The Department of Agriculture was responsible for farming interests, Department of Health, Education, and Welfare for promoting health controls, and Department of the Interior for wildlife and the environment. Administrative reform was recommended by congressional oversight hearings in 1963, resulting in an interagency agreement. Yet, the Mrak Commission report appearing in 1969, carried another recommendation for reform.

Index analysis shows that in the late sixties there was intense concern about specific pesticides and about the ecological consequences of pesticides generally. Executive reorganization in 1970 formed the Environmental Protection Agency. This new agency, high levels of public concern for pesticides being harmful to the environment, and government findings of the ineffectiveness of the 1947 law especially concerning persistent pesticides, led to hearings in 1971 on a new law that would replace FIFRA.

These hearings showed concern over harmful effects of pesticides to wildlife, the environment, and human health. Some concern for farmers and field workers using pesticides was also expressed. These hearings led to the passage of the Federal Environmental Pesticide Control Act of 1972. The act rewrote FIFRA providing for premarket testing for health and environmental effects to meet tolerance standards set by EPA.

3

Values Framework for
Risks, Concerns, and Health:
A Comparative Assessment

Statements of concern are pieces of the puzzle that at any one time is the aggregate of cultural attitudes. It is necessary to review numbers of such statements to reveal the underlying values.

To uncover the values inhering in the social forces leading to legislation in the areas we studied, a values framework (developed at the Center for Policy Alternatives over the last ten years) is first presented and the statements found in the historical review relating to values are mapped to the framework.

We performed the mapping with two types of "value phrases." One type of value phrase, a "framework concept," relates to general parts of the value framework. Examples of these value phrases are <u>fairness</u> or <u>human life</u>. A second type of value phrase, a "critical distinction," relates more specifically to key distinctions that should be considered in light of the value framework. Examples of these value phrases are <u>higher technical capability</u> and <u>irreversibility</u>. As a result of the historical review, a few critical distinctions were added to the framework while the framework concepts remained largely unchanged. (See Sections 3.1.1-3.1.4 for the descriptions of framework concepts and Section 3.1.5 for critical distinctions.)

Section 3.1 discusses the values framework. The following section (3.2) discusses the values as revealed in the historical review. Value phrase references are indicated throughout the section by underlining the phrases. In contrast to Section 2 where reviews were performed by legislative area, this section reviews values within three categories, those expressed: 1) Through the Popular Media; 2) By Advocates, Concerned Scientists, and Congressional Figures; and 3) Through Congressional Action. Finally, the last section (3.3) discusses similarities and differences among these three categories and compares the values revealed in the historical review with the framework.

3.1 A Value Framework for Risks, Concerns, and Health

Background

In a number of recent studies, researchers have attempted to incorporate ethics and morality in regulatory decision-making for health by establishing "moral rules" [Derr, 1981], [Fessenden-Raden & Gert, 1984]. If such rules were established, the legislature could embody them in laws and the process would be completed. Completed, that is, if people could be rational about formulating and following "moral rules".

Instead, what appear to be "moral rules" are at best pieces of a much more complex system of ethics. For example, Derr's proposition of utility is based on the principle of the greatest good for the greatest number. However, from a Rawlsian perspective, this rule violates a justice-as-fairness criterion where members of society might not choose the greatest good for the greatest number if it disadvantaged particular members (see 3.1.1.1). Gert's moral rule directs us not to "deprive individuals of opportunity." In America, citizens can be "deprived" of opportunity by their social position, family background, and income. Application of this "principle" as a general rule would be difficult to apply in practice. Only in circumstances where opportunity is deprived on the basis of race, sex or age has society even approached agreement.

Two recent studies that attempted to apply the Derr rules to explaining "double-standards" for environmental and occupational regulation of lead [Hattis, Goble & Ashford, 1982] and a National Institute of Occupational Health and Safety study on exposure of workers to ionizing radiation [1984], were unable to apply any of the four rules (utility, ability, compensation, & consent) to explaining double-standards in these situations. Instead, they found guidance from legislation, technical factors, and economic factors to explain discrepancies.

Scope of the Framework

In contrast to these rules-based approaches, our study views moral rules as outcomes of a long process of debate among various social groups, legislative factions, and within academic disciplines like philosophy, theology, sociology, and political science. The rules of this process are not universal but reflect the structure and capabilities of the society -- whether it is market oriented, the strengths of its science and medicine, the current idioms of political and moral discussion.

Although we doubt that a values framework derives from moral rules, we believe that there are conceptual structures that can help to formulate moral laws. In particular we have found valuable: Ackoff's values framework as presented in Choice, Communication, and Conflict [1972]; the approach of Rawls' to justice as fairness [1971]; Ladd's ethics of responsibility [1970, 1978]; and Bertocci and Millard's relation of ethics to psychology [1963]. We will identify below the overlap and parallels in these four approaches.

Some readers may have noted that we have thus far ignored the libertarian or "rights" approach to morality and have criticized utilitarian arguments.

In the case of rights, we see a strong similarity between rights, legalism, and the "moral-rules" approach. Like moral rules, we view statements of human rights to be the outcomes of a socio-philosophical process -- not a starting point. Established rights (like established laws) are useful as "sign-posts" of what already has been "agreed" to. They can project the likely agreement on very similar issues. However, because they are descriptive, they cannot provide an ethical basis for future choices. Regarding libertarianism, we agree with Flathman [1976, p. 2] that "contrary to the impression often given by natural rights theorists from Locke to Robert Nozick, rights are not natural, divine, primitive, or brute facts. Nor are they self-justifying or self-evidently justified." Rights reflect social consensus. As for utilitarianism, while we admire it as a means of identifying concepts of value (for example, utility), we find its attempt to apply net social well-being to individuals in a web of social relationships to be abstract and a fundamental weakness.

Approach

We subscribe to three basic principles: 1) For a given society, there is an ideal set of ethics and laws which current laws and morality only approximate; 2) society gradually approaches this "ideal set" by an iterative process of philosophical, theological, and socio-political debate; and 3), a values framework should be functionally based -- i.e. it should be possible to derive the meaning and purpose of principles, morals, and laws from how they serve a needed function. These functions involve values as personal and collective preferences and whose supreme principle is society's continuance.

The first principle is an affirmation of an ideal set of ethics, morality and laws toward which we should strive. The second principle emphasizes the complexity of the process of reaching a better set of ethics, morality and laws. The myriad interactions among members of society and among possible rules requires a long period in which, first, members of society both intuitively (affectively) and rationally perceive problems and opportunities for moral growth in the society (for example, Bockle notes that we experience the out-of-jointness, inequality and injustice of slavery. We then judge it to be wrong [in Haughey, 1979, p. 163]. Second, this perception is communicated by the media, the representational political process, etc. to others. Finally, possible moral rules are proposed and tested in the political, social and intellectual arenas.

The third principle -- that a value framework should be functionally-based -- is a prerequisite to providing a knowable framework. It is an application of a scientific viewpoint that attempts to establish the purpose of ethics, morals, and laws by revealing their relationship to the actions and "desired outcomes" of man, woman, and society. This functional approach is directly addressed in the following sections on the "health qualities model" and the "enumeration of social consequences of illness and death."

Before proceeding to elaboration of the functional approach, the next section describes the particular insights gained from the works of Rawls, Ladd, Ackoff, and Bertocci. These individuals provide key insights for constructing the value framework. In addition, the ethical and moral basis of the responsibilities of government and corporations is addressed.

3.1.1 Approaches to Ethics and Morality
3.1.1.1 John Rawls

Rawls has been acclaimed as one of the most significant philosophers of the century on the idea of the social contract. His approach is valuable in a functionally-based values framework because he provides a touchstone by which various ethical and moral arrangements can be agreed upon and have an objective basis.

Agreement (in the form of a social contract) is reached by imagining all members of society in an "original position" [Rawls, 1971]. In this position there is a veil of ignorance -- while all members are fully aware of the types of institutions and arrangements that are possible in society, they are not aware of their particular position in that society. Thus they "fairly" decide issues of justice (and other ethical positions) that would apply regardless of "station" in society.

In that state, Rawls contends that there are two basic agreements that all members would come to. The first requires equality in the assignment of rights and duties, while the second holds that social and economic inequalities, for example inequalities of wealth and authority, are just only if they result in compensating benefits for everyone.

Rawls' position differs from utilitarianism in that it does not endorse the principle of maximizing net welfare among all members. Net welfare that might be attained by disadvantaging a particular individual would not be permitted (the Caldor-Hicks criteria of compensating the "losers" attempts to remedy this objection in utilitarianism but is rarely achieved.)

The relationship of government to society, then, is straightforward. The members of society would elect to have governmental bodies and laws that all would agree were necessary for attaining justice and other ethical purposes. These institutions would work toward attainment of the two basic agreements listed above and others that a rational group of people would decide in the original position.

Some have criticized Rawls for describing an affirmation of the status quo -- that having made these decisions in the original position, society affectlessly pursues those objectives. This criticism is unfounded, since the concept of the original position is not something that is applied once and then carried out. Rather it is an abstraction that can be applied at any time and, based on new knowledge or new understandings of society, its application can be redirected towards a more successful deployment of the fundamental intent.

A substantive criticism of Rawls is the level of abstraction required to carry out the system of ethics he proposes. If we try to determine what duties a mother has towards her child, we must return to the abstract notion of the original position. In that position all members realize that they will be children at some point in their lives and may be parents at another. They will choose duties between parent and child that "fairly" treat the person at both stages of life. (Some imagine that Rawls is requiring the child to enter into a contract with the mother which they claim is impossible to achieve, but this is a misinterpretation of Rawls' position which asks only for imaginative projection by rational adults).

While Rawls' work provides a plausible basis for ethics, it is short on generating the working rules of ethics. For this we must turn to others who have attempted to distill general notions into useful principles.

3.1.1.2 John Ladd

Ladd emphasizes the notion of the "ethics of responsibility" [Ladd, 1978]. This approach to ethics is strongly oriented toward relationships that are formed in families and other social affiliations. A fundamental goal in this approach is that of moral integrity, which is achieved by recognizing that in everyone has needs, and that a successful society emphasizes the responsibility of people in relationships responding to the needs of others.

The statement "from each according to their abilities, to each according to their needs" can be interpreted in the relational context. Further, if people lack the ability to respond, in order to act responsibly they should seek to develop the capability. Thus ignorance or incapacity is not viewed as relieving a person of having to act responsibly.

The primary strength of Ladd's approach is that it resonates with our intuitive ethical notions about generosity, kindness, charity and other empathic traits that traditionally have been seen as basic to a "good" society.

Ladd's approach contrasts with Rawls' in regard to formal organizations, including governments. Ladd's views on the responsibilities of formal organizations are treated below under Section 3.1.1.5.

3.1.1.3 Russell Ackoff

Ackoff, a management scientist by profession, is an important philosopher on the issues of human behavior and ethics. His perspective is unusually systematic and derives from a behavioral/values approach. In particular, his functional perspective and extensive use of operational definitions add much to the value framework [Ackoff, 1972].

In his approach, the basic human motivation is the "achievement of a desired outcome." This is an important contrast with the utilitarian objective of the "good" defined as the satisfaction of rational desire. It allows for the inclusion of instrumental desired outcomes, outcomes that are valued not for their own sake but for the good they help achieve.

Ackoff's approach does not do much to identify these types of instrumental choices, but concentrates on the behavioral mechanism by which these and other choices are made. A fundamental concept is the efficiency of the individual (or group) in achieving the desired outcome. One's belief structures and capabilities determine the efficiency with which a desired outcome can be achieved.

Further, Ackoff's approach can be used to help generate ethical objectives, viewing ethics as prescriptions for achieving valued outcomes such as respect, material goods, success, etc. For example, virtues, such as courage, can be traced for their "co-productive" instrumentality in relation to the many desired outcomes an individual (and society) hold. What unfolds from this perspective is the function of ethics in establishing a "good" society.

3.1.1.4 Peter Bertocci and Richard Millard

To fill in the gap of specific ethical considerations that perform functions (as described above), we were impressed by the work of Bertocci and Millard in Personality and the Good.

Their approach seeks to answer how ethics and morals enable individuals and groups to attain psychological integrity. The functions of traits and virtues, such as courage, gratitude, and temperance, are examined in relation to individuals attaining a "symphony of values." Moreover their work is a culling of ethical perspectives from man different periods. As such it serves as a reference book on ethical "principles."

3.1.1.5 Moral Responsibilities of Business and Government

In establishing why social forces led to legislation, it is important to consider concepts of government and business responsibility to social concerns. In these areas there are considerable differences of opinion among scholars, government bureaucrats, and business leaders.

As regards government, Max Weber thought the "ethical neutrality" of government was commendable not only because it makes for efficiency and "rationality," but also because it transfers the responsibility for the ethical side of decision-making to persons outside the organization. In so far as the objectives of governmental bureaucracy are set by others, e.g. the elected leaders, accountability to the people as required by the theory of democracy is assured. Ladd, in contrast, notes that the concept of ethical neutrality is based on the presupposition that once the objectives of an organization have been decided, then all subsequent decision-making is merely empirical (factual). This separation of ends and means is illogical "as any reader of Dewey's writings is well aware." [Ladd, 1970, p. 509]. Even the decision-making of subordinate officials will involve some evaluative assessment of alternatives going beyond the mere technological determination of means. Thus, Ladd concludes that the requirement of "ethical neutrality" from bureaucratic officials is one that cannot be met.

The Woodstock Theological Center addressed the issue of government morality more closely in Personal Values in Public Policy [Haughey, 1979]. The format of the discussion is particularly revealing. Papers written at the Center were reviewed and commented on by a number of high-ranking government policy makers. The discussions covered both non-religious morality and Roman Catholic morality (This subject is relevant to the current debate about whether government officials can be against abortion on religious grounds but not carry through this morality in public office.) Smith wrote a rather idealistic paper about how Christian morality was only affirmation through faith of a morality knowable through non-religious means. Further, he describes in "Morally Questionable Policies" procedures by which officials can bring their personal morality to their position. The reactions of the government officials to this paper mainly demonstrated that the reality of bureaucracy was far from Smith's ideal. The officials told many stories about how their lack of security in their jobs forced them to abide by superior's directions rather than risk being outspoken. There was some agreement, however, that the freedom to inject one's own morality was not a constant, but varied from administration to administration.

Ladd sees the ethics of responsibility only applying to moral persons. A formal institution is an aberration in that it divorces individual morality from the aims of the institution. Thus if the institution professes profit maximization as its sole goal, the institution has no direct incentive to behave morally. While individuals in the organization may find its acts to be morally objectionable, they are required to repress their concerns and act in the interest of the organization.

Business favors a stance called "ethical neutrality". Freedman [1982] has noted the high degree of discomfort that company physicians experience with regard to occupational disease. They are continually torn by their oath of responsibility to the patient and their corporate role to serve the company's interests. Ewing [1983] describes twenty stories of individual moral conflict with corporate objectives and observes that those who follow through on their moral convictions typically lose their jobs. Priest [1981] in interviewing managers of asbestos firms asked a vice president, with regard to the moral burden of asbestos disease, whether he ever envied the person in his position thirty years ago (when the connection between asbestos and disease was less visible). The V.P. responded immediately, "everyday."

While the extent to which morality should be exhibited by corporations is not a settled question, accusations of corporate immorality often are raised. For example, with respect to whether employers should inform workers about possible hazards associated with chemicals, Gert states "employers are clearly acting immorally." [Fessenden-Raden and Gert, 1984] From a risk management perspective this is an important issue for if businesses are being accused of immorality when amorality is the case, there can be unnecessary conflict and loss of cooperation.

If "ethical neutrality" is the case for most businesses then non-voluntary approaches such as legislation and regulation are a major means for moving corporations to adopt society's moral concerns. The law formally introduces the objective of the control of occupational disease, for example, into the list of corporate objectives (not to break the law). "Ethical neutrality" similarly undermines the argument for voluntary compliance for unless the corporation can "sell" the product of fewer occupational diseases or deaths, there is little incentive to adopt these actions as corporate objectives. Only the threat of further government control might induce firms to exceed government rules if there is no violation of existing law, but the further any individual firm goes, the less competitive that firm is with respect to its competitors. Some philosophers and decision-makers have argued the value of voluntary compliance as enhancing corporate autonomy. While some have used automony as synonomous with freedom or liberty, its ethical meaning is clear. Autonomy is the "right" to take moral action without outside coercion. But if corporations are essentially amoral they cannot, strictly speaking, be autonomous.

In summary, the problem with formal organizations such as corporations is that they may be amoral and must be controlled through laws and regulations. Perhaps what is missing (and may well be impossible to achieve) is a law that more generally requires morality to be an objective of corporations. Until that can be achieved we are left with the "charity" of some firms and the legislated control of all others. (This view, of course, raises questions about people's feelings that industry should be morally responsible even without legislation: are these feelings a mistaken transference from living with others under ethics-of-responsibility-duties or do these feelings represent an "experienced out-of-jointness" that will give rise to an ethic of corporate responsibility?)

Government suffers many of the same problems of formal organizations but there is agreement that personal morality plays an important but indeterminate role in the function of government.

3.1.1.6 Review

The four approaches described above are remarkably similar. For example, Bertocci's work parallels Ladd's in seeking ethical principles that make a society feel more warm and alive. Ackoff's approach provides a behavioral perspective upon which these two perspectives can be operationally attached. Rawls provides a helpful way to think about the design of an entire system and some generative moral rules.

Government, primarily through the legislative and regulatory process, can be seen as an agent in reducing ethics and morality to laws that help control the achievement of desired outcomes. The critical problem, as Ladd indicates, is whether governments, as institutions, are capable of the task. There is a wide gap between the intricacies of the ethics of responsibility and what legislators can draft as formal rules.

Finally, there is uncertainty about whether firms should be viewed as moral agents or amoral agents. Within Ladd's perspective, firms are amoral agents. Yet, under Rawls' perspective, individuals in an original position might agree to specify moral requirements for firms.

3.1.2 A Health Qualities Model

The approaches to ethics and morality discussed above can provide a general values framework but are not related specifically to the value of health. A useful conceptual approach to understanding the value of health in the lives of individuals and society comes from the decision and behavioral sciences. Researchers in the field [Ackoff, 1972; Rokeach, 1972, 1973; Fischer, 1979] have evolved a functional approach to understanding human behavior that focuses on the role of beliefs, attitudes, and values in producing personal and social well-being.

3.1.2.1 A Description of the Model

This approach suggests that the individual moves through a stream of situations in which choices are made and outcomes achieved. Beliefs provide part of the structure by which a person can "model" situations. Attitudes are complex learned responses to situations in which choice or judgment of action becomes reflexive. Values are achieved for immediate enjoyment, or to aid in achieving other adopted values (by oneself or by others). Achieving values outcomes is accompanied by sensations of well-being that range from immediate satisfaction to an enduring sense of well-being.

When a person tries to achieve a valued outcome, resources such as material goods act as instruments to help produce (co-produce) the valued outcome. The value of a resource therefore is related to its role in gaining a valued outcome. The more valued the outcome, the more valued is the resource. The ultimate determinants of value are the short-run and long-run sensations of well-being (and assurance of cultural continuity).

An important aspect of this approach is that it distinguishes levels of value. The concept of levels or hierarchies of values is common in the literature [Maslow, 1954; Rokeach, 1972]. Lower-level values (consumptive values) contribute to immediate sensations of satisfaction, such as those associated with foods of particular taste or with seeing a particular object. Higher-level values are those that facilitate the achievement of lower-level values. For example, succeeding in employment, a higher-level value, provides income that aids in achieving lower-level valued outcomes. (The accomplishment of a work task may be positively valued for itself and thus be a lower-level valued outcome as well.)

Higher-level values are detached from consumptive values. Traits such as kindness and integrity in many circumstances may be instrumental to achieving consumptive values, but the linkages are complex and their value is rarely apparent to the individual. Values such as freedom or the sense of belonging are related to the achievement of lower order values in so complex a way that it becomes the function of ethics, morality, culture and its religions to uphold these values as inviolate. The "sanctity" of these values must be affirmed and transmitted generationally, as givens, since their function is so oblique to the individual.

To value health in a practical sense, it is necessary to determine how health is valued both as a consumptive value (good health feels good) and as an instrumental value -- health's function in co-producing valued outcomes. Thus, to value health, one must view health in terms of the complex ways through which it relates to all valued outcomes.

At one extreme along the continuum of values concerning health, the individual can have a reasonable idea of the consequences of minor injuries and diseases. For example, a minor cut is likely to be a slight "negative co-producer" (an "instrument" that works against achieving other valued outcomes). There may be occasional discomfort, a small change of local infection, some temporary disfigurement, slight loss of mobility, and insignificant scarring.

At the other extreme are long-term chronic diseases and disabling injuries, which inhibit the achievement of many of a person's most cherished outcomes: autonomy, intimacy, or reproduction. For example, the loss of a leg inhibits thousands of valued outcomes. These outcomes are related to every aspect of a person's activities -- social, vocational, avocational, recreational, parenting, etc. As is further explored in "Enumeration of Social Consequences" (Section 3.1.3), the effect of serious injury and disease on an individual's well-being can be massive. In such situations, an individual can "adjust" -- values and expectations will change slowly over time -- but the individual's well-being is likely to be permanently and severely diminished. For the remainder of this section, health effects that affect many valued outcomes (or a few very important outcomes) will be called "significant" health effects.

An individual cannot evaluate abstractly, cannot imagine clearly such "significant" health effects [Fischer, 1979]. Such a loss would be "tragic" in the sense of Calabresi [1978], and elaboration of its consequences would be difficult. This means that in cases when it is unlikely that an individual can be restored to his original state of well-being, society cannot value adequately his loss by <u>determining the resources required</u> to do so. Thus, the use of hospital costs as a surrogate measure of the value of loss from significant health effects is inadequate.

A person's health is also a co-producer of outcomes that are co-producers of another person's valued outcomes. The ability of a person to earn a living provides the instrument (money) to co-produce the valued outcomes of the spouse and children. Furthermore, husband-wife relationships, and similar relationships, depend on a multitude of valued outcomes that are not directly traceable to earnings (relationships that Ladd shows leads to instrumental values which he terms the "ethics of relationships.") A primary aspect of such relationships is love and when one partner loses health, love and many other valued aspects can be disturbed significantly, producing conflict. While illness occasionally may revitalize a relationship, in the vast majority of situations poor health has a debilitating effect on family, friends, and the community.

The location of health within a hierarchy of values has been debated by philosophers and behavioral scientists. One investigator [Rokeach, 1973] has concluded that health is so high on the hierarchy that it cannot be measured. Mechanic [1968] has argued that despite health's high placement, health is likely to be valued less when values such as national security are seriously threatened.

The accurate placement of health in the value hierarchy is vital since values near the top are protected at nearly all cost while those near the bottom are arbitrated in the market. Yet, we can observe a fundamental difference between the character of health as a value and other higher-level values such as freedom. In our society, the idea of freedom is idolized; health, however, has only become amenable to protection with the advent of modern medicine, public health practices, and government regulation. Having been vulnerable beyond human redress for so long, health has not been as sanctified as some less tangible values.

In recent history, other basic human needs such as sufficient food to prevent malnutrition and starvation have been raised toward a level of sanctity. (The term "merit good" -- a rights-like term -- describes goods that each person, by virtue of his or her existence, is entitled to.) Society appears to be evolving a second tier of guarantees which have the characteristics of first-tier guarantees like freedom but which are influenced by the availability of resources and, in turn, by technological means. Mesthene [1971] has observed that new technology can directly affect the relative values attached to valued outcomes by changing the resources required to achieve them.

Applying Rawls' approach we can imagine deciding between two general situations: 1) Enter society as an individual with a generally high material standard of living, but aware that the "ill-health lottery" may rob you at any time; or 2) Enter society as an individual with a somewhat lower material standard of living, but aware that the "ill-health lottery" has a significantly lower probability of robbing you at any time because society is devoting resources to protecting health. Clearly, there is a trade-off to be made. However, the decision rule appears not to be balancing costs and benefits (since benefits are large but mainly indeterminate) but to establish health as a second tier guarantee, i.e., that loss from significant health effects is to be avoided to the extent of available resources. This decision process and trade-off analysis required an appropriate decision-making framework [Ashford, 1980], not adequately presented in an economically-modeled regulatory analysis. Economic analysis can be used, however, to elucidate the availability of resources.

To support such a decision-making process, indicators are required at least to approximate the benefits achieved by health guarantees. Priest [1982] describes measures of health drawn from sociometrics, psychometrics, economic measures, and factor analysis and, in particular, concentrates on sociomedical health indicators.

3.1.2.2 Valuation as Performed in the Health Professions

One gross measure of a person's ability to achieve valued outcomes is "restricted activity days." A restricted activity day entails the inability to perform at one's job, the inability to enjoy social activities, a likely confinement to one's abode, and interference with family affairs. Of course, with regard to the impact on overall well-being, the index is not linear. That is, fifty restricted activity days are likely to produce a negative effect on well-being that is much greater than ten times the effect of five such days. We might even imagine that a small number of restricted activity days that are not accompanied by significant pain might have a positive effect on well-being.

Mild illness and injuries are a much less serious valuation problem than longer-term, serious illnesses and injuries but the level of seriousness at which the valuation problem becomes difficult is not defined easily. Furthermore, one can imagine situations in which a brief, mild illness might have an unusually unfortunate effect on a person's life, or in which longer-term illnesses might, in rare circumstances, leave the well-being of an individual nearly unscathed. As a point of reference, we can use the term acute illness, defined by the National Center for Health Statistics as a disease of less than three month's duration. Whether this is a useful demarcation for valuation purposes is difficult to say, but the terms acute and chronic certainly conjure distinctly different valuation problems.

One health index of greater discrimination than the restricted activity day index is the "Index of Independence in Activities in Daily Living" [Index of ADL, Katz, 1976]. The index, which was developed about twenty years ago, has been tested and improved in a variety of uses. This approach profiles behavioral levels of six sociobiological functions: bathing, dressing, toileting, transfer, continence, and feeding. The ADL Index is more appropriate for the severe conditions that tend to accompany chronic illnesses or old age. It would be useful in the health legislation and regulation areas in describing the effects of severe, disabling injuries or of chronic illnesses such as cancer. Nevertheless, the measure is still only a rough indicator of well-being, since only six rather specialized areas of dysfunction are used.

Mushkin [1979], who has spent many years developing health measures for policy purposes, suggested a five-level indicator that is addressed more toward the issue of valuation. Her scale ranges from full functioning to varying levels of dysfunction defined by their curtailment of various activities. Her scale is: 1) Cured or in remission; 2) Fully-functioning despite disease or impairment; 3) Functioning with some limitations; 4) Capable of self-care but major and other activities severely limited; and 5) Not capable of self-care. Mushkin's scale is structured to identify policy-relevant health impacts.   She has recommended that an index of health status and function should be able to meet the following criteria:

1) Simple: The index should be easy to understand and to present to policymakers.

2) Comprehensive: The index needs to provide an assessment of the degree to which intended public purposes are being met by resource allocations or program decisions.

3) Able to isolate impacts: The index should change if, and only if, a change in health or functional states occurs due to intervention. In addition, it should record adverse as well as positive impacts.

4) Able to identify target groups: The index should facilitate the identification of impact on special target groups; for example, changes in functional capacity of children.

5) Reproducible: Index information should be collected in a sufficiently simple manner to facilitate repeated samples. Each time that the procedure is reproduced, the same type of information should be gathered; in this way, the information obtained can be compared with that for other groups of individuals or with that for the same individuals in different time periods.

6) Low cost: Collection of information needs to be kept at a cost commensurate with the usefulness of the data.

7) Reasonable: Measures need to be "reasonable" to the diverse groups whose interests are involved in the health policy; for example, consumers, legislators, health providers, and research scientists.

Other indicators of health have been devised that are based on the number of years spent in various states of health. For example, Chiang [1965] proposed a health index based on the expected time in various health states and on the weights assigned to each state.   While this index is attractive from a theoretical point of view, the framework for linking the index to health effects was not provided and the weighting factors are not related to a preference or value scale.

In a similar vein, others [Fanshell & Bush, 1970] have formulated measures of functional years ("well years") or value-adjusted life expectancy. (The concept "quality-adjusted life year" (QALY) is derived from this approach.) Later work by Bush and co-workers [Bush, 1973,1972; Kaplan, 1976] extended this work to develop a general index comprised of a detailed classification of over 40 function levels based on mobility, physical activity, and social activity. The index includes probabilities governing transitions between health states over time that are determined from medical data or expert judgments. Added information includes a table of life expectancy for the different health states. The value of different health states was assessed using psychometric scaling of judgments from respondents.

Perhaps the most comprehensive health profile yet constructed is that by Bergner [1976] and others at the University of Washington. Their Sickness Impact Profile (SIP) is a "behaviorally based measure of sickness-related dysfunction." The SIP consists of about 150 self-administered questions designed to range over 14 categories of behavior.

A similar profile instrument was developed at the Rand Corporation by Brook [1979] and others to help measure the relative effectiveness of health programs to provide information for policy-making on national health insurance. They studied a sample of about 8000 people in 2750 families at six sites across the country. Measures and questions were developed in four major categories: Physical, Mental, Social, and General Health Perception.

Values Implied by Simple Scales

Any list of levels of dysfunction embodies implied judgments regarding valuation. For example, Mushkin's five point list in the previous section is in the order of low to high levels of dysfunction and is also in a valuation order. Generally a person would prefer to be in a lower level of dysfunction than in a higher level. Thus Mushkin's five point scale could be used as a crude indicator of value for a population. One could place each individual in the appropriate level of dysfunction and count the numbers of individuals in each category.

If, due to some action, the number of persons in the lower level categories increased and the number in the upper level categories decreased, the action could be judged as having improved the overall welfare of the population. However, the extent of improvement would not be apparent. To attain more quantitative information about the status of health states one must employ more precise utility assessment measures. The approaches in the behavioral sciences such as Sackett [1978] are useful in this direction.

3.1.2.3 Valuing Life and Health in a Personal, Social, Cultural, and Legal Context

Individual Level

The general health qualities model described in Section 3.1.2.1 can produce some situations that seem to resist cogent valuation. If we ask an individual what sum of money he would demand to die voluntarily, he faces a dilemma since upon his death the money would be of no use to him. From this Mishan [1976] concluded that "no amount of money would induce someone to certain death." Broome [1977] concluded erroneously from this dilemma that "the monetary value of a person's life must be infinite." In fact, there is no logical basis to justify this conclusion. The value of life using this framework is indeterminate.

Social Level

The decision-making model can be applied to an individual's social ties. Each individual is a co-producer of other persons' valued outcomes. Thus, the death of a person represents a loss measured in terms of the value of that person as a co-producer in the other persons' future streams of valued outcomes. As in the case of health, these ties may be simple or complex. The loss of a neighbor may be of small consequence but with some people our interactions are so complex and the person so significant as to be instrumental to thousands of our valued outcomes, and it is beyond our capacity to quantify his/her significance. For example, the value of a husband to a wife in a strong relationship rests on so many valued outcomes that only masterful novels might begin to capture the significance of a loss of the relationship. (Foregone income to the family -- a popular economic measure -- is insignificant in comparison to the value of other lost outcomes, especially since wage insurance, state aid, and relatives often can fill the income gap but not the other losses. Rhoades [1978] notes that Mishan calmly predicts that due to societal trends: "The gradual loosening of family ties and the decline of emotional interdependence should cause the magnitude of bereavement-risk compensation ... to decline." But Rhoades questions whether the proper role of government legislation and regulation is to track the decline of such ties, or to improve those ties by expanding and highlighting lifesaving programs and other valued political goods in a society.)

Community ties often are so diffuse that the value of a constituent individual is not readily apparent. Certain members exercise crucial leadership and support roles, and the well-being of the community is integrally tied to their existence, others seem marginal. But the loss of any member in a tightly-knit community is viewed as an intrusion that affects the sense of security and other shared communal values.

Unfortunately, the significance of community ties require extended discussion or symbolization, information that cannot be condensed to a number entered in a box. For this reason, Section 3.1.3 focuses on sociological and anthropological descriptions of the effects of injury, illness and death.

Cultural Level

We asserted earlier that the value of human life must be sought in terms other than simply its value to the individual. Above we have identified a major component of the value of human life -- its value to others in society. Further, the value of human life is that which "reflects the value that a 'good' culture should value life at, in order that it and its people survive, generation to generation and such that its welfare is optimized [Priest, 1979]. Embodied in each individual of the culture is a sense of the value of living that is not oriented toward the continuation of life of the individual per se but rather the culture -- indeed the species. Since the continuation of the culture depends on the continuation of its members, the sense of the value of life (like the sense of dignity) is a strong component of an individual's value set. This type of value is different from that of preferring pudding to ice cream. It is highly likely that, due to the importance of valuing life to the survival of the species, it has a genetic component. At minimum, there is a cultural aspect of the value of life which government and religious institutions are expected to inculcate in their people, and in the process, to distinguish between values that damage and those that affirm life.

Cultures that undervalue life cease to exist. Cultures that survive put a sufficient value on life so that, despite its vicisitudes and their errors, its members can live. As our society has increased its abilities to prolong life, destroy life (engage in destructive warfare), prevent life (birth control and abortions), and reduce the loss of life, there will be struggles between competing definitions of life-affirming values.

Note that a "right to life" notion makes use of a social definition of right. The "right-to-die" acknowledges individual situations in which death might be preferable to life but then this right is at odds with the social and cultural origins of the value of life. It is in conflicts between cultural values and a purely individual definition of right that discussions of such issues often become deadlocked.

Societies can and have withstood the loss of great numbers of inividual members. Only in cases like plague or total war is society itself threatened with extinction. As demonstrated in the books of anthropologist Colin Turnbull, the essential factor in a society's endurance is its retaining a sense of the sacramental quality of life and its projection of this quality onto the group itself. A society's ability to retain these attitudes of sanctity and bonding may depend on the magnitude of the losses it suffers. In our media-bonded culture, magnitude of loss depends upon coverage or visibility.

In dealing with highly visible losses of life, Mooney [1977] dismisses them as "atypical" and not of use in understanding the value of life. To the contrary, his case of the lone yachtsman who is saved without regard for the expenditure of resources is one of the most revealing aspects of the value of life -- it is a life-saving event because it has the attention of people throughout the world. As Blumstein [1975] notes, "in cases such as that of Karen Quinlan, where public attention is focused on the plight of the unfortunate individual, important symbolic values seem to intercede. The myth of a democratic government, supporting human life at any cost, is a value to which we like to adhere." This was seen again in 1987 in the case of the young girl, Jessica McClure, who was caught in an abandoned well and received national attention by both the media and the country's president. As Havighurst [1975] has noted, "this strong belief in the sanctity of life leads us to reject our usual weighting of benefits and costs when human life appears to be in our hands."

Thus, a crucial factor in assigning resources to saving lives is the visibility of the action (or lack of action), rather than an a priori valuation of life. As a result, many times the resources may be devoted to preserving lives in a highly visible situation while others, with greater suffering, are ignored.

The universalizing aspect of ethics resists the association of value with visibility. Dr. Leo Alexander in the New England Journal of Medicine warned Americans to beware of falling into the same traps as Germans during the Nazi period. He wrote, "Whatever proportions these crimes finally assumed, it became evident to all who investigated them that they had started from small beginnings. The beginnings at first were merely a subtle shift in the emphasis in the basic attitude of the physician. It started with the acceptance of the attitude, basic in the euthanasia movement, there there is such a thing as a life not worthy to be lived. This attitude in its early stages concerned itself first with the severely and chronically sick. Gradually the sphere was enlarged to encompass the socially unproductive, the ideologically unwanted, the racially unwanted, and, finally, the non-Germans. But it is important to realize that the infinitely small wedged-in lever from which this entire trend of mind received its impetus was the attitude toward the nonrehabilitative sick" [Chalmers, 1981].

A parallel danger exists when government publicly states that lives or health can be sacrificed for the "good" of economic production. Once this attitude is adopted, many socially disruptive issues arise: who is expendable and who will decide? What effect on the sensibilities of individuals and the nation will occur as such 'sacrifices' become commonplace? It is in this area that those who attempt to place a monetary value on human life tread to the detriment not only of those individuals first affected but of society as a whole.

Each trade-off of life for scarce resources should be examined so that the pain involved is never forgotten, that is, so that the sanctity of individual and society is affirmed. For this reason, the exchange cannot be reduced to an "acceptable" monetary sum either by explicit valuation or by establishing an automatic cut-off when a pre-set value of life is reached. Once such exchanges are automated, separated from the exercise of individual emotion and the exigencies of individual right and responsibility, then the accelerating devaluation of life may ensue.

Calabresi [1978] has pointed out that some "tragic choices" are finessed by society. This can occur when society's mores and institutions do not require that such choices be formulated and faced explicitly. This in fact is one result of hypothesizing "the market" as a first cause that impersonally and justly shapes economic and social relations. This obscures the choices and responsibilities of those individuals and organizations that move economic activity. In section two of this study, we noted various means by which the nation has attempted to include business within the nation's moral and social fabric in this century. In addition to legislation and citizen pressure, institutions that help avoid obvious breaches of fundamental values are public decision-making bodies, like juries. While in a sense representative, such bodies are not accountable to the public, nor are they compelled to explain their factual conclusions or the values they have applied. This is unfortunate because monetary court awards have been used to value life in wrongful death actions. Moreover, to the degree that juries are constituted anew in each case, they provide varying and often inconsistent valuations. When economic costs are presented to the jury as the means for settling arbitration, their valuations of life are skewed toward economic rather than cultural or religious ones.

Additional Legal Perspectives on the Value of Life

While legal approaches have limited perspective in valuing life, they do illuminate the way societies use law to beg such questions. There are two primary means by which the law protects life. Under criminal law, taking a life is subject to various legal sanctions, depending on the circumstances of the act. Second, the fifth and fourteenth amendments to the Constitution provide certain guarantees regarding the deprivation of life. While it is not possible to assess the quantitative value of life by investigating legal sanctions, such sanctions do provide a sense of the value judgments made in the legislative/political arena about protecting lives since they reflect our social mores (refer to the discussion under Scope in Section 3.1).

The relevance of these legal perspectives depends on the role of the victim in the actions that cause his death. Situations in which a person places his own life in jeopardy are largely outside the domain of law. Situations, however, where one's life is placed at risk by others are very much the subject of law. Thus, the concepts of voluntary and involuntary risk are germane.

As in criminal law, in regulatory statutes the relationship among the parties is a key concept in deciding guilt in legal situations. An employer who directs an employee to work at an intrinsically dangerous task might be viewed in a different light than the automobile manufacturer who produces an automobile that could be made safer. While both entail semi-involuntary* risks, the loss of life from an unsafe automobile is more removed physically from the cause of the loss and, thereby, the manufacturer might be thought less accountable for the death than the employer.**

There are many similarities between tort law (involving wrongful acts against others) and the goals of health, safety, and environmental regulation. For example, the wording of the legislative mandate of the various regulatory agencies is similar to wording used in tort law. Under tort law a person is required to provide "reasonable care under the circumstances." If a person causes damage to another to whom he has a duty without exercising reasonable care, this is a tort offense and the injured party can ask for damages. A regulatory standard likewise can be viewed as similar to a civil injunction to prevent a wrongful loss.

A standard of reasonable care in tort law is determined by what ordinary people in a given community, time, and circumstance might be expected to exercise. Reasonable care is a fluid concept with regard to health, safety, and the environment: as the ordinary person perceives that additional care is warranted based on changing levels of affluence or information, the standard of care demanded in situations may be raised.

----

* Some argue that the employee could change to a lower risk job and that a driver could reduce his/her risk by not driving, presumably using alternative transportation, but the degree to which these are indeed open to free choice is quite small.

** The reverse might be suggested in the case where the worker is highly unionized and the power and information held by the worker and the employer are nearly equal. The driver, in contrast, is not equal in information with regard to hazards of a vehicle and thus some would argue for greater accountability for the automobile manufacturer than the employer.

Various statutes use words similar to those used in tort law. The Occupational Safety and Health Act calls for ensuring a healthy and safe workplace and the General Duty clause of the Act demands care on the part of the employer that mirrors tort concerns. The Toxic Substances Control Act calls for agency action in the case of unreasonable risk. Many of the acts call for action to protect health and property to the extent feasible or within technological capability.

In recent years a category of "unintentional" crime has arisen which approximates the traditional legal standard of taking life "willfully and with malice." An example of an "unintentional" crime would be holding a bartender liable for death resulting from serving intoxicants to a minor. Recently, top managers of a firm working with cyanide were indicted for murder when they defaced labels on the containers to keep the information from a worker who subsequently died.

Returning to our discussion on corporate responsibility, we see that individual morality does matter to the extent that an official of a firm breaks criminal or civil law. In actuality these cases are few in comparison to the number of injuries, illnesses and death caused by corporate acts.

Many decision-makers apply standards of reasonable care when formulating regulations. The more the decision-maker perceives a situation to be tort-like or even criminal, the more stringent will be the regulation. Justice and equity sometimes give monetary cost a secondary role when life or health are considered too sacred to be compromised by cost considerations.

The fifth and fourteenth amendments of the U.S. Constitution require that no person be deprived of life, liberty, or property without due process.* This is not a general entitlement to life but is only a statement that government cannot deprive a person of life without due process. For example, a publicly operated hospital may be required to exercise due process in deciding to discontinue kidney dialysis treatment for a patient. The fact that the government funded the treatment in the first place and the fact that removing the treatment will deprive the person of life may be sufficient to invoke a due process requirement.

Blumstein [1975] explores the implications of these constitutional provisions in relation to health-related life and death decisions. One might argue that once the federal government has intervened by regulation to achieve a lower risk of life loss, this constitutes a sufficient basis for the entitlement to life. Thus, even though government has not set standards strictly enough, it may be required effectively to do so through due process. It might be argued that there is no claim of entitlement from the state, but

----

* Due process pertains to ensuring fairness in the use of legal means of settling claims, including trial and appeal rights.

government is serving only as a mediator between private parties, establishing entitlements between them. The degree to which these provisions are generally applicable to legislative and regulatory decisions for protecting health has not been well explored, although federally mandated caution labels on cigarettes may be contributing to a decline in smoking. One result of this relationship of constitutional law to regulatory decision-making may be to press the decision-maker toward more stringent standards.

The preceding paragraphs indicate how American law reinforces some theoretically derived ethical sanctifications of life. Like other noneconomic approaches, the law protects life at least against immediately identifiable assaults and requires that trade-offs made between life and other resources be performed in the courts or within the political process.

3.1.3 Consequences of Disease and Injury for Individuals and Society

As we noted above, Ladd is among the philosophers who argue that morality stems from responsibilities in relationships. Economics does note deal directly with personal relationships and can assign only monetary, not moral value to the consequences of disease and injury for individuals and society. Disciplines that involve the assessment of social and individual value are anthropology, history, psychology, social work and sociology. This section draws on the literature of these professions and details the types of disruptions to relationships caused by disease and injury. It is particularly concerned with all the consequences of disease and injury that impede the realization of goals valued by affected individuals in the context of their relationships with family, friends, and the larger community. The following section conceptually parallels the Health Qualities Model (Section 3.1.2) and provides more concrete examples of the "negative co-production" associated with ill health.

3.1.3.1 Enumeration of the Social Costs of Disease and Injury

Practioners and researchers in the allied health professions, the humanities and the social sciences have long dealt with the complex social and psychological consequences of disease, injury, or death. Their work, both practical and theoretical, identifies categories of consequences and suggests means for their enumeration.

Impacts on Victims and Their Families

The literature of the allied health professions addresses the impacts on individuals and their families of such health problems as handicaps, chronic disease, disability, terminal illness, and death and dying. They focus on three major areas of consequence: (1) social relationships, within which are included individual psychological effects and changes in family dynamics; (2) the use of time, both for individuals and their associates; and (3) family economy, which includes effects on work and employment.

Serious injury or illness can have important psychological and emotional consequences for victims and their families, including depression, stress, grief, guilt, anger, shame, hostility, pschogenic symptoms, role disruption, feelings of inadequacy and self-reproach, isolation, and altered "life satisfaction."

Impacts on the Family

Several studies consider the impact on family members of a chronically ill or handicapped child, [Peterson, 1972; Dunlap & Hollinsworth, 1977; Friedrich, 1977; Kanof, et al., 1962; Travis, 1976; and Anthony & Koupernik, 1973]. These authors found a high incidence of what Friedrich [1977] has termed "chronic grieving" among parents of these children. This grieving involves feelings of guilt, bereavement, depression, and inadequacy, which can be compounded by feelings of revulsion and rejection when a child is born diseased or disabled. Often these feelings are repressed or sublimated by parents, which can lead to various manifestations of hostility or anger, directed inwardly, toward the partner, or toward the child. While some parents of ill children refuse to punish their children at all, Friedrich has shown that disabled and ill children are abused more frequently than normal children. Marital problems frequently arise when parental hostility remains unmitigated or when, as is often the case, parents do not or cannot communicate their thoughts and feelings.

Siblings of chronically ill or disabled children frequently suffer from parental neglect, sometimes unintended. Moreover, depending on their age and relationship to the ill child, many children blame themselves for their sibling's illness. The consequence of these complex feelings of guilt, jealousy, anxiety, fear, sadness, and anger are significant. Many siblings develop behavioral problems, phobias, psychogenic disorders such as enuresis, and other forms of maladjustment.

Family relationships can be substantially altered when an adult family member suffers a disabling illness or injury [Peterson, 1979; Gibson and Ludwig, 1968; Current Medicine, 1977; Hilbourne, 1973]. In reviewing the literature on marital adjustment to a physical disability, Peterson found evidence of substantial marital discord following a serious illness or injury, much of which he and others attributed to changes in role definitions. That is, disabilities often prevent a partner from fulfilling her or his usual role in the marriage and the resulting role ambiguity can create marital difficulties. The problems of ambiguity are exacerbated when a disability is not readily apparent or is less than total. In such cases, family members are often less tolerant of the person not assuming his/her usual roles. According to Peterson, an impairment that is clearly defined or totally disabling may cause less change in family dynamics than a more subtle disability. Other studies have found that, although the likelihood of marriage is the same for the disabled as for the non-disabled, the marriages of the disabled typically begin later and end earlier. The marriages of the disabled, particularly males, are more likely to end in divorce than those of the non-disabled.

The impact of a disabled or ill parent on children has been studied by Koocher [1978], Graham and George [1972], and Anthony [1969]. Many children of parents with disabling injuries or diseases develop adjustment and behavioral problems. In addition to the overwelming sadness a child often feels about an ill parent and the fears about losing that parent, children are affected deeply by the stress of the familial situation. As a consequence, many suffer from anxiety or express their difficulties by "acting out" in school, at home, and among friends.

Impacts on the Victim

The social and psychological problems encountered by the victims of disabling injuries and illnesses have been studied by Peterson [1972], Anthony [1969], Peterson [1979], Carlson [1979], in Current Medicine [1977], and Friedrich [1977]. For example, chronically ill or handicapped children are often isolated from their peers, either because their illness prevents their joining in the usual activities of childhood, or because they are stigmatized and other children avoid or are prevented from interacting with them. In some cases, disabled children are over-protected and thus have difficulties in coping with maturation or develop dependencies upon their parents. Other children suffer from abuse as parents vent their frustration. Health and social service workers frequently encounter disabled children who are depressed or "chronically sad," other children who harbor hostility and resentment for those around them, and still other children in whom illness and disability produce self-contempt.

Disabled adults frequently must adjust to drastic role changes that threaten their identity and the security of their social relationships. Role disruption, feelings of powerlessness, and social isolation can embitter and thus cause many behavioral problems for a disabled adult. Moreover, disabled adults are not immune to the destructiveness of the stereotypes that isolate them.

Several authors have addressed the social consequences of disability at a more metaphysical level. Park [1975] discusses the concept of the "dignity of risk." In his discussion of the barriers to normality, Park reminds us that normal living includes coping with trouble, strife, trial, and tribulation. He argues that the handicapped have a right to be exposed to the problems of everyday life. Borrowing from Goffman's "courtesy stigma," Hilbourne [1973] describes the effects of a disability on those involved socially with a disabled person as a "courtesy disability" -- the limitations imposed by a disability also constrain those closely associated with the disabled. The constraints discussed here go beyond the necessary changes in schedule, responsibilities, and financial status, to the notion of "being tarred with the same brush" because of the requisite behavioral modifications made by those interacting with the disabled. Similarly, Klarman [1974] points out that friends and relatives, as well as the society as a whole, benefit from programs to avert health loss and the concomitant pain, discomfort, grief, misunderstandings and prejudices.

Impacts on Family Resources

Disabling injuries and illnesses significantly change the use of time by both an affected person and his associates. The possible leisure time activities may change, or the altered responsibilities and obligations of associates may reduce the time available to them for social and community activities. In addition, the environmental requirements of the handicapped person, the time and locational constraints they impose on the family, may preclude job advancement, and in some cases, completely prevent family members from working outside the home. For some families these schedule alterations are a major source of tension. Focussing on changes in use of time facilitates the assessment of the impacts of disablement of persons who tend house or care for children. Often, the loss of this central figure in the household is more disruptive of family dynamics than a comparable loss of income due to the disability of a bread winner.

Income loss and the extraordinary expenses for treatment and rehabilitation of disablement strain the financial resources of a family, which can in turn alter family dynamics. Disability insurance and other transfer payments rarely compensate fully for the loss of earnings due to the disabling of a family's primary wage earner. Disabling accidents and illness can be impoverishing, especially when the caretaking demands of the disabled family member preclude the employment or impede the job advancement of others in the family. The destructive consequences of the stress of poverty are well documented and can compound the severity of the impact of illness or injury.

Impacts on Communities

The consequences of individual disease, injury and death for communities are not so straightforward as for victims and their families. The consequences clearly depend on the frequency of injury, disease or death and on the roles played by the victims in the community. Such consequences as community breakdown or disruption, social alienation, cultural dissolution, and national malaise, are rarely addressed in relation to illness, injury, or death. There is little understanding of the consequences for the larger community when a community member becomes disabled or dies. We have even less understanding of the synergistic effects when several people in a community or workplace become seriously ill or are threatened with serious illness. Moreover, analysts all but ignore considerations such as the long-run effect on the national psyche of such phenomena as accepting, without abhorrence, the fact of over 50,000 highway fatalities a year.

The impact of community consequences such as these can be profound. Such consequences often are ignored by policy analysts because of the difficulties associated with their identification and assessment. The magnitude of these consequences is hinted at by an event such as Love Canal whose consequences extend beyond damaged health. The loss of one's home, one's neighbors and friends, and of the security of familiar surroundings have great impact on the spirit (psyche). When such losses are experienced on a community-wide scale, their impact increases geometrically.

Social impact studies rarely address questions of community structure, intra- and inter-familial relations, local political or religious activities, local social services, or local recreation patterns [Jorgensen, 1980]. An example of an impact affecting these concerns is the effect of the loss of an individual upon his or her neighborhood. This loss will be felt with regard to both the social roles of the individual and the extent to which the illness or manner of injury impinges on the neighborhood. Even the presence of a hazard can contribute to community break-down. The sense of security associated with home and community are eroded when a community increasingly is exposed to hazards beyond local control.

Studies of community dissolution are becoming more common in research on the relationship between mental health and the economy, and in the interdisciplinary literature of social impact assessment [Jorgensen, 1980; Little, 1977; Ferman & Gordus, 1979]. However, most studies of the social consequences of events such as health loss, hazard exposure, economic decline or environmental degradation do not address the full range of impacts upon a community. In an effort to redress this situation, Finsterbusch [1977] has written a comprehensive article on methods of estimating and measuring social impacts as they affect individuals, organizations, and communities.

Several approaches to identifying and describing the social consequences of disease, injury and death have been developed. The method of role theory [Merton, 1957, 1968] postulates that each person plays a number of social roles in society, and that for each of these roles there is an associated set of rights, responsibilities, and socially learned behavior patterns. The theory of relative deprivation [Merton, 1968] suggests that individuals or families suffering a loss will feel less deprived if they are in situations that lead them to compare themselves with others whose losses are more severe. In health, social surveys have been used successfully to assess the effects of existing health programs and to gather data on the probable outcomes of various health policy alternatives [Aday, 1977]. The technique of Bourque and Back [1977] for measuring stressful events in "life graphs" has proven useful. For further measurement approaches consult Katz and Priest [1982].

3.1.3.2 Presenting Social Consequences: The Vignette

This section (3.1.3) has emphasized the need to consider a wide range of individual, family, and community consequences of injury, disease, and death in assessing the benefits of regulation.   It is apparent from the discussion that many of these consequences cannot be valued accurately in monetary terms.   Thus, they challenge the legislative process to convey their nature and importance to congressmen who should inform legislation with these realities.

The most common procedure for presenting such information is to have witnesses appear before congressional committees to present a description of the types of hardships associated with these types of losses.   In the subsequent development of regulations by executive agencies, this information becomes ignored when "regulatory analyses" are performed.   One approach to correcting this is to create a new "currency" of communication whose units would be brief narratives or "vignettes" derived from a package of consequences likely to result from particular kinds of injury, disease or death.   The content of the vignettes would be drawn from case studies, surveys, and interviews of previously affected parties. They would be based on explicit sociological and psychological models of behavior, such as role theory or family dynamics. They would need to be sufficiently detailed to convey their actual intensity and sufficiently succinct to permit effective integration by decision-makers.

Priest [Katz and Priest, 1982] describes the process of constructing and using vignettes.   Vignettes would be constructed for differing demographic loss situations (such as age, sex, etc.) and matrixed by levels of dysfunction (e.g. low, high).   Katz provides a sample vignette of the consequences of an industrial accident. The approach was presented in Congressional hearings conducted by Rep. George Miller on the "Costs of Not Regulating" in 1981. It is anticipated that such an approach would be useful in the legislative process as well as in promulgating regulations under law.

3.1.4 Use of Economic Approaches to Valuation under
Some Conditions

Under some conditions, economic approaches can be used for valuing losses from injury and disease. Economic analysis has been widely applied to the costs of regulation and has played a central role in the development of cost-benefit analysis [Mishan, 1976] and policy analysis [Stokey and Zeckhauser, 1978].   The major focus of economic approaches to valuing reduced losses in health and death is on the consequential indirect costs, or opportunity costs, associated with loss of health or life.   Hospital treatment costs and foregone earnings usually do not represent personal losses (direct costs) to a person or family but are monetary losses to insurance systems or society in general. However, these indirect costs are often substantial and their reduction represents a significant value to society.

3.1.4.1 Opportunity Costs of Capital

When a person becomes ill or injured, resources must be diverted from some other use to his/her care. These diverted resources represent the "opportunity cost" of expenditures used to respond to the health loss. These expenditures can often be viewed as rehabilitation costs or costs that reverse, arrest, or mitigate health damage, pain and suffering. Major studies done for regulatory agencies contain extensive documentation of the opportunity costs of health loss related to consumer products [Stone, 1976, 1980], railroad accidents [Priest and Knoblauch, 1978], and automobile accidents [Faigin, 1975].

The usual approach is to identify a list of cost items associated with health loss and to assign as values of legislation or regulation the reductions in each health loss. Since these benefits extend into the future and are in monetary units, future benefits are discounted to permit a presentation of the "present value" of the savings. Typical cost categories associated with injury and illness are medical and hospital costs; lost wages (foregone earnings), taxes, and worker benefits; costs incurred by others in hospital visits and home care; insurance claims, legal and accident investigation costs; and lower industrial productivity. Also considered are the opportunity costs associated with "premature death," such as wage and life insurance costs, and legal and funeral expenses. (Actually, the latter costs are adjusted to reflect the additional cost of a death that occurs earlier than the average life expectancy.)

3.1.4.2 The Human Capital Approach

The human capital approach long has been a widely used economic measure of the loss of life. A typical monetary figure is computed by taking the average age at which death of people killed by a certain type of disease or accident occurs and computing what their expected future income would have been if they had lived a normal life span. The future income is discounted to arrive at a present-value figure. Depending on the group studied and the discount rate used, the figure ranges from $100,000 to $400,000 per life. This figure is interpreted as an output loss from early death, and this is an individual's direct contribution to the GNP and the marketplace.

The human capital approach formed the basis for public policy analysis within Health, Education and Welfare in the 1960's, the Federal Aviation Administration, the National Highway Traffic Safety Administration, and numerous other agencies and groups. Despite Mishan's objection that the figure should be at least net of consumption, the measure is still popular today. Further, while often described as a measure of human life, it should be more properly called simply a measure of the cost of removing an individual from production since discounted foregone earnings are the same whether a person has been killed or fully incapacitated.

3.1.4.3 Willingness-to-Pay

In the late 60's and 70's, growing concern about the validity of the human capital approach prompted economists to explore the use of willingness-to-pay measures. Mishan [1976] has stated "the worth or value of a thing is determined simply by what a person is willing to pay for it." According to this view, the value of life and health can be arrived at by determining what persons are willing to pay for them. In the case of valuing life, the willingness-to-pay question is not typically stated as a willingness-to-pay to prevent certain death but rather a willingness-to-pay to reduce the risk of death. While some analysts attempt to compute a "value of human life" from the monetary sum people are willing to pay to reduce the risk of death (by dividing the monetary sum by the probability of the risk), this approach is generally viewed with great suspicion. Willingness-to-pay approaches have also been applied to valuing morbidity in addition to mortality.

There are two general approaches to determining willingness-to-pay. Willingness-to-pay can be inferred by analyzing selected marketplace decisions or it can be elicited by polling or questionnaires. Those analysts who choose the inferred approach prefer it, arguing that polling techniques are inaccurate because people's response to a stranger's question may have little relation to actual value. Other economists are leary of inferred approaches, arguing that in the case of the use of the wage differential (the premium paid workers for risky work), the approach depends on the unrealistic assumptions of worker mobility and effective worker bargaining power.

Willingness-to-pay figures for human life have ranged from as low as $16,000 to over $1,000,000. Seven studies of risk premiums have been performed since 1973. The following table shows the risk premium computed per increment in the probability of death by 1/1000.

Author of Study	Year	Risk Premium for Risk of Death Only (in current dollars)
Dillingham	1979	168
Thaler and Rosen	1975	200-300
Brown	1980	400-600
Viscusi	1978	1,500
Smith	1973	2,000
Olson	1978	3,500
Graham	1982	237*

Source: Graham, 1982
* Primary labor market value. The risk premium is negative for the secondary labor market

The seventh study performed at Clark University demonstrates what some [Ashford, 1976] strongly suspected -- the existence of a dual labor market for the compensation of hazardous work. While the primary market (characterized by high wages, job stability and skilled labor) does show a positive risk premium, the secondary market (characterized by low wages, poor job stability and unskilled labor) shows a negative risk premium! Thus, assumptions of labor mobility and bargaining power of workers must be carefully considered in using wage differentials to infer the value of risk reduction.

Of additional concern is what willingness-to-pay is actually measuring in the case of risks to death. While the economic studies cited in the above table assume the wage differential to be a measure of the value of (reducing) the risk of death, the measure may well include (or be) the valuation of reducing the risk of injury and/or disease since all situations that cause premature death can also cause injury (and usually extreme injury) to health. Further, while risk premiums are considered reasonable measures of willingness-to-pay for valuation of acute injury, they are vigorously rejected by economists as measures applied to chronic health problems [Smith, 1981].

3.1.4.4 Summary of Economic Approaches

Economic valuation applies market concepts to phenomena that are not marketable values. As a consequence, its utility is limited by unresolved and, perhaps, unresolvable, problems.

The human capital concept has conceptual faults. As mentioned above, the computed results should be net of consumption. Unlike monetary capital, human capital has always been in excess supply (as evidenced by unemployment). While it is acknowledged that a supply of unemployed is not of the same quality of input as the employed, a marginal analysis provides a very different perception of what happens when a worker is killed or incapacitated. When a worker is lost, that input is not lost to society because another worker fills the opening. This produces a chain of openings as workers leave the job. Aside from depressing wages, the final result of this rippling process would be an opening for the marginally unemployed. The economic benefit of employing this person should be significant since the unemployed cost society in terms of unemployment insurance and welfare payments. In a narrowly economic sense, the death or incapacitation of a worker might be a net positive value to society. Further, if the death occurred to an unemployed person, the method clearly implies that this would be of net positive value to society since the unemployed have a negative earnings stream. For reasons discussed in the preceding section, a methodology whose full implications suggest that the loss of members of society is beneficial is unfit to assess the value of life.

Willingness-to-pay measures also are problematic. As mentioned above, Smith states that willingness-to-pay measures should be limited to acute injuries and not used to value chronic conditions. This limitation follows logically from the distinction in the health qualities model between acute and chronic conditions.

The use of wage differentials for valuing reduced risks to loss of life is accompanied by numerous difficulties. As mentioned above, it is not clear whether wage differentials are measures of life or health. And to the extent that they are measures of willingness-to-pay for reductions for severe injuries and disease, it is not clear how these measures stand in light of Smith's concern. The data by Graham showing a negative valuation for secondary labor markets further places this method under suspicion. If the measure can be this severely skewed by worker demographics, what validity does it have as a measure of the value of risk reduction?

What becomes apparent from these limitations is that economics can do little to measure the "value of human life" and can contribute substantially only to valuing acute, not chronic, illness and disease.

3.1.5 Critical Distinctions

The above discussion of our values framework has been systematic but purposefully general in keeping with our second principle: that the complexity of relationships and institutions does not permit conclusions about current morality to be drawn readily from a value system.

Nevertheless, it is possible to illuminate areas of special sensitivity in the legislative and regulatory process. The means for so doing have appeared in the public policy literature and in a number of publications from our Center.

As described previously (Section 3.), there are two types of "value phrases" that we used to map the findings of the historical review to the value framework. Concepts such as fairness are phrases that apply to the general framework. Critical distinctions such as voluntary versus involuntary are phrases that apply to specific, key distinctions

3.1.5.1 Ex Post versus Ex Ante Valuation

The latin terms ex post and ex ante refer to assessment of a situation after the situation occurs (ex post) or before the situation occurs (ex ante). In cases of injury, disease, or death, many valuations are performed when the legislator or decision-maker has not personally experienced the situation -- ex ante.

Studies have shown that ex post valuations are more sensitive and show greater concern for prevention than ex ante valuations. Individuals tend to undervalue the potential loss in a future situation until they themselves have experienced it.

To reduce this undervaluation, it is important to gain information from those who have suffered. As described in 3.1.3.2, testimony by afflicted persons and the use of vignettes can infuse ex post valuations with ex ante experience.

3.1.5.2 Reversibility of the Harm

Considering the reversibility of harm helps divide valuation into two useful categories. Where harm is reversible, the negative co-production of the harm is present for a limited duration. An injury that will heal "completely" differs significantly than one that will leave permanent disability. Where harm is irreversible, negative co-production continues through a person's lifetime, greatly affecting all subsequent valuations. Irreversible harm enduring through many generations (such as would accompany the destruction of a major ecological chains) engenders concerns we refer to by the term "uncertainty caution" (discussed in 3.1.5.4).

3.1.5.3 Presence of Risk Aversion

So far we have referred mainly to the certain loss of health or life. In most situations loss is not certain but is statistically described by a risk of harm. The value of reducing exposure to uncertain harm is greater than that for certain harm by an amount proportional to an individual's aversion to risk. A typical individual who sees the expected value of the loss (probability of loss times the value of the health loss if certain) as X is willing to give up X+x resources to eliminate the risk where x is the risk premium.

The quantity x, the risk premium, is partly related to the value of reducing anxiety about the loss. In the health qualities model, there are two sources of impact on well-being when health is at risk: from actual illness and from fears that unknown risks may be damaging one's health (interfering with future valued outcomes). This emotive element raises the value of protecting an individual from risk above the expected value of the loss. (For further discussion see Priest & Ashford, 1982, p. 9-69 to 9-72.)

3.1.5.4 Uncertainty Caution

In valuing reduced damage from injury or disease, there can be uncertainty that damage will occur as well as about the level of damage. When outcomes are uncertain, it is important to think in terms of an estimated mean value and uncertainty ranges.

Often when the risk of health loss is estimated, the mean value is computed and the uncertainty terms are omitted. However, if the range of uncertainty is great, there is the potential for harm much more severe than a mean value would suggest. Therefore, situations involving large uncertainty, such as destruction to ecological chains, should be treated differently from situations with less uncertainty.

In addition to risk-aversion (discussed earlier), people tend to be cautious about unknown outcomes unless there is a promise of sizable rewards. We call this phenomenon "uncertainty caution." We might wish to exercise greater uncertainty-caution today regarding, for example, the development of new chemicals as the positive returns to such development diminish and the chance of catastrophic illness as a result of their production, use, or disposal increases.

A society's conservatism is tied integrally to its degree of uncertainty-caution. Greater conservatism reduces gains from change but also reduces exposure to unexpected consequences. Conservatism prefers to invest in prevention than to suffer losses of health and life with the associated economic disruptions.

3.1.5.5 Statistical Life versus an Identified Life

Since the legislation of the late 60's and early 70's, regulatory activity has attempted to bring a rational approach to evaluating the costs and benefits of regulatory action. It is stated often that regulation evaluates "statistical" life rather than the value of an individual life. However, if 1,000,000 persons are exposed to a .1% chance of death, 1000 individuals will lose their lives. Thus, the statistical approach can only pretend to ignore the value of an individual life, for if action is taken to regulate the loss, it will be possible to compute the amount spent per life.

There are two fundamental valuation reasons why the "statistical life" approach is excessively sterile and always undervalues human life. First, the statistical approach removes lives from their circumstances and relationships and thus glosses the moral dimension of death. Second, the visibility of the loss of life, as discussed in section 3.1.2.4, is important in affirming the sanctity of life. A statistical death is abstract and, in that sense, invisible, and therefore unlikely to engage cultural strictures about the sanctity of life.

Unfortunately, regulatory legislation of recent decades did not direct government to think of a human life in terms of its relationships nor to think about the value of our cultural continuity. As a result, we have a crisis of moral responsibility in government (as discussed in 3.1.1.5). Administrators who themselves respect human life may or may not be able to inject this moral sense into the regulatory process depending on the moral outlook of their superiors (which changes with every administration).

3.1.5.6 Choice of Discount Rates

Choosing the best means to evaluate the reduction of future losses is a serious problem for government. The economic approach is to convert a future stream of value to a net present value. OMB circular A-94 establishes a standard discount rate to be used in evaluating measurable benefits of programs or projects when they are distributed over time. It is clear that this technique is valid when dollars and benefits can be interchanged at any point in time, because in a financial market a dollar today is worth more than a dollar a year from now.

The discounting of benefits that are not valued in monetary terms is related to the concept of the "time-rate-of-preference" of goods. Often people prefer "present consumption" to "future consumption" and as a consequence will trade an amount of future consumption for fewer units of present consumption of the same good. This provides an approach to discounting future desired outcomes relative to current desired outcomes of the same type.

In cases where dollars cannot be exchanged for desired outcomes at every point in time, the discounting approach loses utility. For example, if a level of health in the future can be purchased only with a current expenditure, and future expenditures cannot restore future health to that level after intervening damage, then the discounting approach doesn't help. This situation holds for incurable chronic diseases with latency between exposure and disease onset. To prevent the future illness, a certain sum must be spent today. If the illness were to occur in the future, no level of medical expenditure would be able to restore the person's prior health and for most incurable chronic diseases no amount of compensation could restore the original level of well-being.

If we wish to use time-rate-of-preference to resolve such dilemmas, we note that one cannot determine what level of present consumption is worth some future level of consumption corrupted by disease. So the time-rate-of-preference approach to obtaining a discount rate is inapplicable.

Henderson [1965] has suggested that some positive discount rate is "rationally implied by the inevitability of death." (People are willing to gamble that they may not survive to experience future harm.) Present consumption is to be preferred over future consumption, simply on the basis that future consumption may not be attainable. Henderson suggests that this component of the discount rate would be about 1 percent. If one accepts this argument, it still leaves a question about the other components of the rate. To date, no conceptual or analytical means has been developed to determine the total discount rate for health damage. Consequently, there is no justification for applying a discount rate greater than 1%. The legislator or decision-maker must make a personal judgment about the value of future health.

3.1.5.7 Voluntary versus Involuntary Assumption of Risk

Assumption of risk by an individual may be voluntary or involuntary. An example of involuntary risk assumption is a worker exposed to a dangerous chemical without his knowledge. An example of voluntary risk assumption is the skier who knowingly commits himself to a dangerous trail.

Tied to the concept of voluntary/involuntary is that of consent. In general, those who subject themselves to voluntary risks have exercised consent; those who are unaware or coerced into assuming risks (involuntary) have not given consent.

From an ethical perspective, the issue relates to whether a person is put at risk by someone else or elects it himself. More explicitly, the issue is whether the risk is taken by the individual, fully knowing the advantage of taking the risk, and having assessed for him or her self whether the risk was worth taking. But it does not necessarily follow that voluntary risk assumption is always better than involuntary assumption (see Section 3.1.5.8

on Bounded Rationality). A person may voluntarily assume the risk of sky-diving and the decision may actually not be worth the consequences. Also a person may be placed in involuntary risk and the risk may be well worth the consequences.

Thus, while the notions of willingness and consent suggest potential ethical problems, they indicate potential rather than necessary problems. Furthermore, the principle of autonomy suggests that, other things being equal, it is desirable that an individual make moral decisions for himself rather than have an external agent impose a decision. Ethics and autonomy (freedom) favor voluntary risk assumption.

It is sometimes difficult to distinguish voluntary from involuntary situations. Does a worker who is aware of the hazards of his job submit voluntarily or involuntarily when he or she is transferred? In actuality, there is a continuum from voluntary to involuntary.

In summary the voluntary/involuntary category alerts us to possible problems in decision-making situations. Legislation, informed by an implicit cultural-ethical consensus, is more likely to protect people from involuntary as opposed to voluntary risks.

3.1.5.8. Presence of Bounded Rationality

Economic theory recently has recognized a limitation in decision-making that had been noted previously in behavioral science, management science, and philosophy. The economic term, bounded rationality, refers to a buyer's inability to assimilate and use all the information needed to make an appropriate decision.

The concepts of bounded rationality and paternalism are closely entwined. It is because of phenomena that we refer to as bounded rationality, that parents and government have exercised control over children and citizens, respectively. Bounded rationality limits an individual's autonomy but it is not only children or the "common citizen" whose behavior it describes. In complex situations or in high risk, low probability situations, it is often impossible for individuals to draw a correct conclusion.

In the terminology of market-failure, bounded rationality is one of several fundamental reasons that a market is not always an efficient market. Health decisions are particularly susceptible to problems of bounded rationality since, as suggested by the health qualities model, the co-productive relationship of health to thousands of desired outcomes is so complex.

3.1.5.9 Presence of Externalities

Externalities are said to exist when a person or organization does not take responsibility or interest in some outcome(s) of an action. An example of a negative externality is pollution of a water supply by an upstream papermill. A positive externality is the employment created by the mill. These facts are called "externalities" because they are not objectives of the operation of the papermill.

In the terminology of market-failure, externalities are another reason a market is not always an efficient market. A major objective of social legislation is to "internalize" externalities by making them, legally, important to corporations. Occupational Health and Safety Legislation was directed toward internalizing the externalities of worker injuries and deaths. (Firms, within this theory, will have already taken into account the non-external effects of injuries and deaths on productivity and morale and have achieved safety and health up to the point where the last dollar spent on health and safety equaled the savings in increased productivity.)

3.1.5.10 Lack of Information

Informed decisions require available information. In the terminology of market-failure, lack of information is another reason markets may not be efficient. A major component of social legislation is to improve the information available to all concerned parties.

3.1.5.11 Presence of Monopoly

Some activities have such significant "economies of scale" that they interfere with competition. These activities become monopolies unless there is government intervention.

In the terminology of market-failure, markets depend on many independent competing firms to keep prices down and quality up. A monopoly does not meet the requirement for perfect competition and is therefore not likely to be efficient without economic regulation. In cases of occupational health and safety, monopoly power over employment can create undesirable consequences such as higher levels of injury and deaths. In such cases an objective of social legislation is to overcome such monopoly power and rebalance the situation.

3.1.5.12 Visibility

A prominent characteristic related to the value of life and the connection between good health and relationships is visibility (discussed in 3.1.2.3). Part of what motivates legislation that seeks to protect life is the visibility of the loss of life. The Coal Mine Safety Act was motivated in large part by the visibility of tragic coal-mine accidents. Aviation safety legislation is also highly motivated by the visibility of airline crashes involving hundreds of people.

Visibility in the way that the loss of health and life effects individual relationships is important to focus on the "negative co-productive" effects of such losses on family, friends, and communities. These effects have been described at length in 3.1.3 on the Social Consequences of Injury, Illness and Death.

Further Distinctions --

The next four critical distinctions relate to four plausible trends in industrial society. They are listed as much as hypotheses as critical distinctions.

3.1.5.13 Increased Risk

The first distinction is that the risk of harm in particular situations or occupations may have increased in an absolute way (e.g. higher number of accidents per worker or greater numbers of airline deaths per traveller.)

The hypothesis is that social legislation to control such risks would be more likely when the risk has increased in absolute numbers.

3.1.5.14 Increased Awareness

The second of these four distinctions refers to an overall increase in the social perception of risk. The hypothesis is that as the social perception of risk increases, so will the social forces to control risks through legislation.

3.1.5.15 Improved Standards of Protection

The third of these critical distinctions is that demand by society for an overall decrease in the real degree of risk present has increased. This may have occurred due to increased information about risks and their effects, a greater willingness to devote resources to their reduction, and because of the expectation that risks can be reduced.

3.1.5.16 Higher Technical Capability

The last of these four critical distinctions is that the presence of higher technical capability to reduce risks may have motivated social legislation. As our ability to control risks increases, our expectations for the control of risks increases.

3.1.5.17 Non-Compensability

Much of our basic law as well as early forms of social legislation were directed toward achieving fairness through compensation. For example, workers' compensation has various dollar amounts that are to be paid the worker for specifically listed injuries and diseases.

The health qualities model challenges the fairness of compensability for irreversible harms and for harms accompanied by extended family impacts. The term "non-compensability" is used to refer to such situations.

3.1.5.18 Intertemporal Equity

Intertemporal equity includes the obligation of societies to preserve future generations. The term, however, goes further by indicating an obligation of fairness between generations.

Employing the approach of Rawls, we can imagine being a member of any generation. From this position, not knowing which generation will be ours, we will contract a fair situation where no generation is disadvantaged relative to any other.

Some have noted that the concern for future generations is clouded by technology. The "technological fix"* is more likely available to future generations and might be used to remedy any problems passed on by past generations (such as low-level radiation waste). Since the efficacy of these solutions ("fixes") is unknown, there is considerable disagreement about the extent to which any one generation should consider equity for another generation.

----

* The term "technological fix" refers to a solution to a social problem that either accompanies the progress of technology or that requires technological innovation. One irony is that technology sometimes generates problems as it solves or seeks to solve others. For some problems such as the buildup of heat in the atmosphere, there may be no practical solution other than moderation in the use of energy.

3.2 Values Revealed in the Historical Review

The historical review (Section 2.) presented the context for concerns expressed in indexes, hearings, and the secondary literature. To appreciate how these expressions of concerns reflect values, a list of 47 "value phrases" were developed from the value framework. These phrases were matched with expressions of concern. Figure 3.2-1 shows: the list of the value phrases; whether the phrase is a "framework concept" or a "critical distinction"; and where in the framework discussion (Section 3.1) the value phrase can be found.

The following sections present values found in the historical review under three categories of actors: 1) Media; 2) Advocates, Concerned Scientists, and Congressional Figures; and 3) Congressional Action. These values are presented by describing the expressions of concerns found in the historical review in terms of the value phrases. These phrases are highlighted by underlining them in the text.

3.2.1 Values as Found in Media Voiced Concerns

The analysis of the media was accomplished by tracking expressions of concern over time. The details of this method were discussed in section 2.1. It is in light of that discussion that the description of the values found from interpreting media-voiced concerns is presented here.

Consumer Product Safety

In the area of consumer products, the indexes told somewhat different stories. The Index to Legal Periodicals emphasized mechanisms of redress (fairness and non-compensable) and the liability of manufacturers (responsibility). The concept of government regulation (fairness) was only a significant issue in the late 1960s and early 1970s in this index. The New York Times Index only showed concern in the 1970s, and the major emphasis was on stories related to government regulation. Apparently The New York Times was more interested in the currency of consumer product issues than in value-laden expressions of concern. Concerns discovered in the Public Affairs Information Service were related to liability (responsibility), regulation (fairness), and specific household products (information). The Readers' Guide was dominated by expressions of concern about specific household products (information) and specific hazards (information) through the entire time period studied. Interest in regulation (fairness), and other forms of consumer protection (fairness, bounded rationality, information, and increased risk) became significant after 1960. Although it is possible that many of the concerns were related to children, the first substantial

Key Value Phrases, Their Use, and Where Described

Value Phrase	How Used	Where Described
Autonomy	Framework concept *	Section 3.1.5.7
Bounded Rationality	Critical distinction *	Section 3.1.5.8
Coproduction	Framework concept	Section 3.1.1.3
Discount rates	Critical distinction	Section 3.1.5.6
Duty	Framework concept	Section 3.1.1.2
Environment	Concept treated elsewhere	See chapter 10, [Mitchell, 1982]
Ex post / Ex ante	Critical distinction	Section 3.1.5.1
Experienced out-of-jointness	Framework concept	Section 3.1.1 (Approach)
Externality	Critical distinction	Section 3.1.5.9
Fairness	Framework concept	Section 3.1.1.1
Government Responsibility	Framework concept	Section 3.1.1.5
Health	Framework concept	Section 3.1.2.3
Health qualities model	Framework concept	Section 3.1.2
High level value	Framework concept	Section 3.1.2.1

* See notes at end of figure

Figure 3.2-1

Value Phrase	How Used	Where Found
Higher technical capability	Critical distinction	Section 3.1.5.16
Human life	Framework concept	Section 3.1.2.3
Improved standards	Critical distinction	Section 3.1.5.15
Increased Awareness	Critical distinction	Section 3.1.5.14
Increased risk	Critical distinction	Section 3.1.5.13
Industry responsibility	Framework concept	Section 3.1.1.5
Inequity	Framework concept	Section 3.1.1.1
Information	Critical distinction	Section 3.1.5.10
Injustice	Framework concept	Section 3.1.1.1
Intertemporal equity	Critical distinction	Section 3.1.5.18
Involuntary	Critical distinction	Section 3.1.5.7
Justice	Framework concept	Section 3.1.1.1
Limitation of economics	Framework concept	Section 3.1.4
Market failure	Critical distinction	Sections 3.1.5.8 thru 3.1.5.11
Monopoly	Critical distinction	Section 3.1.5.11
Negative coproduction	Framework concept	Section 3.1.2.1
Non-compensability	Critical distinction	Section 3.1.5.17
Physiological effects	Concept treated elsewhere	See Chapter 5 [Hattis, 1982]

Figure 3.2-1 (Cont.)

Value Phrase	How Used	Where Found
Quality of life	Framework concept	Section 3.1.3
Relationship	Framework concept	Section 3.1.1.2
Responsibility	Framework concept	Section 3.1.1.2 and Section 3.1.1.5
Reversibility	Critical distinction	Section 3.1.5.2
Right	Framework concept	Section 3.1
Risk aversion	Critical distinction	Section 3.1.5.3
Sanctity of life	Framework concept	Section 3.1.2.3
Social consequences	Framework concept	Section 3.1.3
Societal costs	Framework concept	Section 3.1.3
Statistical versus identified life	Critical distinction	Section 3.1.5.5
Uncertainty caution	Critical distinction	Section 3.1.5.3
Value of life	Framework concept	Section 3.1.5.3
Visibility	Critical distinction	Section 3.1.5.12
Voluntary versus involuntary	Critical distinction	Section 3.1.5.7
Voluntary compliance	Framework concept	Section 3.1.1.5
Welfare	Framework concept	Section 3.1.2.3

Framework Concept: A term introduced in the text during the general development of a framework that relates human values to issues of health and life.

Critical Distinction: A term introduced in the text that specifically relates to key areas of legislative concerns and were critical considerations in public decision-making.

Figure 3.2-1 (Cont.)

appearance of such concerns were about specific children's products (information), such as toys, was in the 1970s. As discussed in section 2.1.2.3 The Washington Post Index only covered the 1970s. In this case, The Washington Post Index seemed to follow where the analysis of The Readers' Guide left off. The concerns about toys (information) were high in the early 1970s. The other typical concerns relating to regulation (fairness), other forms of protection (fairness, bounded rationality, information, and increased risk), and concern about physical phenomena (information) were present through most of the rest of the 1970s.

Occupational Safety and Health

The expressions of concern relating to occupational safety and health were fairly similar in all the indexes. All the indexes showed strong concern about redress (fairness and non-compensable). The Index to Legal Periodicals also showed a great concern for liability (responsibility). Concern relating to government regulation (fairness) appeared primarily in the 1970s, except in The Readers' Guide, where it was present throughout the time period studied. Also The Readers' Guide showed great concern relating to specific hazards (information), specific industries (information, responsibility, and fairness), specific diseases (information, and fairness), the desire or need for increased safety (increased risk, improved standards, information, increased awareness, and fairness), and other expressions about inequity (fairness). The concern about occupational safety was predominantly stated in the 1930s and steadily declined in strength to almost insignificant in the 1970s. This must be remembered when including these concerns with those of other areas. Also the concern expressed in The Washington Post Index should be interpreted in light of the fact that concern about occupational safety and health issues had dwindled to almost nothing before the beginning of that index.

Pesticides

Concerns relating to the use of pesticides responded similarly to specific historical events in all the indexes. Prior to 1945 the concerns were primarily about protecting the farmer from fraud etc. (fairness), protecting the consumer (information), and some general concern about the need for more effective pesticides and a better pesticide industry. From 1945 through 1960 concerns increased about the need for better pesticides. Pesticides and monoculture had made pests more virulent and technology seemed able to provide more potent weapons for the "war on pests." Although concerns about the actual harmful effects of pesticides themselves (information, increased risk, and increased awareness) started in the late 1940s and built in the 1950s, it was not until the 1960s that this became the dominant concern. In the 1960s the concern about pesticides changed dramatically in character to one about the ecology (information, increased awareness, uncertainty caution, irreversibility of harm, and coproduction), and the long term effects on the food chain and consumers health (information, involuntary harm, and negative coproduction). By the 1970s the concern about pesticides had finally embraced the concept of government regulation to limit their use (fairness, increased awareness, increased risk).

Air Quality

From the 1950s on, the indexes studied all told similar stories regarding concerns about air pollution. There was early strong concern about air pollution as a nuisance (information, increased awareness, externalities, and fairness), which was thought to be handled best by state and local government (responsibility), found in The Readers' Guide. This concern was strongest in the 1930s and died away in the 1940s. That air pollution was still a major problem (information, increased risk, externalities, increased awareness, and fairness) of national proportions (responsibility), was found in all the indexes studied after the 1950s. This new concern primarily manifested itself as concern about specific pollutants (information, and negative coproduction), physiological effects (information), concern for the environment (responsibility), specific industries (fairness, and responsibility), the best way to control the problem (responsibility, information, and fairness), and discussions over the degree of the problem in the present and the future (information). There were also expressions about the horror generated from classic cases (information, and increased risk), damage to property etc. caused by air pollution (negative coproduction), and about the fact that air ought to be pure (coproduction, and uncertainty caution).

Aviation Safety

The indexes studied showed different emphasis of concern with respect to air traffic safety issues. These differences in emphasis did not conflict, so much as they reflected the nature of the periodicals involved. The New York Times Index and The Washington Post Index were the most similar to each other in that they concentrated on the reporting of aircraft accidents (visibility). This was to be expected since accidents are popular newspaper stories. Of course these periodicals also covered the issues more substantively. Concerns were expressed through statements about unsafe situations (information, increased awareness, and improved standards), causes or blame in accident situations (responsibility), safety improvements (information and increased awareness), and administrative and political issues (responsibility and fairness). Concern about legal technicalities such as liability (responsibility, fairness, and non-compensable) tresspass (fairness, responsibility, and relationship), and (fairness and responsibility) were primarily found in the Index to Legal Periodicals, however there was some similar concern about who is harmed (fairness and responsibility) found in The Washington Post Index. The Readers' Guide provided the most complete picture. Most of the above expressions of concern appeared in this index with the possible exception that legal concerns were primarily related to generic insurance issues (responsibility, fairness, and non-compensable). In addition, there were early concerns about the need for progress (fairness, responsibility, and externalities), strong concern about what are the best societal mechanisms to achieve safety (fairness, responsibility, and externalities) throughout most of the time period studied, and healthy concern relating to specific unsafe situations and safety improvements (information, increased risk, increased awareness, improved standards) throughout most of the time period studied. These additional concerns made The Readers Guide uniquely inclusive on concerns expressed about air traffic safety. Concerns found in the Public Affairs Information Service largely confirmed what was found in The Readers' Guide.

3.2.2 Values as Presented by Advocates, Concerned Scientists, and Congressional Figures

Rachel Carson

Biologist Rachel Carson became a publicly recognized advocate for pesticide control with the publication of her book Silent Spring in 1962. The ensuing controversy not only put her in the spotlight, but brought the issue of pesticides' harmful effects on man and the environment to the forefront of public concern. Miss Carson was a concerned scientist trying to convey to others her concerns about the potential dangers of pesticides.

Primarily, she spoke of the need for caution in using pesticides, further research into their harmful effect (information), and minimization of their use by developing other forms of pest control (higher technical capability). All of these were important to her because of the uncertainty she felt was involved with large scale use of these poisons.

Rachel Carson valued the complex workings of nature and was distressed at man's disruption of these processes (increased awareness). She writes of the contamination of soil and water and the persistence and intensification of certain pesticides in the food chain (negative coproduction). A chapter of her book is devoted to diseases attributable or aggravated by pesticides abundant in the environment. Milk from dairy cows being contaminated by the government's spraying of grazing pastures to kill fire ants is an example given.

In describing the milk contamination Carson asks the question "who is safeguarding the consumer...?" [Carson, p.169] Governmental responsibility for safe and cautious use of pesticides underlies her pleas for more consideration in USDA pesticide programs and advice given to farmers. The government is obviously not carrying out responsibly its duty to or relationship with citizens.

Concern for pesticides hastening the extinction of particular species is a reflection of the irreversible harms pesticides can have. Environmental poisons definitely cause undesirable effects in other wildlife as exemplified by the instances of fishkills discussed in Silent Spring (negative coproduction).

At the Ribicoff hearings in 1963, Miss Carson gave testimony reflecting another aspect of her concerns. She states that every citizen has the right to be secure in his or her own home without having to be involuntarily subjected to the effects of private and government sprayings. Her testimony shows her concern that individuals should have some control over harms affecting them (autonomy) as well as an element of government's responsibility to protect citizens. Further she discusses the need for more information to help the individual users make informed decisions and to warn people of what is being sprayed into their immediate environment.

The capability of pesticides to be a negative coproducer to health and the environment led to Rachel Carson's call for caution in their use. She felt government had certain responsibilities to citizens to help insure that citizens are not involuntarily subjected to pesticides and have more information.

Kenneth Hahn

As a supervisor for the county of Los Angeles, Kenneth Hahn not only experienced the problem of air pollution, but was in a position to do something about it. Accepting that challenge, he made an ongoing effort to induce the major automobile manufacturers to develop a control device for autos to decrease their contribution to air pollution (externality) in Los Angeles.

To achieve this goal, Hahn wrote to the presidents of the major automobile manufacturers, every year from 1953 until 1968. The content of this correspondence is contained in a Los Angeles County publication. [Hahn, 1968] This document, as well as his distribution of it to various US Senators, the President and Vice President, is testimony to the urgency with which he viewed the problem. The content of his letters reflect some of his underlying moral concerns regarding this subject.

In 1953, Mr. Hahn states that these manufacturers would be rendering a "great public service" to the people of Los Angeles by inventing and installing a device to control air pollution on new cars. At that time he expressed a desire that the problem be solved without the need for "forcing" legislation. By October, 1954, he had strengthened his language saying, "the automotive industry must assume the responsibility of rapidly finding a solution." This responsibility is reiterated in virtually every piece of his correspondence. In a letter to the President of Ford Motor Company in 1965, he extends his argument to "it is my belief that you owe it to the citizens who have purchased your products to return to them in a positive manner some assistance in preserving their health."

Health and welfare is Supervisor Hahn's major argument for government regulation. He asserts that an air pollution control device for autos is imperative for the health and welfare of the people of his county. Stressing the urgency of the problem, he reiterates the specific diseases auto exhaust leads to (negative coproduction). He calls exhaust from cars a "serious health menace."

Incorporated with Supervisor Hahn's feeling that the automotive industry has "sole responsibility" for this type of pollution, is an underlying concern for fairness. "Under our system of government and free enterprise, I believe that the industry which causes a problem should be the first to correct it without regulations." Industry responsibility is not merely an obligation from seller to buyer, but also an obligation of the agent of harm to society (see discussion in 3.1.1.5 on business responsibility).

When auto manufacturers did not respond voluntarily, Hahn wrote to Congress saying they must pass legislation to force the industry to assume its responsibility. In these requests, a certain role of responsibility is seen for government.

Over time, Hahn perceived the problem of air pollution getting worse (increased risk). The need to correct the problem therefore became more urgent, as did his words stressing this need.

Ralph Nader

Ralph Nader was one of the most well-known advocates for health and safety in the sixties. His book Unsafe at Any Speed brought public attention to the issue of automobile safety in 1965. Nader, and the Center for Study of Responsive Law he established, have also worked in the areas of consumer product safety, air pollution, food and drug safety, water pollution, occupational safety and health and many other areas of consumer protection. His statements regarding occupational health and safety taken from the introduction of Bitter Wages, a Nader Study Group report to which he was special consultant, and his testimony before the US Senate Subcommittee on Labor on December 15, 1969 give some idea of Nader's moral values.

Respect for the individual worker (monopoly) and dismay at the insensitivity with which the rest of society views worker health and safety (responsibility) are basic to Ralph Nader's actions in this area. Charting the extent of occupational hazards and counting the workers harmed each year is primary to his work. He speaks of under-reported statistics that can "never convey the agony of the injured, the anguish of the family" (social consequences and Statistical versus Identified Life). Nader argues that purely statistical means of measuring the problem minimizes public concern for the issue in general and for the specific individuals at risk.

As a means to correct this shortcoming, Nader asserts that legislators considering this issue should visit workplaces, talk to workers and allow them to testify at the hearings (fairness, visibility, and ex post versus ex ante). Nader says in the 1970 hearings, "if workers came in and testified from their own experience, you (the Senate Subcommittee on Labor) would see the deep pathos and the tragedy and the injustice that is being proliferated every day... ." Examining the problem on this individual worker level would produce more genuinely useful legislation.

In the hearings, Nader describes the drive for new legislation as necessary and humane, pointing to spotty coverage created by varying state laws (fairness). He describes industry and government as having responsibility for worker safety. His call that legislation should seek to prevent rather than to compensate for accidents (which is "a sign of a catch-up, not a humane, society"), amply demonstrates his concern for health. Government and employer duty is not merely to give monetary payments which cannot correct the injustice (irreversibility and non-compensable).

Ralph Nader also is concerned that the worker's views be represented. Unions are not doing well in this area according to Bitter Wages, and industry tries to dodge the issue of job safety. Nader encourages the Senate Subcommittee to give those citizens which he calls the "silent majority," a voice. Society is in a way responsible for not giving enough attention to this issue (information and improved standards), the seriousness of which he expresses by calling industrial disease and accidents a form of violence comparable to street crime (social consequences).

Nader argues that the evaluation of an individual's worth should consider all factors, even non-economically quantifiable ones (health qualities model). Government has a responsibility to protect the health and safety of citizens through effective, fair legislation.

Michael Pertschuk

As a staff member for Senator Warren Magnuson, who chaired the Senate Commerce Committee, and as member of the National Commission on Product Safety, Michael Pertschuk was heavily involved with consumer safety issues in the latter part of the sixties and early seventies. Holding these positions, he was a moving factor in consumer product safety legislation. From discussion with him and from his book Revolt Against Regulation, some insight into his thoughts on the subject can be obtained.

Pertschuk calls himself a consumer advocate. His work toward passage of many consumer bills, especially the Consumer Product Safety Act, reveal a belief that there are situations in this country that cause harm to citizens, are wrong, and need to be corrected (fairness). He says there was a need for consumer safety legislation and that there are "certain moral and ethical constraints on a society" that make correction necessary (responsibility).

Calling himself a "cost-benefit draft resister," Pertschuk conveys a belief that economics is not only inadequate for capturing the total problem of harm (limitation of economics), but leads to injustice and inequity. He recognizes the benefit of an economic approach in that it raises appropriate questions, and he speaks of "regulatory humility" in understanding what the market can and cannot do. Yet, his statements and actions basically reflect a belief that government has a responsibility to perceive what the need in society is, evaluate the harms adequately, and answer the need through legislation and regulation.

Through working for legislation and being a regulator, Michael Pertschuk learned the importance of public support in governmental action. But he extends this importance to a strong belief in the "inelegant passion of moral outrage" (experienced out-of-jointness) as a necessary part of our political system. His concern that the individual express his anger is coupled with concern that our political system does not always provide appropriate channels for this outrage to help government identify and correct societal problems. These concerns combine his concern for fairness and justice with government's challenge and responsibility to the society.

David L. Behncke

David L. Behncke was president of the Air Line Pilots Association, representing ninety percent of the airline pilots in the country, from the mid-thirties to the late-forties. This period was formative for the airline industry and civil aviation legislation. With acute professional and personal concerns for safety, Mr. Behncke's testimony in 1936 and 1947 before the Senate reveals some of his views as an advocate for government regulation.

As a representative of airline pilots, he showed great concern for the increasing number of airplane crashes in general and specifically the deaths of airline pilots (increased risk). He placed responsibility for correcting this problem on the government and the airlines. Safety is compromised by stretching equipment, underpaying personnel involved in maintaining safety, and the lack of copilots, all for economic reasons which Behncke felt should not be placed above safety (value of life). These economic concerns would not have to be placed higher than safety if government regulation were effective and enforced (responsibility and externality) which would help airlines keep passengers, save money, provide a greater safety margin, and require better practices.

Behncke argued that better regulation would come from an independent Air Safety Board that would conduct more thorough accident investigations to correctly assess the cause of an air crash, not simply "put the blame on the pilot as the easy answer" so others do not have to take their share (fairness and information). He wants to insure "fair accurate investigations."

The importance of aviation safety to him is embodied in the lives of those he represents and the increasing risk they face if action is not taken. He argues for action by airlines as their responsibility but encouraged and supervised by government.

Congressional Figures

Often individual legislators hold positions of authority and influence that allow them to have a significant effect on the process of passing legislation. Their values illuminate their work and its social context.

Senator Warren G. Magnuson, first elected to the Senate in 1946, was Chairman of the Senate Commerce Committee during the sixties. He pushed for creation of the National Product Safety Commission and fought for the Consumer Product Safety Act, as well as being involved in many other consumer issues. In the book The Dark Side of the Marketplace, which he coauthored with Jean Carper, Senator Magnuson writes about his concern for the consumer.

In 1967 hearings, he stated "the consumer has a <u>right</u> to reasonable safety of purchased products." His belief that products should be made as safe as technically possible (<u>higher technical capability</u>) reflects the idea that industry has a <u>responsibility</u> to consumers. He viewed government's role as promoting regulations that will "help private industry live up to its responsibilities."

Related to his belief that comprehensive product safety legislation was necessary, he often talked about the need for prevention rather than after-the-fact or patchwork remedies (<u>non-compensable</u>). This view reflects his feeling that the problem is "bad and should be corrected before it gets worse" (<u>improved standards</u> and <u>increased risk</u>) and hazards should be corrected before they cause injury or death (<u>value of life and health</u>). He made consumer problems "his issue" in the sixties and his position helped to get laws passed. [Pertschuk, 1984]

Other legislators that had an important part in congressional action on safety and health were Senator Ralph Yarbourough, chairman of the Senate Subcommittee on Labor, and Representative James O'Hara, chairman of the house Subcommittee on Labor in 1968. Both of these men were important in regard to federal occupational safety and health legislation being considered by Congress. Their experiences before that time, and personal feelings toward this issue aided this legislation.

First concerned with public health (he ran on this issue for governor), Yarbourough became more interested in worker legislation after seeing the <u>inequity</u> of the worker's situation in Texas (<u>fairness</u>). As a lawyer he had been involved in workmen's compensation cases where he saw maimed injured workers and learned about occupational safety and health problems (<u>social consequences</u> and <u>health qualities model</u>). With the chairmanship of the labor subcommittee, he could call hearings on this issue and present it to the Senate as a federal <u>responsibility</u>. Yarborough said he "wanted to see it [OSHA] enacted" because he it was a "just law." He gave very high priority to protection of the worker, even though he claims there is no political benefit to supporting labor. His strong feelings on this subject are exemplified by the fight he had to undertake to support this legislation in the face of much opposition in Congress.

James O'Hara also had strong feelings about worker health and safety. He was involved in other laws on this subject. He was identified by outside health and safety interests as a congressional proponent of this issue. He was angered by the inadequate <u>information</u> given to workers using dangerous substances. What he called the "chamber of horrors" conditions of some workplaces reflects his concern for the worker (<u>fairness</u> and <u>social consequences</u>). He held extensive hearings to learn about this problem and modified and introduced the Labor Department's bill to "take both sides into account" (<u>fairness</u>). Even considering both sides, he supported the legislation and was not pleased with some of the weakening compromises in the enacted law (government responsibility).

3.2.3 Values as Stated in Congressional Action

The process of examining Congressional documents for expressions of concern is described in an earlier section (2.1.3). Studying these hearing records reveal both the values of individual Congressmen as well as widely shared social values of the period.

Air Quality

Tracking air quality hearings from 1955 to 1970 shows the clear trend of increased awareness and increased risk. Information gathered over this period enabled an improved establishment of danger thresholds and better assessment of the extent of air pollution (negative coproduction).

Analysis of the 1955 Senate Public Works Committee hearings indicate the forming of a consensus that the Federal Government was responsible for the control of air pollution because increasing risk and possible irreversible harm was making the social costs unbearable. Improved standards were sought but the technical information was not available. Concern about the known physiological effects of air pollution (value of life and negative coproduction) is stated numerous times, and the public's increased awareness of the menace of contaminated air becoming a dangerous problem in many parts of the country is evident.

The 1958 hearings focused on the specific problem of unburned hydrocarbons discharged at dangerous levels by motor vehicles (increased risk and value of life). The specific pollutants and the specific source of the problem had been determined; society's concerns about health and environment demanded that the Federal Government act to improve standards. These demands are voiced in both the 1958 and the 1963 House hearings. Expressed fears about the growing proportions of the problem (increased risk) in the future (uncertainty caution) were frequent in the 1963 hearings.

Physiological effects from air pollution (health concern and health qualities model) continued to be a major topic of debate during the 1963-64 Senate Special Subcommittee on Air and Water Pollution hearings. The societal costs due to the air pollution problem and the Federal Government's responsibility to clean the air were discussed at great length. By 1968 there was ample evidence to justify air pollution control and it was no longer necessary to prove harm to health from air pollution (physiological effects) as a justification for control.

The 1970 hearings marked continued public discussion about the <u>health</u> and <u>environmental</u> effects and the <u>costs to society</u> from air pollution. Concern for the <u>quality of life</u>, especially that of the children and the elderly, is quite pronounced. As Dr. Aaron J. Teller of Teller Environmental Systems, Inc., suggests, the solution to the pollution problem involves considerations about the value of <u>human life</u>, the value of the <u>environment</u>, and the value of raw materials to future generations (<u>intertemporal equity</u>).

Aviation Safety

The historical trend for air safety shifts from concerns for military safety and for the development of safe air machines by the private sector to growing Federal <u>responsibility</u> in regulating commercial airplane safety. As early as the 1920s, the general public consensus was that government regulation would accelerate the progress of air traffic safety (positive coproduction). The nation's defense also would benefit from aviational progress. The general sentiment was that government-sponsored safeguards (<u>responsibility</u>) were necessary to bolster public confidence.

The lack of government support had forced the airlines to large expenditures for safety. The Air Transportation Association president stated that the companies should not have to operate at a loss for safety's sake. The 1958 House hearings grappled with the increasing frequency of midair accidents (<u>increased risks</u>) and the possibility that the introduction of jets would make a bad problem-- air traffic control-- worse. There was also concern on the part of small aircraft owners and pilots who feared regulations would increase cost, complication, and restrictions.

The 1961 Senate hearings attempted to determine the specific <u>responsibility</u> of the Federal Government in air traffic safety. The 1967-68 House hearings centered on efforts to address specific dangers such as congestion in the airways and disorganization at the airports. Increased traffic was aggravating the amount of pressure air traffic controllers faced (<u>negative coproduction</u>). The subject of the 1969 Senate hearing was the role of general aviation in the overall transportation system. The general opinion was that the Federal Government should not attempt to reduce demand but should provide a system able to handle efficiently the demands placed upon it. (<u>responsibility</u>)

Consumer Product Safety

Values present in the 1953 and 1956 hearings under consumer product safety included <u>social consequences</u>, and <u>sanctity of life</u>. <u>Increasing awareness</u> of the failure of industry to protect the public had made many people believe that the Federal Government should undertake a new responsibility. Specifically, many witnesses testified on the hazards of abandoned iceboxes and refrigerators and asserted that mandatory restrictions should be imposed on manufacturers to prevent the deaths of young children. On the other hand, some industrial advocates claimed manufacturers could arrive at satisfactory solutions if they were left unrestricted. (voluntary compliance) The need for information resulted in calls for more extensive consumer education programs.

In the 1967 hearings considering the establishment of the National Commission on Product Safety (NCPS), Senator Warren Magnuson stated that consideration of two 'essential rights' is paramount: (1) the consumer has a right to reasonable safety of products and (2) the manufacturer is entitled to reasonable uniformity in laws. In addition, technology could and should provide solutions to product hazardousness (higher technology capability). The hazards of flammable clothing and action to spare people from painful burns were major topics in the 1967 House hearings regarding the amendments to the Flammable Fabrics Act (social consequences). There was also some concern for consumers who might not be able to afford higher priced products with more safety features (fairness).

Protecting children from a specific harm was the main concern of the 1970 House hearings. Voluntary compliance had failed to provide adequately safe containers, but supporters of the bills frequently expressed confidence that laws would spur the manufacturers to resolve the problem. In 1971 the chairman of the NCPS stated that the laissez-faire approach to consumer product safety had hurt the American public and that Federal regulation was necessary to reduce hazards. Many other witnesses agreed that it was a matter of consumer right that hazards be limited. Technological complexity (increasing risk) in products was denounced for causing unreasonable numbers of deaths and injuries.

Occupational Safety and Health

There was much dissatisfaction in the late 1960s with the insufficient attention paid to worker's safety. The general sentiment in the testimony on occupational health and safety was that society could do better in making the workplace safer (responsibility and higher technical capability). During the 1968 House Committee on Education and Labor hearings, several of the witnesses voiced a concern for fairness because society was not making an adequate effort in eliminating the problem of occupational hazards and injuries as compared to efforts made in some other areas. The National Consumers League asserted that assurance of safe and healthful working conditions was the right of every worker.

The general facts (14,000 workers killed annually and $1.5 billion in wages lost) illustrated the magnitude of the social and economic costs. Furthermore, not only were many of the existing standards outdated and inadequate, they were poorly administered because of insufficient staffing. Experts like Ralph Nader pointed out that the toll of job-related accidents had never been quantified accurately but that public concern had been numbed by "mass statistics" (statistical versus identified life).

During the 1969-70 Senate hearings, the AFL-CIO claimed the States had performed poorly in protecting its workers and supporters of OSHA urged the Federal Government to exercise more leadership position in occupational health and safety (responsibility). Social attitudes had changed drastically so that it was generally conceded that the worker could not secure his own health and safety because of the complexities of the modern workplace (voluntary versus involuntary and information).

Pesticides Control

Early Congressional action on pesticides primarily focused on eliminating fraudulent products from the market. Due to the dearth of information, farmers were being defrauded (negative coproduction). Farmers welcomed the legislation because it protected them against loss or damage (fairness) before they occurred. The pesticide industry supported a labelling requirement but balked at establishing strict standards.

By the 1947 House hearings, fears about damage to the environment were beginning to surface. A major concern of the 1954 House hearings was the safeguarding of public health against dangerous pesticides. Several witnesses expressed concerns about the inadequate testing procedures for pesticides. However, some witnesses, asserting the necessity of pesticides, expressed concern for aiding food producers. The 1954 Senate hearings stressed the effects of pesticides on human life and on the environment.

The 1969 House hearings examined the deficiencies in Federal regulation (responsibility). The House Committee on Government Operations disapproved of the way the Agricultural Research Service of USDA had tested new products for hazards to the environment and human health. Both the 1971 House and Senate hearings were concerned with irreversible harm to the environment and the natural resources. Threats to human life were examined because the health of the people was considered paramount (high level value). Some witnesses claimed that we still know little about the long-term effects of pesticides on human life and ecosystems.

There was fear that the environment had been saturated with deadly poisons that endanger man and other organisms (increased risks and uncertainty caution).   Because sickness, injury, and death had struck some workers handling pesticides, there was concern for farmers and field workers who came into contact with pesticides.   The need for more selective control of pesticides was emphasized by EPA officials.

3.3 Comparison of the Value Framework with Values from the Historical Review

The historical review (Section 2.) presented findings on concerns expressed in indexes, hearings, and the secondary literature. The relationship between expressions of concern and values is close but not self-evident (See the discussion in the Approach to the Historical Review [2.1.1]).   Thus we developed a means to translate expressions of concern into values (Section 3.2).

The form of this translation was to use a set of 47 "value phrases" to characterize the values embedded in the expressions of concern.   These were highlighted by underlining the phrases in the text.

The content analysis of the indexes and the hearings provided precise counts of expressions of concern over periods of time.   In contrast, the translation from these expressions of concern to values revealed in the historical review was not a quantitative process.   Rather, the researchers who had the greatest experience with each of the three categories of information sources (media, advocates, and congressional action) composed the sections on values (3.2.1, 3.2.2, & 3.2.3) in a way that best expressed the values they saw in the expressions of concern.

Content analysis was performed on these sections of writing to gain perspective on the relative importance of different value phrases.   Figure 3.3-1, "Value Phrase Prevalence by Three Categories of Actors," shows the results of the analysis.   The value phrase is displayed down the left column and counts of the occurrence of the value phrases are shown with the three categories of actors.*   Down the right side are the totals across all three categories.

----

* The "actors" under the category Hearings is narrower than it might first appear.   While there are witnesses from many interested parties, including industry, only those expressions of concern for health, safety and the environment were extracted.   Thus, the counts under this category primarily reflect those of witnesses testifying in favor of the legislation.

Value Phrase Prevalence
by Three Categories of Actors

Value Phrase	Occurence in			
	Media	Advocates	Hearings	Total
Autonomy	0	1	0	1
Bounded Rationality	2	0	0	2
Coproduction	2	0	0	2
Discount rates	0	0	0	0
Duty	0	1	0	1
Environment	0	0	5	5
Ex post / Ex ante	0	1	0	1
Experienced out-of-jointness	0	1	0	1
Externality	4	2	0	6
Fairness	27	6	6	39
Government Responsibility	0	0	1	1
Health	0	1	7	8
Health qualities model	0	1	2	3
High level value	0	0	1	1
Higher technical capability	0	1	3	4
Human life	0	0	2	2

Figure 3.3-1

Value Phrase	Occurence in		
	Media	Advocates	Hearings
Improved standards	3	1	3	7
Increased Awareness	9	1	3	13
Increased risk	8	3	8	19
Industry responsibility	0	1	0	1
Inequity	0	1	1	2
Information	26	5	6	37
Injustice	0	1	0	1
Intertemporal equity	0	0	1	1
Involuntary	1	2	0	3
Justice	0	1	0	1
Limitation of economics	0	1	0	1
Market failure	0	0	0	0
Monopoly	0	1	0	1
Negative coproduction	3	4	4	11
Non-compensability	4	1	1	6
Physiological effects	0	0	1	1
Quality of life	0	0	1	1
Relationship	1	1	0	2

Figure 3.3-1 (Continued)

Value Phrase	Occurence in Media	Advocates	Hearings	
Responsibility	18	13	13	44
Reversibility	1	2	2	5
Right	0	0	4	4
Risk aversion	0	0	0	0
Sanctity of life	0	0	1	1
Social consequences	0	2	5	7
Societal costs	0	0	3	3
Statistical versus identified life	0	1	1	2
Uncertainty caution	2	4	2	8
Value of life	0	1	3	4
Visibility	1	1	0	2
Voluntary versus involuntary	0	0	1	1
Voluntary compliance	0	0	2	2
Welfare	0	1	0	1

Figure 3.3-1 (Continued)

Framework Concepts and Critical Distinctions Affirmed by the
Historical Review

The most prevalent value phrase was responsibility (44). This affirms
the importance of John Ladd's perspective on ethics-of-responsibility. The
use of this phrase was evenly divided across the three categories of actors.
The second most prevalent value phrase was fairness (39). This affirms
the importance fairness in general, and lends support to John Rawls'
perspective on justice as fairness. In contrast, justice and
injustice were referred to only twice and both times only by the
advocate group. The reference to fairness is predominantly from the media
sources (27) and less from the advocates (6) and the hearings (6).

The third most used value phrase was information (37). Most of these
uses came in the media (26). The phrase refers both to providing information on specific hazards and the need to acquire information on hazards.
The need for information affirms the use of the Health Qualities Model in
which information is a necessary component for individuals to make choices
about hazards.

The group of "hypothesized distinctions" were substantially affirmed:
improved standards (7), increased awareness (13), increased risk
(19), and higher technical capability (4). Thus, over time, the country's
awareness of hazards was increasing, there was a perception of increasing
numbers of hazards, there was a desire for improved standards in dealing
with hazards, and there was a perception that there was a greater technical
capability of society to deal with hazards.

The concept of negative co-production (11) (part of the Health
Qualities Model, see Section 3.1.2) was affirmed. There was a recognition,
evenly distributed across the three categories of actors, that health was
instrumental for people to achieve desired outcomes in their lives.

The social consequences (7) of hazards were also found to be a
significant value concern. The impacts on individuals, families and
communities are an important driving force in the passage of legislation.

Also, uncertainty caution (8) was a driving social force. Society was
not certain about the possible effects of hazards, especially newly created
hazards, on their futures.

Other significant value phrases included value of life (4),
irreversibility/reversibility (5), rights (4), non-compensability (6), health
(8), externality (6), the environment (5), involuntary/voluntary (3), and
societal costs (3).

Framework Concepts and Critical Distinctions Unaffirmed by the Historical Review

In general, economic gain was not significant among the concerns that drove health and safety legislation. There were no references to market failure per se. There were few references to the monetary costs of hazards. There was an appreciation of externalities (6) and information (37) but these terms are less reflective of economic values than they are of impacts and needs within the Health Qualities Model.

Summary

Values such as responsibility, fairness, and adequate information are the major driving forces for legislation in the five areas studied. Both the Health Qualities Model and the Social Consequences perspective on the role of health was highly affirmed. Economic values, such as the monetary costs of illness, disease, and death were not found to be driving forces for the legislation.

4

Conclusions and Recommendations for Further Work in the Field

Conclusions

Historical review of the social forces leading to legislation in the health and safety area provides considerable information about the concerns and values that prompted legislation. In most instances, the concerns of the public expressed through popular articles closely tracked the activities of advocates, concerned scientists, congressional figures, and legislation. In the case of Occupational Safety and Health, however, a substantial lag was observed between the expression of concerns in the 30's to the passage of legislation in 1970. The reasons for this discrepancy are not fully apparent. Perhaps reasons of class played a factor.

Our value framework was found to be highly consistent with the results of the historical review. Content analysis of the values we found mapped closely to the key elements of the framework. The framework emphasizes the function of ethics in society in contrast to a "moral-rules" approach.

We discovered that health is a newcomer to the upper regions of the nation's value hierarchy. Only in this century have we gained a degree of control over disease and environmental dangers. Because of the newness of these capabilities, society has not yet integrated fully its ethical assumptions with commitments to maintain health (including the right to a natural death).

Thus our regulatory statutes do not yet map a coherent position on health and safety issues. As citizens perceive that additional care is warranted by growing levels of affluence, information, or technical capability, the standard of care demanded will rise.

The values found in the historical review were highly consistent with the ethical approaches discussed in 3.1.1, with the Health Qualities Model discussed in 3.1.2, and the Social Consequences of Injury and Disease for Individual and Society discussed in 3.1.3. The values did not reflect economic definitions of health and life (Section 3.1.4).

The relatively new concept of "negative co-production" (the instrumentality that health serves in enabling individuals and society to achieve desired outcomes) was found particularly useful in explaining the function of health. The concept also was validated by content analysis of the values revealed in the historical review.

The values framework validated by our research can serve in future as a prescriptive model when health risks are discussed in the political arena. It will be useful in clarifying issues and formulating solutions.

Our study indicates that government and business, as major expressions of our culture's activity, have a basic responsibility in reducing hazards. These responsibilities can be addressed effectively by use of the values framework we have charted.

Recommendations for Further Research

There are two interesting areas that the current research did not address: first, the role of the courts in arbitrating the regulatory decisions made under the five areas; second, the question of whether there is consistency in the stringency of hazard legislation. The courts have an important role in making decisions in light of the statutes that were passed. These decisions occur when government attempts to implement these statutes and reflect both the values embodied in the legislation and other "competing" values such as the costs of implementation. The question of consistency also has been raised often. Researchers have found a wide variance in the funds expended under various laws to prevent loss of life. Are these differences arbitrary or do they coherently relate to issues such as the visibility of the loss and other value considerations?

The use of vignettes to present social consequences of injury, illness, and death (Section 3.1.3.2) has been relatively unexplored prior to this study. There exists a need, however, to supplement the current form of regulatory impact analysis with data from first-person accounts.

Finally, the value framework is applicable to social issues including health policy on abortion, euthanasia, and patient consent. The concept of the ethics-of-responsibility should be extended to study the emerging computer information systems which will affect human relationships. Further, the framework moves toward attaining "operational" approaches to value problems (see Section 3.1.1.3 on Ackoff) which can help individuals and groups clarify their values choices.

Bibliography and References

Abelson, Philip (1966). "Are the Tame Cats in Charge?," Saturday Review, January, p. 100.

Ackoff, Russell L. and Emery, Fred E. (1972). Choice, Communication and Conflict (Published under the title of "On Purposeful Systems"). Chicago: Aldine-Atherton.

Adams, Franklin S. (1971). "Environmental Decision Making: Retrospect and Prospect," The Midwest Quarterly, vol. 13, no. 1, October, p. 101.

Aday, Lu Ann, Andersen, Ronald, and Anderson, Odin W. (1977). "Social Surveys and Health Policy: Implications for National Health Insurance," Policy Studies Review Annual, vol. 92, Nov/Dec, pp. 545-553.

Adler, Robert (1984). "Private Conversation with Robert Adler," MIT Center for Policy Alternatives [Cambridge, MA], July.

Alderson Reporting Company, Inc., Statement of Louis Harris, Chairman, Louis Harris and Associates, Inc., before Congress. Washington, D.C.: Alderson Reporting Company, Inc.

American Association for the Advancement of Science (1965). Air Conservation. Washington, D.C.: American Association for the Advancement of Science.

American Chemical Society (1925). "Occupational Diseases and Hazards in the Chemical Trades," American Chemical Society.

American Public Health Association, Inc. (1968). Local Health Official's Guide to Occupational Health. New York: American Public Health Association, Inc.

Anderson, John P., Bush, James W., and Berry, Charles C. (1978). Performance Versus Capacity: A Conflict in Classifying Function for Health Status Measurement (unpublished draft). San Diego, CA: University of California. Dept. of Community Medicine. Div. of Health Policy.

Anderson, Nancy N. and Robins, Leonard (1976). "Observations on Potential Contributions of Health Planning: Debate on Health Planning in the United States," International Journal of Health Services, vol. 6, no. 4, pp. 651-681.

Anderson, Odin W. (1976). "Foreword to International Journal of Health Services Monograph on Health Care Policy," International Journal of Health Services, vol. 6, no. 3, p. 383.

Andrews, John B. (1940). "Mine Tragedies Dramatize Need for Prompt Action," The American Labor Legislation Review, vol. 30, no. 2, June, p. 51.

Anthony, E. James (1969). "The Mutative Impact on Family Life of Serious Mental and Physical Illness in a Parent," Canadian Psychiatric Association Journal, vol. 14, no. 5, October.

Anthony, E. J. and Koupernick, C. (1973). "Child in His Family - Impact of Disease and Death" in International Association for Child Psychiatry and Allied Professions Yearbook (Volume II). New York: John Wiley and Sons, Inc.

Ashford, N.A., Zolt, E.M., Hattis, D., Katz, J. I., Heaton, G.R., and Priest, W. Curtiss (1979). Evaluating Chemical Regulations: Trade-off Analysis and Impact Assessment for Environmental Decision-Making. MIT Center for Policy Alternatives.

Bartell, Joyce J. (ed.) (1980). Rights and Responsibilities: International, Social, and Individual Dimensions (Proceedings of a Conference Sponsored by the Center for Study of the American Experience, Annenberg School of Communications, University of Southern California, November 1978). Los Angeles: University of Southern California Press.

Becker, Howard S. (1963). Outsiders: Studies in the Sociology of Deviance. New York: The Free Press.

Bell, Marion V. and Bacon, Jean C. (1957). Poole's Index Data and Volume Key. Chicago: Association of College and Reference Libraries.

Bergner, Marilyn, Bobbitt, Ruth A., Kressel, Shirley, Pollard, William E., Gilson, Betty S., and Morris, Joanne R. (1976). "The Sickness Impact Profile: Conceptual Formulation and Methodology for the Development of a Health Status Measure," International Journal of Health Services, vol. 6, no. 3, pp. 393-415.

Bergner, Marilyn, Bobbitt, Ruth A., Pollard, William E., Martin, Diane P., and Gilson, Betty S. (1976). "The Sickness Impact Profile: Validation of a Health Status Measure," Medical Care, vol. 14, no. 1, January, pp. 57-67.

Berry, Charles C. and Bush, James W. (1978). "Estimating Prognoses for a Dynamic Health Index - The Weighted Life Expectancy Using the Multiple Logistic with Survey and Mortality Data," American Statistical Association. Proceedings of the Social Statistics Section, pp. 716-721.

Bertocci, Peter A. and Millard, Richard M. (1963). Personality and the Good: Psychological and Ethical Perspectives. New York: David McKay Company, Inc.

Bice, Thomas W. (1976). "Comments on Health Indicators: Methodological Perspectives," International Journal of Health Services, vol. 6, no. 3, pp. 509-520.

Blake, Roland P., ed. (1943). Industrial Safety. New York: Prentice-Hall, Inc.

Blischke, W.R., Bush, J.W., and Kaplan, R.M. (1975). "Successive Intervals Analysis of Preference Measures in a Health Status Index,"

Health Services Research, vol. 10, no. 2, Summer, pp. 181-198.

Blodgett, John E. (1974). "Pesticides: Regulation of an Evolving Technology" in The Legislation of Product Safety (Volume II). Cambridge, MA: The MIT Press.

Bloom, Sandra C. and Degler, Stanley E. (1969). Pesticides and Pollution. Washington, D.C.: Bureau of National Affairs.

Bourque, Linda Brookover and Back, Kurt W. (1977). "Life Graphs and Life Events," Journal of Gerontology, vol. 32, no. 6, November.

Bowman, James S. (1977). "Attitudes and Orientations of Environmentally-concerned Citizens," Environmental Conservation, vol. 4, no. 4, January, p. 259.

Brindley, Thomas A. (1977). "Environmental Education and the Philosophy of Education," Journal of Thought, vol. 12, April, p. 152.

Brodeur, Paul (1968). "A Reporter at Large: The Magic Mineral," New Yorker, vol. 44, October, p. 117.

Brodeur, Paul (1973). "Annals of Industry: Some Nonserious Violations," New Yorker, vol. 49, November, p. 44.

Brodeur, Paul (1973). "Annals of Industry: That Dust Has Ate Us Up," New Yorker, vol. 49, November, p. 92.

Brodeur, Paul (1973). Expendable Americans. New York: The Viking Press.

Broome, John (1978). "Trying to Value a Life," Journal of Public Economics, vol. 9, pp. 91-100.

Brook, Robert H., Davies-Avery, Allyson, Greenfield, Sheldon, Harris, L. Jeff, Lelah, Tova, Solomon, Nancy E., and Ware, John E., Jr. (1977). "Assessing the Quality of Medical Care Using Outcome Measures: An Overview of the Method," Medical Care (Supplement).

Brook, Robert H., Ware, John E. Jr, Davies-Avery, Allyson, Stewart, Anita L., Donald, Cathy A., Rogers, William H., Williams, Kathleen N., and Johnston, Shawn A. (1979). "Overview of Adult Health Status Measures

Fielded in Rand's Health Insurance Study," Medical Care (Supplement).

Broun, Heywood (1937). "Child Labor," The Nation, vol. 144, no. 12, March, p. 325.

Brunswick, Ann F. (1976). "Indicators of Health Status in Adolescence," International Journal of Health Services, vol. 6, no. 3, pp. 475-491.

Bunch, Snowden E. and Jacobs, Philip (1979). "Health Costs Due to Environmental Hazards: A Survey of Estimates," Journal of Environmental Health, March/April, pp. 267-269.

Burkhardt, Robert (1967). The Federal Aviation Administration. New York: Frederick A. Praeger.

Bureau of National Affairs (BNA), Inc. (1971). The Job Safety and Health Act of 1970. Washington, DC: Bureau of National Affairs (BNA), Inc.

Bush, James W., Chen, Milton M., and Zaremba, Joseph (1971). "Estimating Health Program Outcomes Using a Markov Equilibrium Analysis of Disease Development," American Journal of Public Health, vol. 61, no. 12, December, pp. 2362-2375.

Bush, James W., Fanshel, Sol, and Chen, Milton M. (1972). "Analysis of a Tuberculin Testing Program Using a Health Statuss Index," Socio-Economic Planning Sciences, vol. 6, no. 1, February, pp. 46-68.

Bush, James W., Chen, Milton M., and Patrick, Donald L. (1973). "Health Status Index in Cost-Effectiveness: Analysis of PKU Program" in Health Status Indexes (edited by Robert L. Berg). Chicago: Hospital Research and Educational Trust, pp. 172-194.

Bush, J.W., Blischke, W.R., and Berry, C.C. (1975). "Health Indices, Outcomes, and the Quality of Medical Care in Evaluation in Health Services Delivery (edited by R. Yaffe and D. Zalkind). New York: Engineering Foundation, pp. 313-339.

Bush, James W., Kaplan, Robert M., and Berry, Charles C. (1980). "A Standardized Quality of Well-Being Scale for Cost-Effectiveness and Social Decision Analysis" in Health: Reliability and Generalizability. La Jolla, CA: University of California - San Diego. Dept. of Community

Medicine.

Business Week (1937). "Curbing Job Diseases," Business Week, October.

Business Week (1938). "Telling the Public: Air Hygiene Foundation Urges More Publicity for Industrial Health Movement," Business Week, November, p. 22.

Calabresi, Guido and Bobbitt, Philip (1978). Tragic Choices. New York: W.W. Norton and Company.

Carlson, Carolyn E. (1979). "Conceptual Style and Life Satisfaction Following Spinal Cord Injury," Archives of Physical Medicine and Rehabilitation, vol. 60, no. 8, pp. 346-352.

Carr, Donald E. (1965). The Breath of Life. New York: W.W. Norton & Company, Inc.

Carr, Willine and Wolfe, Samuel (1976). "Unmet Needs as Sociomedical Indicators," International Journal of Health Services, vol. 6, no. 3, pp. 417-430.

Carson, Rachel (1962). Silent Spring. Boston: Houghton Mifflin Company.

Carter, Charles Frederick (1919). "Putting 'Safety First' in the Skies," Illustrated World, vol. 31, no. 5, July, p. 699.

Carter, William B., Bobbitt, Ruth A., Bergner, Marilyn, and Gilson, Betty S. (1976). "Validation of an Interval Scaling: The Sickness Impact Profile," Health Services Research, Winter, pp. 516-528.

Chalmers, Thomas C. and Stern, Alfred R. (1981). "The Staggering Cost of Prolonged Life," Business Week, February 23, pp. 19-20.

Cheit, Earl F. (1961). Injury and Recovery in the Course of Employment. New York: John Wiley and Sons, Inc.

Cheit, Earl F. and Gordon, Margaret S. (1963). Occupational Disability and Public Policy. New York: John Wiley and Sons, Inc.

Chen, Milton M., Bush, James W., and Zaremba, Joseph (1975).

"Effectiveness Measures" (Chapter 12) in Operations Research in Health Care - A Critical Analysis (edited by L. Shuman, R. Speas, and J. Young). Baltimore, MD: Johns Hopkins University Press, pp. 276-301.

Chen, Milton M., Bush, J.W., and Patrick, Donald L. (1975). "Social Indicators for Health Planning and Policy Analysis," Policy Sciences, vol. 6, no. 1, March, pp. 71-89.

Chen, Milton M. and Bush, James W. (1976). "Maximizing Health System Output with Political and Administrative Constraints Using Mathematical Programming," Inquiry, vol. 13, no. 3, pp. 215-227.

Chen, Milton M. and Bush, James W. (1976). "Maximizing Health System Output with Political and Administrative Constraints Using Mathematical Programming," Inquiry, vol. 13, no. 3, September, pp. 215-227.

Chen, Milton M. and Bush, James W. (1979). "Health Status Measures, Policy, and Biomedical Research" (Chapter 1) in Health: What is it Worth? Measures of Health Benefits (edited by Selma J. Mushkin and David W. Dunlop). New York: Pergamon Press, pp. 15-41.

Chemical Week (1981). "Management: How to Limit the Rising Costs of Stricter Regulation," Chemical Week, January 21.

Chiang, C.L. (1965). "An Index of Health: Mathematical Models," National Center for Health Statistics, Vital and Health Statistics.

Cicourel, Aaron V. (1964). Method and Measurement in Sociology. New York: The Free Press.

Clearinghouse on Health Indexes (Public health Service) (1978). "Bibliography on Health Indexes," Clearinghouse on Health Indexes (Public health Service).

Clearinghouse on Health Indexes (Public Health Service) (1978). "Bibliography on Health Indexes," Clearinghouse on Health Indexes (Public Health Service).

Clearinghouse on Health Indexes (1979). "Bibliography on Health Indexes," Clearinghouse on Health Indexes.

Clearinghouse on Health Indexes (1979). "Bibliography on Health Indexes," Clearinghouse on Health Indexes.

Clowes, Ernest S. (1927). "Poison in Small Doses," Hygeia, vol. 5, no. 9, September, p. 458.

Commoner, Barry (1963). Science and Survival. New York: The Viking Press.

Commoner, Barry (1971). The Closing Circle: Nature, Man, and Technology. New York: Alfred A. Knopf.

Conn, Joanne, Bobbitt, Ruth A., and Bergner, Marilyn (1978). Administration Procedures and Interviewer Training for the Sickness Impact Profile. Seattle, WA: University of Washington. Department of Health Services.

Corn, Jacqueline K. (1975). "Historical Perspective to a Current Controversy on the Clinical Spectrum of Plumbism," Milbank Memorial Fund Quarterly, vol. 53, no. 1, January, p. 93.

Crown, Paul (1963). Legal Protection for the Consumer. Dobbs Ferry: Oceana Publications.

Current Medicine for Attorneys (1977). "Disruption of Domestic Relations as a Result of Disability," Current Medicine for Attorneys, vol. 24, no. 97, p. 2.

Daniels, Norman (1981). Cost-Effectiveness and Patient Welfare. New York: Alan R. Liss, Inc.

Daniels, Norman (1982). "Am I My Parent's Keeper?," Midwest Studies in Philosophy, vol. 7, p. 517.

Davidson, D., Suppes, P., and Siegel, S. (1957). Decision Making: An Experimental Approach. Stanford University Press.

Davidson, Ray (1970). Peril on the Job: A Study of Hazards in the Chemical Industries. Washington, D.C.: Public Affairs Press.

de Bell, Garrett, ed. (1970). The Environmental Handbook. New York: Ballantine Books, Inc.

Derr, P., Goble, R., Kasperson, R. E., and Kates, R. W. (1981). "The Double Standard," Environment, September.

Diamond, Edwin (1963). "The Myth of the 'Pesticide Menace'," Saturday Evening Post, vol. 236, no. 33, September, p. 16.

Dickerson, F. Reed, ed. (1968). Product Safety in Household Goods. New York: The Bobbs-Merrill Company, Inc.

Dubos, Rene (1959). Mirage of Health: Utopias, Progress, and Biological Change. New York: Harper and Brothers.

Dubos, Rene (1968). "Adapting to Pollution," Scientist and Citizen, vol. 10, no. 1, January, p. 1.

Dunlop, David W. (1979). "Returns to Biomedical Research in Chronic Diseases: A Case Study of Resource Allocation" (Chapter 11) in Health: What is it Worth? Measures of Health Benefits (Edited by Selma J. Mushkin and David W. Dunlop). New York: Pergamon Press, pp. 247-271.

Dunlap, William R. and Hollinsworth, J. Selwyn (1977). "How Does a Handicapped Child Affect the Family? Implications for Practitioners," Family Coordinator, vol. 26, no. 3, July, pp. 286-293.

Edwards, Linda N. and Grossman, Michael (1979). "The Relationship Between Children's Health and Intellectual Development" (Chapter 12) in Health: What is it Worth? Measures of Health Benefits (edited by Selma J. Mushkin and David W. Dunlop). New York: Pergamon Press, pp. 273-314.

Ehrlich, Dr. Paul R. and Harriman, Richard L. (1971). How to Be A Survivor. New York: Ballantine Books, Inc.

Ehrlich, Dr. Paul R. (1971). The Population Bomb. New York: Ballantine Books.

Ehrlich, Paul R. and Ehrlich, Anne H. (1972). Population, Resources, Environment: Issues in Human Ecology. San Francisco: W.H. Freeman and Company.

Eisen, Marvin, Ware, John E., Jr., Donald, Cathy A., and Brook, Robert H. (1979). "Measuring Components of Children's Health Status," Medical

Care, vol. 17, no. 9, September, pp. 902-921.

Elinson, Jack (1976). "Introduction to the Theme: Sociomedical Health Indicators," International Journal of Health Services, vol. 6, no. 3, pp. 385-391.

Epstein, Kenneth A., Schneiderman, Lawrence J., Bush, James W., and Zettner, Alfred (1980). The "Abnormal" Screening Serum Thyroxine (T4) Analysis of Physician Response, Outcome, Cost and Health Effectiveness (to be published in Journal of Chronic Disease). La Jolla, CA: Univ. of California, San Diego, School of Medicine (c/o James Bush).

Esposito, John C. and Silverman, Larry J. (1970). Vanishing Air: The Ralph Nadar Study Group Report on Air Pollution. New York: Grossman Publishers.

Ewing, David (1983). "Do It My Way or Your Fired.". New York: John Wiley & Sons.

Faigin, Barbara Moyer (1976). 1975 Societal Costs of Motor Vehicle Accidents. Washington, D.C.: United States National Highway Traffic Safety Administration.

Fanshel, S. and Bush, J.W. (1970). "A Health-Status Index and its Application to Health-Services Outcomes," Operations Research, vol. 18, no. 6, Nov/Dec, pp. 1021-1066.

Ferman, Louis A. and Gordus, Jeanne P. (eds.) (1979). Mental Health and the Economy. Kalamzoo, MI: W. E. Upjohn Institute for Employment Research.

Fessenden-Raden, June and Gert, Bernard (1984). A Philosophical Approach to the Management of Occupational Health Hazards. Bowling Green, OH: Social Philosophy & Policy Center.

Finkhauser, G. Ray (1973). "Trends in Media Coverage of the Issues of the '60s," Journalism Quarterly, vol. 50, Autumn, pp. 533-538.

Finsterbusch, Kurt and Wolf, C. P. (eds.) (1977). Methodology of Social Impact Assessment. Strudsberg, PA: Dowden, Hutchinson, and Ross, Inc.

Flathman, Richard E. (1976). The Practice of Rights. Cambridge, England: Cambridge University Press.

Freedman, Audrey (1982). Industry Response to Health Risk. New York: Conference Board.

Friedrich, William N. (1977). "Ameliorating the Physiological Impact of Chronic Physical Disease on the Child and Family," Journal of Pediatric Psychology, vol. 2, no. 1, pp. 26-31.

Frisbie, Walter S. (1936). "Federal Control of Spray Residues on Fruits and Vegetables," American Journal of Public Health, vol. 26, no. 4, April, p. 369.

Fuller, John G. (1972). 200,000,000 Guinea Pigs New Dangers in Everyday Foods, Drugs, and Cosmetics. New York: G.P. Putnam's Sons.

George, Dr. John L. (1957). The Pesticide Problem: A Brief Review of Present Knowledge and Suggestions for Action. New York: The Conservation Foundation.

Gibson, Geoffrey and Ludwig, Edward G. (1968). "Family Structure in a Disabled Population," Journal of Marriage and the Family, vol. 30, no. 1, pp. 55-63.

Gilson, Betty S., Gilson, John S., Bergner, Marilyn, Bobbitt, Ruth A., Kressel, Shirley, Pollard, William E., and Vesselago, Michael (1975). "The Sickness Impact Profile: Development of an Outcome Measure of Health Care," American Journal of Public Health, vol. 65, no. 12, December, pp. 1304-1310.

Gilson, Betty S., Bergner, Marilyn, Bobbitt, Ruth A., and Carter, William B. (1978). The Sickness Impact Profile: Final Development and Testing 1975-1978. Executive Summary.. Baltimore, MD: U.S. Public Health Service. National Center for Health Services Research.

Goldman, Marshall I., ed. (1967). Controlling Pollution: The Economics of a Cleaner America. Englewood Cliffs: Prentice-Hall.

Gould, William and Thaler, Richard (1982). "Public Policy Toward Life Saving: Should Consumer Preferences Rule?," Journal of Policy Analysis and Management, vol. 1, no. 2, p. 223.

Graham, Frank, Jr. (1970). Since Silent Spring. Boston: Houghton Mifflin Company.

Graham, John D. and Vaupel, James W. (1980). The Value of a Life: What Difference Does it Make? (manuscript). Washington, D.C.: National Academy of Sciences Committee on Risk and Decision Making.

Graham, P. and George, S. (1972). "Children's Response to Parental Illness: Individual Differences," Journal of Psychosomatic Research, vol. 16, no. 4, p. 251.

Greenfield, Meg (1961). "The Great Morality Play," The Reporter, June, pp. 13-18.

Grossman, Gary M. and Potter, Harry R. (1977). A Trend Analysis of Competing Models of Environmental Attitudes. West Lafayette: Institute for the Study of Social Change, Purdue University.

Grossman, Michael (1972). The Demand for Health: A Theoretical and Empirical Investigation. Occasional Paper 119 of the National Bureau of Economic Research. New York: Columbia University Press.

Hahn, Kenneth (1968). A Factual Record of Correspondence Between Kenneth Hahn Los Angeles County Supervisor and the Presidents of General Motors, Ford, and Chrysler Regarding the Automobile Industry's Obligation to Meet Its Rightful Responsibility in Controlling Air Pollution from Automobiles. Los Angeles, CA: County of Los Angeles, February.

Hamilton, Alice (1943). "Exploring the Dangerous Trades," The Atlantic Monthly, vol. 171, no. 3, March, p. 132.

Harrison, James R. (1984). "Private Conversation with James Harrison," MIT Center for Policy Alternatives [Cambridge, MA], July.

Hart, Hornell (1933). "Changing Opinions about Business Property: A Consensus of Magazine Opinion in the U.S.," The American Journal of Sociology, vol. 38, March, pp. 665-687.

Hattis, Dale R., Goble, Robert, and Ashford, Nicholas (1982). "Airborne

Lead: A Clearcut Case of Differential Protection," Environment, vol. 24, no. 1, Jan./Feb., pp. 14-42.

Hattis, Dale B. (1982). "From Presence to Health Impact: Models for Relating Presence to Exposure to Damage" in Analyzing the Benefits of Health, Safety, and Environmental Regulations. Cambridge, MA: MIT Center for Policy Alternatives, September, pp. 5-1/5-66.

Haughey, John C. (ed.) (1979). Personal Values in Public Policy: Essays and Conversations in Government Decision-Making. New York: Paulist Press.

Hayhurst, Emery R. (1925). "Values in the Maintenance of Health of the Worker," American Journal of Public Health, vol. 15, no. 2, February, p. 116.

Hays, Samuel P. (1959). Conservation and the Gospel of Efficiency: The Progressive Conservation Movement, 1890-1920. Cambridge: Harvard University Press.

Hays, Samuel P. (1981). "The Structure of Environmental Politics Since World War II," Journal of Social History, vol. 14, no. 4, June, p. 719.

Heaton, George R. (1975). The Regulatory Framework for Pesticides. Cambridge, MA: MIT Center for Policy Alternatives.

Henderson, P.D. (1965). "Notes on Public Investment Criteria in the United Kingdom," Bull. Oxford Univ. Inst. Econ. Stat..

Hilbourne, John (1973). "On Disabling the Normal: The Implications of Physical Disability for Other People," British Journal of Social Work, vol. 3, no. 4, Winter, pp. 497-507.

Hohenemser, C., Kates, R.W., and Slovic, P. (1983). "The Nature of Technological Hazard," Science, vol. 220, April, p. 378.

Hood, O.P. (1930). "Progress and Possibilities in the Abatement of Smoke," The American City, vol. 43, no. 3, September, p. 125.

Jackson, Charles O. (1970). Food and Drug Legislation in the New Deal. Princeton: Princeton University Press.

Jones, Charles O. (1975). Clean Air: The Policies and Politics of Pollution Control. Pittsburgh: University of Pittsburgh Press.

Jones, Ellen W., McNitt, Barbara J., and Densen, Paul M. (1979). "An Approach to the Assessment of Long-Term Care" (Chapter 2) in Health: What is it Worth? Measures of Health Benefits (edited by Selma J. Mushkin and David W. Dunlop). New York: Pergamon Press, pp. 43-57.

Jones-Lee, M.W. (1976). The Value of Life: An Economic Analysis. Chicago: University of Chicago Press.

Jorgensen, Joseph G. (1980). Environmental Policies of Government and Industry and the Responsibilities of Social Scientists. Lawrence, KA: University of Kansas, Public Policy Research Institute.

Kane, Robert M. and Vose, Allan D. (1977). Air Transportation. Dubuque, IA: Kendall/Hunt Publishing Company.

Kanof, Abram, Kutner, B., and Gordon, Norman (1962). "The Impact of Infantile Amaurotic Familial Idiocy (Tay-Sachs Disease) on the Family," Pediatrics, vol. 29, no. 1, January, pp. 37-45.

Kaplan, Robert M., Bush, J.W., and Berry, Charles C. (1976). "Health Status: Types of Validity and the Index of Well-Being," Health Services Research, vol. 11, no. 4, Winter, pp. 478-507.

Katz, Cindi and Priest, W. Curtiss (1982). "The Consequences of Disease and Injury for Individuals and Society" in Analyzing the Benefits of Health, Safety, and Environmental Regulations. Cambridge, MA: MIT Center for Policy Alternatives, September, pp. 8-1/8-43.

Katz, Elihu et al. (1973). "On the Use of the Mass Media for Important Things," The American Sociological Review, vol. 38, April, pp. 164-181.

Katz, Sidney and Akpom, C. Amechi (1976). "A Measure of Primary Sociobiological Functions," International Journal of Health Services, vol. 6, no. 3, pp. 493-507.

Kearney, Paul W. (1955). I Smell Smoke: How to Fight and Prevent Fires. New York: Simon and Schuster.

Kelman, Howard R. (1976). "Evaluation of Health Care Quality by Consumers," International Journal of Health Services, vol. 6, no. 3, pp. 431-442.

Klarman, Herbert E. (1974). "Application of Cost-Benefit Analysis to the Health Services and the Special Case of Technological Innovation," International Journal of Health Services, vol. 4, no. 2, pp. 325-352.

Kneese, Allen V. and Schulze, William D. (1981). "Risk in Benefit-Cost Analysis," Risk Analysis, vol. 1, no. 1, p. 81.

Komesar, Neil K. (1974). "Toward a General Theory of Personal Injury Loss," Journal of Legal Studies, vol. 3, pp. 457-486.

Koocher, G. P. (1978). "Listen to the Children - A Study of the Impact on Mental Health of Children of a Parent's Catastrophic Illness (Book Review)," Journal of Child Psychology and Psychiatric and Allied Disciplines, vol. 19, no. 4, p. 407.

Kudlich, Rudolf (1922). "The Soot Burden on American Cities," The American City, vol. 27, no. 1, July, p. 12.

Ladd, John (1970). "Morality and the Ideal of Rationality in Formal Organizations," The Monist, p. 488.

Ladd, John (1975). "The Ethics of Participation" in Participation in Politics (edited by J. Roland Pennock and John W. Chapman). New York: Lieber-Atherton, pp. 98-125.

Ladd, John (1978). "Legalism and Medical Ethics" in Contemporary Issues in Biomedical Ethics (edited by John W. Davis, Barry Hoffmaster and Sarah Shorten). Clifton, NJ: The Humana Press.

Ladd, John (ed.) (1979). Ethical Issues Relating to Life and Death. New York: Oxford University Press.

Law and Contemporary Problems (Duke University. School of Law) (1976). "Valuing Lives," Law and Contemporary Problems (Duke University. School of Law).

Lawler, John (1950). The H.W. Wilson Company: Half a Century of

Bibliographic Publishing. Minneapolis: University of Minnesota Press.

Leiser, Burton M. (ed.) (1981). Values in Conflict: Life, Liberty, and the Rule of Law. New York: MacMillan Publishing Co., Inc.

Lewis, Howard R. (1965). With Every Breath You Take. New York: Crown Publishers, Inc.

Lieberman, Jethro K. (1970). The Tyranny of the Experts: How Professionals Are Closing the Open Society. New York: Walker and Company.

Lindsay, Dr. Dale (1984). "Private Conversation with Dale Lindsay," MIT Center for Policy Alternatives [Cambridge, MA], July.

Lipscomb, Joseph (1979). "The Willingness-to-Pay Criterion and Public Program Evaluation in Health" (Chapter 5) in Health: What is it Worth? Measures of Health Benefits (Edited by Selma J. Mushkin and David W. Dunlop). New York: Pergamon Press, pp. 91-139.

Little, Ronald L. (1977). "Some Social Consequences of Boom Towns," North Dakota Law Review, vol. 53, no. 3, pp. 401-425.

MacLaury, Judson (1981). "The Job Safety Law of 1970: Its Passage Was Perilous," Monthly Labor Review, vol. 104, no. 3, March, p. 18.

Magnuson, Warren G. and Carper, Jean (1972). The Dark Side of the Marketplace. Englewood Cliffs: Prentice-Hall, Inc.

Mayer, Milton S. (1937). "Slow Death in Illinois," The Nation, vol. 144, no. 16, April, p. 432.

McEwen, F.L. and Stephenson, G.R. (1979). The Use and Significance of Pesticides in the Environment. New York: John Wiley and Sons.

McMillen, Wheeler (1965). Bugs or People?. New York: Appleton-Century.

Mechanic, D. (1968). Medical Sociology: A Selective View. New York: Free Press.

Merton, Robert K. (1957). "The Role-Set: Problems in Sociological Theory," The British Journal of Sociology, vol. 8, June, pp. 106-120.

Merton, Robert K. (1968). Social Theory and Social Structure. New York: The Free Press.

Mesthene, E.G. (1970). Technological Change. New York: Mentor/ New American.

Miller, Alan S. (1978). A Planet to Choose. New York: The Pilgrim Press.

Miller, Alan S. (1978). A Planet to Choose: Value Studies in Political Ecology. New York: The Pilgrim Press.

Mitchell, Clifford S. (1982). "Valuing the Benefits of Environmental Goods" in Analyzing the Benefits of Health, Safety, and Environmental Regulations. Cambridge, MA: MIT Center for Policy Alternatives, September, pp. 10-1/10-40.

Mooney, Gavin H. (1977). The Valuation of Human Life. New York: MacMillan Press Ltd.

Morrison, Denton E. (1973). "The Environmental Movement: Conflict Dynamics," Journal of Voluntary Action Research, vol. 2, no. 2, April, p. 74.

Moscow, Alvin (1961). Tiger on a Leash. New York: G.P. Putnam's Sons.

Mrak, Dr. Emil (1984). "Private Conversation with Emil Mrak," MIT Center for Policy Alternatives [Cambridge, MA], July.

Mueller, John (1970). "Presidential Popularity from Truman to Johnson," The American Political Science Review, vol. 64, pp. 18-34.

Muller, Charlotte, Jaffe, Frederick S., and Kovar, Mary Grace (1976). "Reproductive Efficiency as a Social Indicator - Measures Related to Life Stage," International Journal of Health Services, vol. 6, no. 3, pp. 455-474.

Mushkin, Selma J. (1979). "Health Indexes for Health Assessments" (Chapter 13) in Health: What is it Worth? Measures of Health Benefits (edited by Selma J. Mushkin and David W. Dunlop). New York: Pergamon Press, pp. 315-338.

Mushkin, Selma J. and Dunlop, David W. (1979). Health: What is it Worth? Measures of Health Benefits. New York: Pergamon Press.

Nadel, Mark V. (1971). The Politics of Consumer Protection. Indianapolis: The Bobbs-Merrill Company, Inc.

Nader, Ralph (1971). Beware. New York: Law-Arts Publishers, Inc.

National Institute of Occupational Safety and Health (1984). Unpublished study on Ionizing Radiation. Cincinatti, OH: National Institute of Occupational Safety and Health.

Naughton, James R. (1984). "Private Conversation with James Naughton," MIT Center for Policy Alternatives [Cambridge, MA], July.

Newsweek (1934). "Air Mail: Nation Protests Deaths of Army Postmen, as Congress Plays out Drama of Contracts," Newsweek, vol. 3, no. 9, March, p. 9.

Newsweek (1934). "Air Mail: Ten Army Deaths Cause President to Alter Policy And Ask Congress to Expedite New Bids From Private Lines," Newsweek, vol. 3, no. 11, March, p. 1.

O'Hara, James (1984). "Private Conversation with James O'Hara," MIT Center for Policy Alternatives [Cambridge, MA], July.

Page, Joseph A. and O'Brien, Mary-Win (1973). Bitter Wages. New York: Grossman Publishers.

Park, Leslie D. (1975). "Barriers to Normality for the Handicapped Adult in the U.S." in The Physiological and Social Impact of Physical Disability (R. P. Marinelli and A. Dell Orto, eds.). New York: Springer Publishing Co., pp. 25-33.

Patrick, Donald L., Bush, J.W., and Chen, Milton M. (1973). "Methods for Measuring Levels of Well-Being for a Health Status Index," Health Services Research, vol. 8, no. 3, Fall, pp. 228-245.

Patrick, Donald L., Bush, J.W., and Chen, Milton M. (1973). "Toward an Operational Definition of Health," Journal of Health and Social Behavior, vol. 14, March, pp. 6-23.

Patrick, Donald L. (1976). "Constructing Social Metrics for Health Status Indexes," International Journal of Health Services, vol. 6, no. 3, pp. 443-453.

Payne, J. (1976). "Task Complexity and Contingent Processing in Decision Making: An Information Search and Protocol Analysis," Organizational Behavior and Human Performance, vol. 16, pp. 366-387.

Pertschuk, Michael (1980). Revolt Against Regulation: Rise and Pause of the Consumer Movement. Berkeley: University of California Press.

Pertschuk, Michael (1984). "Private Conversation with Michael Pertschuk," MIT Center for Policy Alternatives [Cambridge, MA], July.

Peskin, Henry M. and Seskin, Eugene P. (1975). Cost-Benefit Analysis and Water Pollution Policy (edited by Henry M. Peskin and Eugene P. Seskin, UI 169-5006-1). Washington, D.C.: Urban Institute.

Peterson, Evan T. (1972). "The Impact of Adolescent Illness on Parental Relationships," Journal of Health and Social Behavior, vol. 13, no. 4, December, pp. 429-437.

Peterson, Yen (1979). "The Impact of Physical Disability on Marital Adjustment: A Literature Review," The Family Coodinator, vol. 28, no. 1, pp. 47-51.

Priest, W. Curtiss and Knoblauch, Karl (1978). Railroad Safety Economics - A Guidebook for the Analysis of Regulations, Including Effectiveness Analysis, Benefit-Cost Analysis, Economic Impact Analysis, Use of Data Resources, Methods of Presentation. Prepared for the Office of Rail Systems Analysis and Information. Federal Railroad Administration. U.S. Dept. of Transportation. Cambridge, MA: IOCS Inc. Transportation Systems Division.

Priest, W. Curtiss (1979). "The Cost-Benefit Charade (Letter to the Editor)," Wall Street Journal, June 18.

Priest, W. Curtiss (1979). "Problems of Cost-Benefit Analysis," Journal of Hazard Prevention, November.

Priest, W. Curtiss and Ashford, Nicholas A. (1982). "Valuing Human

Disease, Injury and Death" in Analyzing the Benefits of Health, Safety, and Environmental Regulations. Cambridge, MA: MIT Center for Policy Alternatives, September, pp. 9-1/9-92.

Rabin, Edward H. and Schwartz, Mortimer D. (1972). The Pollution Crisis: Official Documents. Dobbs Ferry: Oceana Publications.

Rawls, John (1971). A Theory of Justice. Cambridge, MA: The Belknap Press of Harvard University Press.

Reich, Robert B. (1981). "Looking Back at Regulation: Business is Asking for Trouble Again," New York Times, November 22.

Rokeach, Milton (1972). Beliefs, Attitudes, and Values: A Theory of Organization and Change. San Francisco: Jossey-Bass Inc.

Rokeach, Milton (1973). The Nature of Human Values. New York: Free Press.

Sackett, David L. and Torrance, George W. (1978). "The Utility of Different Health States as Perceived by the General Public," Chron Dis, vol. 31, pp. 697-704.

Schneyer, Solomon (1979). "Allocation and Priority Setting in Research" (Chapter 10) in Health: What is it Worth? Measures of Health Benefits (edited by Selma J. Mushkin and David W. Dunlop).. New York: Pergamon Press, pp. 237-245.

Schulze, William, Ben-David, Shaul, Crocker, Thomas D., and Kneese, Allen (1979). "Economics and Epidemiology: Application to Cancer" (Chapter 9) in Health: What is it Worth? Measures of Health Benefits (edited by Selma J. Mushkin and David W. Dunlop). New York: Pergamon Press, pp. 219-234.

Schweig, Barry B. (1979). "Products Liability Problem," Annals of the American Academy of Political and Social Sciences, vol. 443, May, p. 94.

Showalter, Stuart W. (1978). "Sampling from the Reader's Guide," Journalism Quarterly, June, p. 346.

Siegmann, Athilia E. (1976). "A Classification of Sociomedical Health Indicators: Perspectives for Health Administrators and Health Planners,"

International Journal of Health Services, vol. 6, no. 3, pp. 521-537.

Simpson, George Gaylord (1967). "Biology and the Public Good," American Scientist, vol. 55, no. 2, June, p. 161.

Small, Melvin (1975). "When Did the Cold War Begin?: A Test of an Alternative Indicator of Public Opinion," Historical Methods Newsletter, vol. 8, March, pp. 61-73.

Smith, Robert S. (1978). Compensating Wage Differentials and Public Policy: A Review (to be presented at the 1978 I.R.R.A./A.E.A. Meetings, Chicago IL, August 1978). Draft. Ithaca, NY: Cornell University, New York State School of Industrial and Labor Relations, July.

Stewart, Ethelbert (1920). "A Plea for More Adequate Comp- ensation Rates," Monthly Labor Review, vol. 11, no. 6, December, p. 1121.

Stewart, Richard B. (1977). "Paradoxes of Liberty, Integrity and Fraternity: The Collective Nature of Environmental Quality and Judicial Review of Administrative Action," Environmental Law, vol. 7, no. 3, April, p. 463.

Stewart, R. and Krier, J. (1978). "Environmental Law and Policy," Publisher not known.

Still, Henry (1967). The Dirty Animal. New York: Hawthorn Books, Inc.

Stone, Robert F., Fenton, Chester G., Musselman, Charles, and Priest, W. Curtiss (1976). Injury Costs Project. Final Report. Submitted to Consumer Product Safety Commission. Contract CPSC-C-75-0102. Cambridge, MA: Technology and Economics Inc.

Thaler, Richard and Rosen, Sherwin (1974). The Value of Saving a Life: Evidence from the Labor Market. Upton, NY: University of Rochester Department of Economics.

Thaler, R. and Rosen, S. (1975). "The Value of Saving a Life: Evidence from the Labor Market" in Household Production and Consumption - NBER Studies in Income and Wealth - Vol. 40 (edited by N. Nerleckyj). New York: Columbia University Press, pp. 265-297.

The American City (1922). "The Need for a Federal Air Law," The American City, vol. 27, no. 4, December, p. 542.

The Environmental Pollution Panel, U.S. President's Science Advisory Committee (1965). Restoring the Quality of Our Environment. Washington, D.C.: The Environmental Pollution Panel, U.S. President's Science Advisory Committee.

The Literary Digest (1919). "Saving 13,000 Workers' Lives Yearly," The Literary Digest, vol. 61, no. 4, April, p. 21.

The Literary Digest (1921). "Dangers of Some Common Things," The Literary Digest, vol. 71, no. 5, October, p. 23.

The Literary Digest (1927). "The Outcry for a Curb on Death Flights," The Literary Digest, vol. 904, no. 13, September, p. 5.

The Literary Digest (1930). "Air-Crash Secrecy," The Literary Digest, vol. 104, no. 9, March, p. 10.

The Literary Digest (1937). "Gas Death Lurks On Unseen Wings," The Literary Digest, June, p. 16.

The Nation (1934). "A Needed Amendment," The Nation, vol. 138, no. 3576, January.

The Outlook (1909). "Are the Miners Worth Saving?," The Outlook, November, p. 638.

The Outlook (1912). "Human Lives or Commercial Profits?," The Outlook, vol. 100, no. 7, February, p. 349.

Time (1942). "Catastrophe: Aerial Traffic Cops Needed?," Time, vol. 40, no. 19, November.

Touhey, James (1984). "Private Conversation with James Touhey," MIT Center for Policy Alternatives [Cambridge, MA], July.

Travis, G. (1976). Chronic Illness in Children: Its Impact on Child and Family. Stanford, CA: Stanford University Press.

Turner, James S. (1970). The Chemical Feast. New York: Grossman Publishers.

U.S. Dept. of Health and Human Services. National Center for Health Statistics (1980). Clearinghouse on Health Indexes. Cumulated Annotations 1978. Hyattsville, MD: U.S. Dept. of Health and Human Services. National Center for Health Statistics.

U.S. Dept. of Health and Human Services. National Center for Health Statistics (1980). Clearinghouse on Health Indexes. Cumulated Annotations 1977. Hyattsville, MD: U.S. Dept. of Health and Human Services. National Center for Health Statistics.

U.S. Senate Committee on Commerce (1937). "Safety in the Air," U.S. Senate Committee on Commerce, March, p. 1.

University of Washington. Department of Health Services (1977). Sickness Impact Profile. Seattle, WA: University of Washington. Department of Health Services.

University of Washington. Department of Health Services (1978). The Sickness Impact Profile: A Brief Summary of its Purpose, Uses, and Administration. Seattle, WA: University of Washington. Department of Health Services.

U.S. Congress. Office of Technology Assessment (1980). The Implications of Cost-Effectiveness Analysis of Medical Technology. Washington, D.C.: U.S. Congress. Office of Technology Assessment.

U.S. Congress. Office of Technology Assessment (1980). The Implications of Cost-Effectiveness Analysis of Medical Technology. Background Paper #1: Methodological Issues and Literature Review. Washington, D.C.: U.S. Congress. Office of Technology Assessment.

U. S. Congress (92nd Congress, 1st Session) (1971). Safe Drinking Water (Legislative History in 5 Volumes). Washington, D.C.: U. S. Congress (92nd Congress, 1st Session), May.

U. S. Congress (93rd Congress, 1st Session) (1973). Safe Drinking Water Act -- 1973 (Legislative History in 4 Volumes). Washington, D.C.: U. S. Congress (93rd Congress, 1st Session), March.

U. S. Congress (94th Congress, 1st Session) (1975). Legislative History of the Federal Coal Mine Health and Safety Act of 1969 (P.L. 91-173) As Amended Through 1974, Including Black Lung Amendments of 1972. Part 2: Appendix (Legislative History in 6 Volumes). Washington, D.C.: U. S. Congress (94th Congress, 1st Session), August.

U. S. Congress (94th Congress, 1st Session) (1975). Legislative History of the Federal Coal Mine Health and Safety Act of 1969 (P.L. 91-173) As Amended Through 1974, Including Black Lung Amendments of 1972. Part 1 (Legislative History in 5 Volumes). Washington, D.C.: U. S. Congress (94th Congress, 1st Session), August.

U. S. Congress (94th Congress, 1st Session) (1975). Waste Control Act of 1975 (Legislative History in 9 Volumes). Washington, D.C.: U. S. Congress (94th Congress, 1st Session), April.

U. S. Congress (95th Congress, 1st Session) (1977). Oversight of the Administration of the Black Lung Program, 1977 (Legislative History in 5 Volumes). Washington, D.C.: U. S. Congress (95th Congress, 1st Session), April.

U. S. Congress (96th Congress, 1st Session) (1979). Safe Drinking Water Act Authorization (Legislative History in 4 Volumes). Washington, D.C.: U. S. Congress (96th Congress, 1st Session), March.

U. S. Congress (91st Congress, 1st & 2nd Sessions) (1969). Occupational Safety and Health Act, 1970. Part 1 (Legislative History in 11 Volumes). Washington, D.C.: U. S. Congress (91st Congress, 1st & 2nd Sessions), September.

U.S. Congress (91st Congress, 2nd Session) (1970). Authorize Appropriations for Flammable Fabrics Act and Fire Research and Safety Act of 1968 (Legislative History in 4 Volumes). Washington, D.C.: U.S. Congress (91st Congress, 2nd Session), June.

U. S. Congress (91st Congress, 2nd Session) (1970). Federal Coal Mine Health and Safety Act, Legislative History (Legislative History in 3 Volumes). Washington, D.C.: U. S. Congress (91st Congress, 2nd Session), March.

U. S. Congress (93rd Congress, 2nd Session) (1974). Implementation of the

Federal Water Pollution Control Act (Legislative History in 9 Volumes). Washington, D.C.: U. S. Congress (93rd Congress, 2nd Session), February.

U. S. Congress (95th Congress, 2nd Session) (1978). Legislative History of the Federal Mine Safety and Health Act of 1977 (Legislative History in 6 Volumes). Washington, D.C.: U. S. Congress (95th Congress, 2nd Session), July.

U. S. Congress (95th Congress, 2nd Session) (1978). Nuclear Siting and Licensing Act of 1978 (Legislative History in 5 Volumes). Washington, D.C.: U. S. Congress (95th Congress, 2nd Session), July.

U. S. Congress (95th Congress, 2nd Session) (1978). National Traffic and Motor Vehicle Information and Cost Savings Authorization of 1979 and 1980 (Legislative History in 4 Volumes). Washington, D.C.: U. S. Congress (95th Congress, 2nd Session), March.

U. S. Government Printing Office (1970). Final Report of the National Commission on Product Safety. Washington, DC: U. S. Government Printing Office, June.

United States Public Health Service. National Center for Health Care Technology (1980). Conference on Maternal Serum Alpha-Fetoprotein: Issues in the Prenatal Screening and Diagnosis of Neural Tube Defects (Program, Summary, and ethics paper by LeRoy Walters). Rockville, MD: United States Public Health Service. National Center for Health Care Technology.

Veatch, Robert M., Branson, Roy, (editors) (1976). Ethics and Health Policy. Cambridge, MA: Ballinger Pub. Co.

Vierthaler, Erich A. (1974). Wholesale Content Analysis: Using the Readers' Guide to Periodical Literature for Studying the Twentieth Century History of American Interest in Social Issues (Technical Report). Pittsburgh: University of Pittsburgh, Department of Sociology.

Vierthaler, Erich A. (1981). The Social Origins of American Interest in Public Health, 1900-1974: A Modern Public Issue and Its Transformation into Federal Policy (Doctoral Dissertation). Pittsburgh: University of Pittsburgh, Department of Sociology.

Wan, T.H., Weissert, William G.,   and Livieratos, Barbara B. (1980). "Geriatric Day Care and Homemaker Services: An Experimental Study," Journal of Gerontology, vol. 35, no. 2, pp. 256-274.

Ward, Barbara and Dubos, Rene (1972). Only One Earth: The Care and Maintenance of a Small Planet. New York: W.W. Norton and Company, Inc.

Ware, John E., Jr. and Young, JoAnne (1979). "Issues in the Conceptualization and Measurement of Value Placed on Health" (Chapter 6) in Health: What is it Worth? Measures of Health Benefits (edited by Selma J. Mushkin and David W. Dunlop). New York: Pergamon Press, pp. 141-166.

Ware, John E., Jr., Brook, Robert H., Davies-Avery, Allyson, Williams, Kathleen N., Stewart, Anita L., Rogers, William H., Donald, Cathy A., and Johnston, Shawn A. (1980). Conceptualization and Measurement of Health for Adults in the Health Insurance Study. (8 volumes). Vol. I: Model of Health and Methodology. Vol. II: Physical Health in Terms of Functioning. Vol. III: Mental Health. Vol. IV: Social Health. Vol. V: General Health Perceptions. Vol. VI: Analysis of Relationships Among Health Status Measures. Vol. VII: Power Analysis of Health Status Measures. Vol. VIII: Overview R-1987/1-8-HEW. Santa Monica, CA: Rand Corporation.

Weekly Compilation of Presidential Documents (1968). "To Earn a Living: The Right of Every American The President's Message to Congress," Weekly Compilation of Presidential Documents, vol. 4, no. 4, January, p. 104.

Weekly Compilation of Presidential Documents (1968). "To Earn a Living: The Right of Every American The President's Message to Congress," Weekly Compilation of Presidential Documents, vol. 4, no. 4, January, p. 104.

Weekly Compilation of Presidential Documents (1969). "Occupational Safety and Health The President's Message to Congress," Weekly Compilation of Presidential Documents [Washington, D.C.], vol. 5, no. 32, August, p. 1082.

Weissert, William, Wan, Thomas, Livieratos, Barbara,   and Katz, Sidney (1980). "Effects and Costs of Day-Care Services for the Chronically Ill," Medical Care, vol. 18, no. 6, June, pp. 567-584.

Wellford, Harrison (1972). Sowing the Wind. New York: Grossman Publishers.

Westman, Walter E. (1977). "How Much are Nature's Services Worth?," American Association for the Advancement of Science.

Whitten, Jamie L. (1967). That We May Live. New York: D. Van Nostrand and Company, Inc.

Williams, Alan (undated). Measuring the Quality of Life of the Elderly. Alan Williams, pp. 282- 297.

Wu, S.Y. (1979). "Measuring Returns to Technical Innovation in Health Care: The Utility Theory Approach" (Chapter 8) in Health: What is it Worth? Measures of Health Benefits (edited by Selma J. Mushkin and David W. Dunlop). New York: Pergamon Press, pp. 203-218.

Wyer, R.S., Jr. (1975). The Role of Probabilistic and Syllogistic Reasoning in Cognitive Organization and Social Inference - in Human Judgment and Decision Processes (edited by M.F. Kaplan and S. Schwartz). New York: Academic Press Inc.

Yarbourough, Ralph (1984). "Private Conversation with Ralph Yarbourough," MIT Center for Policy Alternatives [Cambridge, MA], July.

Zeckhauser, Richard (1975). "Procedures for Valuing Lives," Public Policy, vol. 23, no. 4, Fall, pp. 419-464.

Zeckhauser, Richard and Shepard, Donald (1976). Where Now for Saving Lives?. Cambridge, MA: Harvard University. JFK School of Government. Discussion Paper.

Zimmerman, O.T. and Lavine, Irvin (1946). DDT: Killer of Killers. Dover: Industrial Research Service.

Subject and Author Index